THE AGE
OF MARTYRS

"How long, O God, shall the enemy reproach:
is the adversary to provoke thy name for ever?"
—Psalm 73:10

THE AGE
OF MARTYRS

CHRISTIANITY FROM DIOCLETIAN (284)
TO CONSTANTINE (337)

By

Abbot Giuseppe Ricciotti

Translated By

Rev. Anthony Bull, C.R.L.

"Will God then cast off forever? Or will he never be more favourable again? Or will he cut off his mercy forever, from generation to generation? Or will God forget to show mercy? Or will he in his anger shut up his mercies? And I said, 'Now have I begun: this is the change of the right hand of the most High.'" —Psalm 16:8-11

TAN BOOKS AND PUBLISHERS, INC.
Rockford, Illinois 61105

easily, in time, assume the imperial power; plus, he was popular with the Army. Instead, he was allowed to leave the Eastern Empire to hasten to his father's sick-bed, and upon the death of his father (306), the Army in the West proclaimed him Augustus, despite the fact that Galerius had exerted his will with the aging Diocletian and had selected his own Augustus for the West, as well as the two Caesars that were to serve under the Augusti. Needless to say, Constantine was not one of them. But, as Abbot Ricciotti points out, when the Army made a selection for Emperor, the recipient had better not turn it down, lest he himself be killed by the Army and they choose another. This is how Constantine came to be launched on his career to power—by a move that was not of his own doing.

But then, *fourth*, Constantine lived through a number of major battles and was never killed. In one of these battles, he well might have taken a lance or a sword blow that could easily have ended everything for him, or an assassin could have killed him. Instead, he succeeded through all vicissitudes to gain complete control of the government by 324. And *fifth*, it was only *at that time* that religious persecution throughout the Empire was brought to a close; persecution was not ended simply with the abdication of Diocletian (305), or with the death of Galerius (311), and not even with the Edict of Milan (313), but with the second and final defeat of Licinius (324), when Constantine assumed complete power in the Roman Empire.

There are many other historical object lessons to be learned from *The Age of Martyrs*. For example, we see Diocletian's failed attempt through the Tetrarchy to end the problem of succession to the throne; we see the difficulty the Roman government had in managing so vast an empire; we see many epochal events and movements occurring in the same time frame—such as the Edict of Milan (313), the Arian heresy, the Council of Nicea (325), the Donatist heresy and the efforts to quell it, the attacks against the Empire by the barbarians and so forth. Indeed, this book covers a host of events in an orderly and in-depth manner that is both enlightening and inspiring. In the process of also recounting the stories of many famous martyrdoms, the author has woven an historical tapestry that will give the reader great food for thought, largely because it was through the agency of one man that history was turned and Christianity began to exercise its influence upon governments and peoples and, from that time on, to reach out to affect, more and more, the entire world. Thus, *The Age of Martyrs* is not about just *any* era of history, but about a time that affects us all, right down to the present day.

Just to have moved the Imperial seat from Rome to Constantinople was brilliant enough to warrant Constantine's being called "The Great," for the Empire in the East was thereby helped to last until 1453, almost a thousand years longer than in the West. But when one analyzes the entirety of his life, he has to admit that Constantine was obviously chosen by God to do great things. And he did them. And Abbot Giuseppe Ricciotti has caught the whole panoply of events in a most absorbing and highly unlikely study. Yet here it is, *The Age of Martyrs*, a book about an incredible time and an incredible man.

Thomas A. Nelson, Publisher
March 8, 1999
St. John of God

PREFACE

Before it was the general custom to count the years from the birth of Christ many Christian communities used a system which reckoned from the age of the martyrs — beginning with the first year of Diocletian's rule. Though this system was found especially in the East many other learned writers used it, among them Ambrose and Bede. It is said that among certain communities of the Copts in Upper Egypt this system is still in use. The choice of such a name for the period was most suitable, for under Diocletian the *Great Persecution* raged. This was the last and most cruel of the sufferings of the Christians, and the innumerable victims who fell in those years claim for the era without any rival the description *of the martyrs*.

The usual reaction followed the persecution. Calm came after the storm, liberty and triumph succeeded oppression, Diocletian changed for Constantine.

This is the period about which this book is written.

The book is not intended to be a critical study but a critical narration of the facts. The bases of the story are those historical documents which will stand careful and impartial examination. The method used is that of exposition after the example of the ancient masters of history writing. There are many critical researches today and many of them are very learned and acute, but they are of interest usually only to the specialists for they do not present the over-all development of the story.

This book is intended for historians and generally educated people, and so the author is sure they will welcome the absence of footnotes which allows the book to be read continuously. The rights of criticism have been respected and the documents on which the story is based will be found listed at the end of the book. Only occasional references will be found in the body of the work.

The cross references of paragraphs will help the reader to connect persons and facts as they reoccur in the story.

It is my happy duty to express my gratitude to the Very Rev. Antonio Casamassa, O.E.S.A., for the useful advice he gave me after reading the manuscript.

G. R.

Rome, October 15, 1953

TRANSLATOR'S NOTE

It was a great honor when Abbot Ricciotti asked me to translate his *Era dei Martiri* and I hope that the version I have made takes as little as possible from the quality of the original. A long time ago, however, I spent four pleasant years in his community and I know that Don Giuseppe will view any blunders of mine with a kindly eye.

I should like to thank those who have helped me in various ways especially my colleague Fr. George Rowe, C.R.L., who corrected the proofs and Fr. Francis Wharton, C.R.L., for his considerable assistance in finding English versions of obscure places in North Africa.

TABLE OF CONTENTS

LIST OF ILLUSTRATIONS

THE AGE OF MARTYRS

"Help us, O God, our Saviour, and for the glory of thy name, O Lord, deliver us; and forgive us our sins for thy name's sake: Lest they should say among the Gentiles: Where is their God? And let him be made known among the nations before our eyes." —Psalm 78:9-10

York

BRITAIN

London

Isle of Wight

English Channel

FRISIA

GESORIACUM

R. Rhine

TREVIRI

R. Danube

RAETIA

LAURIACUM

CARNUNT

BOIODUM

RIPENSE

NORACUM

MEDIA

SUEVIA

CABILLORUM

GAUL

AUGUSTODUNUM

SAINT-MAURICE

MILAN

SISCIA

OCTODURUM

VERONA

SEGUSIO

RAVENNA

ARLES

R. Po

SALONA

MASSILIA

CORSICA

ROME

ZARAGOZA

SPAIN

SARDINIA

LUCANIA

ELVIRA

CARTENNA

CALARIS

SICILY

CATANI

RUSICADE

CARTHAGE

MAURETANIA

TINGITANA

CIRTA

MAURETANIA

CAESARIENSIS

NUMIDIA

BAGORA

MASCULA

THEVESTE

CONSULAR AFRIC

QUINQUEGENTIANI

Medit

TERRITORY of CONSTANTIUS

TERRITORY of MAXIMIAN

TERRITORY of GALERIUS

TERRITORY of DIOCLETIAN

the ROMAN EMPIRE
DURING THE FIRST TETRARCHY —

SINGIDUNUM

VIMINACIUM
R. UPPER
MOESIA

R. Danube

LOWER
MOESIA

Black Sea

THRACE

SERDICA

ADRIANOPLE
BYZANTIUM
CHRYSOPOLIS

NEOCAESAREA

PONTUS

ARMENIA MAJOR

PERSIA

MACEDONIA

THESSALONICA

HERACLEA

NICOMEDIA

BITHYNIA

ZELA

MEDIA

EPIRUS

Hellespont

ANCYRA

GALATIA

CAPPADOCIA

MELITENE

CAESAREA

R. Tigris

ASIA

PHRYGIA

LYCAONIA

LYSTRA

TYANA

CILICIA

NISIBIS

CONSTANTIA

APAMEA

SELEUCIA

TARSUS

SAMOSATA

EDESSA

MESOPOTAMIA

R. Euphrates

CYPRUS

EPIPHANIA
EMESA

PALMYRA

CRETE

BEIRUT

HELIOPOLIS

PHOENICIA

-ranean Sea

TYRE

SYRIA

PHILIPPOPOLIS

CAESAREA

JERUSALEM

Syrtis
Major

ALEXANDRIA

GAZA

PALESTINE

ELEUTHEROPOLIS

JOVIA

PELUSIUM

PHOENO

LIBYA

R. MEMPHIS

EGYPT

HERCULEA

LYCOPOLIS

THEBAID

BLEMMYES

closed litter. By the time the army reached the Bosphorus the litter contained a corpse.

The soldiers were fond of their leader and when they learned of his death, they blamed it on Aper, prefect of the praetorian guard and brother-in-law of the dead man. Since he was thought to have committed the crime with the intention of taking Numerianus' place they immediately elected, in Chalcedon, a new emperor. He was an official called Diocletian. Aper was put in chains and the soldiers demanded a court-martial. It was held before the whole army but was very short: Diocletian took his place as the judge, called on the god Sol to witness his personal innocence in the matter of the death of Numerianus, and, having announced Aper as the murderer, he drew his sword and killed him.

It was not certain that Aper was guilty; on the other hand, all the soldiers laid the crime at his door, perhaps because they suspected that he was in secret accord with Carinus, ruler in the West, whom they did not like. With this support from the army the deed of Diocletian did not bring with it any of the dangers that would normally be expected in those times, while he gained even more favor from the soldiers by a show of apparent justice. For the rest, people could already see a divine predisposition in what had happened. In fact, it is told — rather later — that a druid priestess of Gaul had already predicted imperial dignity for Diocletian, on condition that he should have killed a boar: it happens that this is the meaning of the Latin word *aper*.
3. Carinus remained in the West although he had great resources and, a large army. He does not seem, however, to have been so unwarlike or so attached to pleasure as ancient tradition says, for in the following spring he was already leading a strong army against the troops who supported Diocletian. On his way he put down, near Verona, another pretender, Aurelius Julianus; in Moesia he had a number of successful engagements with Diocletian's troops; finally, in a battle near Viminacium, everything was again going well for Carinus until a tribune he had offended killed him, and left Diocletian without a rival.

And so Diocletian found himself at the head of the Roman Empire. He was of very humble origins. Son of a freedman of the Senator Anulinus, he was born in Dalmatia, perhaps in the neighborhood of Salona, where he retired after his abdication. Like so many of his countrymen in search of their fortune, he had taken up a military career as a young man. His true name was Diocle, but according to the custom of the time he lengthened and decorated it, calling himself Marcus Valerius Diocletianus. Entirely dedicated to his military service, he took part in the campaigns of Aurelianus, Probus, and Carus where he showed how valuable he could be to a general. At the time of his election as emperor he had reached the high position of Comes Domesticorum — Commander of the Imperial Guard.

Although without cultural background, Diocletian was intelligent in affairs and had plenty of common sense. Everything he did was motivated by a profound veneration for the majesty of the Roman Empire which he, as a provincial from Dalmatia, regarded in an almost religious light. In any case, it is apparent from many of his acts that he was neither greedy for power nor a lover of quarreling and war. His final abdication and the fact that even before this he had shared his rule with others show that he was not really a fanatical lover of power.

Even his killing of Aper was probably prompted more by a veneration for the majesty of the Empire than by personal ambition. Diocletian was intelligent and had certainly been convinced for some time that even if the Empire were not gravely threatened by barbarians from the outside, it was gravely injured within by the incessant struggles of claimants to the imperial throne. The first of these claimants which came to his hand was Aper and he treated him in the summary manner we have seen — a manner which showed up both his natural rusticity and his loyalty to the Empire.

4. When his only competitor, Carinus, had been eliminated for him, Diocletian began to carry out his plan of protecting the Empire from both internal and external dangers. As a matter of fact, the two were often closely connected. One emperor alone was not enough to defend such immense frontiers, and the supreme commander of the Empire was practically forced to select faithful helpers as Valerian and Carus had done. Such assistants must share in the imperial power; otherwise it might well happen that a general victorious in some campaign against the barbarians would become, almost without realizing it, a rival merely because his army acclaimed him.

Once Diocletian had formed his plan, he began to act. First he chose an assistant called Marcus Aurelius Maximian on whom he placed the duty of defending the frontiers. He was an old companion at arms of Diocletian who had been helped and protected by him, and was therefore very attached to him. Maximian was the son of country tradespeople in Pannonia. Though he had no culture or spiritual formation, he had acquired a reputation for military efficiency and organizing power. Ancient authors, generally unfavorable to him, show him as a man of unclean habits, violent, cruel, and ambitious. Diocletian, who had weighed him well, knew how to use his qualities, bad as well as good, to best advantage. Above all he knew that he was absolutely loyal. In 285 Diocletian nominated him "Caesar" which meant that he was worthy of the supreme command but not yet decorated with it. Soon afterward, when Maximian had again proved his value in the campaigns in Gaul, on April 1, 286, the Emperor nominated him "Augustus" associating him with himself in the government of the Empire. In theory Diocletian and Maximian had equal powers, dividing supreme rule between them. In practice Diocletian was the elder Augustus and his new colleague continued to show him that careful deference which had proved so useful in the past.

In this way the first step toward the *restauratio imperii* in Roman territories was made. The second step was still to be made. A rule must be fixed for the succession to the two Augusti, thus putting a stop to revolutions and competition. For this, however, there was no hurry, and Diocletian postponed a decision until more experience should give him a better idea of how it should be made (par. 11).

5. There is no record that the Roman Senate was consulted about these steps or that it gave its approbation. Even so, Senate approval would have been a pure formality with no influence on the course of events. Instead, right from the beginning one can see evidence of Roman religiosity guiding the decisions of Diocletian.

When in 286 Diocletian made Maximian Augustus, he took for himself the name of Jupiter and called his colleague Hercules. Jupiter and Hercules, divinities of Ancient Roman veneration, were mirrored now in the two Augusti who labored to restore the Empire. The elder Augustus was Jupiter, father of the gods, and the younger was Hercules, who labored at the orders of Jupiter. Curiously more than two centuries before this something similar had happened to the Apostles Barnabas and Paul when, during their stay at Lystra in Lycaonia, they had been taken by the people of the town as Zeus (Jupiter) and Hermes (Mercury) respectively (Acts 14:11–12).

It was at this time that there began in the court of the Augustus the rather foolish imperial ceremonial, which later became much more involved. This ceremonial, though abhorrent to ancient Roman tradition, fitted in quite well with the mentality of Orientals who had always been accustomed to see their monarch surrounded by divine light (par. 13).

6. Maximian's first task as Caesar was to solve a problem which had existed for a long time. Gaul had been in a state of the utmost desolation for many years; the large country estates had become so unproductive that they barely sustained a few small holders. Periodic attacks by barbarians from across the Rhine thinned out the scanty harvests, while along the coast of the English channel German pirates cut off communications with Britain. The populations of the north, who in the past had been looked after by Rome for economic and strategic reasons, were now left to their own resources because of the instability of the central government. Meanwhile, more and more tribute was demanded. Degradation and hunger, only a step from despair and rebellion, resulted from this action.

Among these unfortunate people, shepherds without flocks and peasants without land, revolt now broke out. It was to be a grim contest, for they had everything to gain and nothing to lose, except their lives. They quite quickly formed a *multitudo*, and by this name which in the Celtic language is *Bagad* or *Bagat*, the rebels came to be called. They are the Bagauds of contemporary documents. But the movement, although very large, was not organized or even united; and its leaders were inefficient. Bravery and individual valor were not wanting, however, and two rebels, Aelianus and Amandus, were elected as Augusti. Even with the imperial cloak on their shoulders, however, they lacked the power to transform the *multitudo* into an efficient army.

To put down this insurrection Diocletian sent Maximian from Nicomedia in all haste, since although the rebellion was dangerous the news from the East was even more alarming. When Maximian arrived on the scene he soon saw that the opposing rabble could be easily broken and dispersed by his disciplined veterans. Between the last months of 285 and the first of 286 the rebellion was more or less crushed, though many parties who had fled from military defeats and routs temporarily prolonged the hardly glorious campaign of the Caesar. Along the imperial roads gloomy reports usually became gloomier; this time a few skirmishes became a victory, and by the time the news got to Nicomedia, people were talking of a glorious lightning campaign which could only hasten the day when the conqueror would be named an Augustus.

7. To put down the insurrection Maximian had gathered his forces not from the legions guarding the German borders but from those in the districts north of the Po and around the Alps where detached sections of larger formations could be stationed. These troops were not likely to have been weakened by the war of nerves which was always alive along the frontiers.

With this is connected the martyrdom of the Theban Legion according to the *Passio* which was written in the seventh century, probably by a monk of that region (Saint-Maurice). According to this document, before Maximian set off against the Bagauds, he assembled at Octodurium (today Martigny in the Swiss Vallais) either other troops or a Theban legion brought from the East and then stationed at Agaunum (today Saint-Maurice, also in the Vallais) and commanded all the soldiers to share in the pagan sacrifices, demanding also their oath that they would fight against the Bagauds and the Christians. They refused to obey this order, and after having suffered decimation they were all slaughtered at Agaunum.

More ancient is the story of Eucherius of Lyons (first half of the fifth century) who made detailed investigations and seems to have visited the church which had been erected over the tombs of the martyrs as early as the fourth century. According to this story the martyrdom took place during the persecution of Diocletian but the exact date is not given. The whole Christian Theban legion was executed at Agaunum. Their highest officers were Maurice (who had the rank of *primicerius*), Esuperius (*campiductor*), and Candidus (*senator militum*). He relates that these Christian legionaries quite naturally refused to join in a general persecution of the Christians; and that they were therefore twice decimated; and that when they still persisted in their refusal, they were all executed.

8. There are some discrepancies between the two stories and both of them contradict, here and there, known historical facts. From the chronological standpoint, the later *Passio* seems more authoritative. This places the martyrdom under Maximian on the occasion of the campaign against the Bagauds and not under Diocletian who, at that time, was favorable to the Christians and who began his persecution of them only later. Maximian was indeed quite entitled to act as he did against Christian soldiers, not by right of any anti-Christian edict, but in support of general military discipline. Since he was due to go into action against the Bagauds, he might quite easily have suspected

some sympathy for the rebels among his soldiers, and therefore required from them participation in pagan sacrifices and oaths just as had been done on other occasions in like situations. If this is the kernel of truth in the matter, it is easy to see how the oral tradition on which Eucherius depends should have confounded the provisions of Maximian with the later well-known persecution of Diocletian, mixing up the dates and making the usual amplification of the facts.

Certainly the entire legion was not slaughtered. And only a small number of Christians belonging to a legion was martyred. In reality the oral tradition which came to Eucherius, one hundred and fifty years later, has not been repeated in other sixth-century Romano-Gallic writers such as Avitus of Vienna, Gregory of Tours, and Venantius Fortunatus. These knew all about the veneration given to the martyrs at the place of their sufferings, but they never spoke of Thebans and they expressed themselves so vaguely that they obviously lack real information. In conclusion it can be said that we have an event which without doubt has historical foundation but which has in its relation suffered some chronological changes and some exaggerations, none of which are unusual in popular legends.

9. Though Gaul was now pacified, many other territories of the Empire were in danger. The North Sea and the English Channel were infested with pirates who brought ruin to the coast of Gaul and Britain and made communication difficult. Therefore, according to the plans of Diocletian, the fleet in those parts was strengthened and concentrated at Gesoriacum (Boulogne-sur-Mer) under the command of a valiant Gallo-Roman, Carausius. He was most capable; not indeed of dislodging the pirates from their strongholds but of feathering his own nest, for he hoped eventually to make himself independent of Rome and to set up his own kingdom on both sides of the Channel. He got on the right side of the local population, especially of the Franks, fought those pirates who were not favorable to his plans, and, after detaching a good share for himself, handed out the booty thus acquired to his allies. His center of operations was Gesoriacum whence he maintained undisturbed relations with the Britons whom he controlled absolutely.

His game was soon discovered by Maximian who had direct responsibility for those regions, and sicarii were sent to dispose of the traitor. But Carausius was not asleep. He cut off all approach to the harbor of Gesoriacum, left a powerful garrison there, and sailed with his faithful rabble to Britain where he was proclaimed emperor at the beginning of 287.

Since he lacked sufficient naval forces to pursue and punish the rebel, Maximian had a fleet constructed. This came into action in 289; it had no great success and Carausius remained unpunished. Diocletian and Maximian by now were faced by other dangers and so they recognized the usurper and gave him the government of Britain. On this occasion Carausius took the names of Marcus Aurelius Valerius to show himself the brother of Maximian and struck money showing three Augusti with the inscription *Pax Auggg., Laetitia Auggg., Carausius et fratres sui.* But the *Pax* was obviously a fictitious peace and the two first Augusti only tolerated their new colleague. An occasion to get rid of him came within a few years (par. 14).

10.   Although the quarrel with Carausius was suspended for the moment, the rest of the Empire was by no means quiet. Barbarian pressure on the German frontiers had been increased by the treachery of Carausius. Over the whole of northern Africa, from Egypt in the east to Mauretania in the extreme west, there passed a shudder of rebellion. The economic restrictions on a once prosperous Egypt, the turbulent character of the multiracial population of Alexandria brought about a rebellion led by another would-be Augustus — one Achilleus who took the name of Lucius Domitius Domitianus. (It may be that there were really two leaders whose names have somehow fused into one.) In upper Egypt south of the delta, the savage tribes of the Blemmyes made their way into the country around the cataracts of the Nile. To the west of the delta, riots broke out at Carthage and even further west, while the Quinquegentiani and other barbarian nations threatened the rest of the Mediterranean coast as far as Mauretania. To the east lived the traditional enemy of Rome — the Persians. There the Sassanian dynasty which had succeeded the Parthian Arsacids in 227 had had its last conflict with Rome a few years before in the time of Carus (par. 2) and the sudden death of this emperor had left affairs as they were for the time being. There was neither legal peace nor actual war. But the Sassanian kings cherished great ambitions and especially planned to take back from Rome the lands which had been occupied during the late war. The most contested region was Armenia which lay to the east of the Roman Empire and to the north of Persia. This mountainous and almost impassable country was of great strategic importance for both powers. As long

as it was in the grasp of the Roman legions, Rome was able to menace Persia from the north and to take in the rear Persian armies which might have advanced against Roman Syria; on the other hand, if it were occupied by the Persian "King of Kings" this would protect the right flank and the rear of his armies in any operations against the Roman Empire. Augustus had already put a high value on possession of Armenia; and Trajan had conquered it and made it a province; Hadrian allowed the Armenians to choose a king for themselves. He turned out to be a devoted client of Rome. After the defeat and capture of Valerian in 260, however, Armenia fell into the hands of the Persians who killed King Chosroes. His son, Tiridates, was able to flee and take refuge in Rome where, in the shelter of the Empire, he prepared for revenge. He was sent back secretly to Armenia and profited from the discontent of the people, whose religious susceptibilities were offended by the intolerant Persian magians, besides being burdened by ruinous taxation. Tiridates raised his banner, and the Armenian nobility who had taken refuge in the mountains flocked to his side; favored by good fortune, he won back his own kingdom and then invaded Persia. After all this success, however, he could not withstand the counterattack of Narse, the Persian king, who drove him once more from Armenia. Naturally he again took refuge with the Romans where he did his best to increase the hostility between Rome and the "King of Kings." The matter would have to come to a head sooner or later.

11.   This threat, coupled with the weakness of the eastern frontiers of the Danube, made Diocletian decide to continue the *restauratio imperii* which he had already begun with the nomination of Maximian as Augustus. By now, however, the two Augusti were not sufficient and needed other active helpers. Indeed, it was now possible to provide a stable norm for their succession so as to stop usurpations. This was part of the original plan of the far-seeing Diocletian (par. 4).

In the first months of 291, the Augusti had met at Milan and probably the principal lines of action were decided at that time. These arrangements were made public on March 1, 293. The two Augusti each elected a Caesar of their own (Maximian had begun as a Caesar; par. 4). Gaius Valerius Galerius Maximinianus was chosen by Diocletian and Gaius Flavius Valerius Constantius by Maximian.

Galerius had begun his active life as a plowman in his native Illyria, a task for which he had all the physical and mental requirements. He was of enormous size and even when he became an important official in the Empire remained a brutal and ignorant man. He was well supplied with courage and practical sagacity and was particularly expert in Persian affairs, so much so that in concert with King Tiridates, once again under Roman protection, he had prepared a possible plan to restore him his kingdom.

Constantius, surnamed Chlorus (green face or pallid), was also an Illyrian, and according to the authorities seems to have been a descendant of Emperor Claudius II, the Goth; but it may be that such descent was a complacent invention in honor of his celebrated son, Constantine. He was a brave officer and prefect of the praetorian guard under Maximian; his character was mild and his constitution weak. This ill-health led to his surname.

The two new Caesars were under the strong influence of two women. Galerius was guided by his mother Romula, a priestess of mountain gods imported probably from Germany and a fanatical enemy of Christianity. Constantius was influenced by Helena, the woman with whom he lived before he was elected Caesar and by whom he had had a son, Constantine, in 280 or a little earlier. Helena did not come from the top of the social ladder. St. Ambrose (cf. *De obitu Theodos.*, 42) says that she was a *stabularia*, that is, she kept a "hostelry." Remembering the customs of the period this was probably not a very honorable occupation. After his election as Caesar, Constantius was forced to put her away to uphold his new dignity which carried with it an implication of relationship to his Augustus. He now married Theodora, Maximian's stepdaughter.

Although Constantius was a pagan tending toward a rather vague monotheism, Helena even at the time of her association with Constantius felt some sympathy for Christianity; we do not know, however, when she finally did embrace it. The assertion of Eusebius (cf. *De Vita Constantini III*, 47) that Helena was led by Constantine to the adoration of the true God whom she had not known before is certainly worthless flattery. On the other hand, not much faith can be attached to the contrary statement of Theodoretus (cf. *Hist. Eccl.*, i. 18) according to which after Helena had brought Constantine into the world, she administered to him the "food of piety." In any case, however, Helena certainly had great influence on the mind of Constantine who honored her until her death and gave her the title of "Augusta."

12. By a kind of *fictio iuris* a relationship arose among the four rulers: the two Augusti were brothers and the two Caesars were their respective sons. Thus the succession was assured since each "son" automatically succeeded his "father," while the two "fathers" were linked in "brotherhood." In their turn, each of the Caesars, when they had become Augusti, would choose a new Caesar as his "son." By this, the supreme power would be transmitted peacefully without any of the disturbances and rivalries which had so disturbed the Empire during the century just ending. Under this system, the praetorian guard, who too often in the past had decided on the next emperor, lost all importance. The Roman Senate was deprived of its powers both of nomination and of confirmation, and remained an empty symbol of its glorious past.

The "tetrarchy" thus brought into being seemed to suit the changed times with its new dangers, but later experience showed that it was only a happy theoretical dream with no connection with reality. The succeeding Augusti and Caesars were not the impersonal and impassive beings that Diocletian dreamed of, but men of flesh and bones with all their passions and egotistic propensities. These qualities made a peaceful continuance of the tetrarchy impossible. But even aside from this fact, there were many forces outside this system of succession which would one day or another threaten its existence. At the beginning, the tetrarchy bore good fruit precisely because it was intended as a cure for the actual dangers of the time.

13. As was to be expected from the religious mentality of Diocletian the tetrarchy thus constituted was surrounded by an aura of religiosity and clothed with a substantially religious ceremonial. The Augustus — especially Diocletian who was held unanimously to be the head of the tetrarchy — was invested with sacred majesty. He thus moved away from the true Roman tradition and approached the Oriental. The first sovereigns to receive divine honors were in the East — the Seleucids and the Lagidae, while in Rome during the first years of the Empire the Quirites were disturbed by the idea of an emperor being given divine honor while he was still alive. The prudent Augustus had *in Urbe quidem pertinacissime* refused the honor of temples and altars (cf. Suetonius, *Divus August.*, 52); he had thrust away even the title of *dominus* (cf. *ibid.*, 53), which in Rome meant the "master" of slaves, but which in the East was also valid as an epithet of divinity, while, for the Christians, the essence of the Christian confession consisted in applying this title to Jesus Christ (cf. 1 Cor. 8:5–6; 12:3; Rom. 10:9, etc.). Diocletian, however, played heavily on his concept of the sacred and divine Emperor. The Augustus had the official title of *dominus* over all; he was draped in rich purple edged with gold, wore precious slippers on his feet, and on his head bore the sacred diadem sparkling with gems. In his presence a subject — who was granted an audience only for very special reasons — had to prostrate himself and adore the divine majesty. Very detailed regulations governed the ceremonial of the court and an interminable hierarchy of officials and courtiers trailed down from the sacred throne until they finally reached the common mortals.

We must, however, discount any consideration that Diocletian acted thus through vanity or personal ambition; he wished to magnify the four dynasts in the eyes of his subjects so that even the external apparatus might inspire a trembling veneration.

As a common man, Diocletian could laugh at all this. He showed his true nature clearly a few years later when he had abdicated and retired to Salona; when urged to take back his power he would remark that no one would wish him to do this if they had seen the magnificent cabbages he grew. For Diocletian, the man, the magnificence of the imperial court was worth less than his beloved cabbages.

The immense Empire was divided between the four dynasts and each one chose a place of residence for himself suitable for the territories he governed. The Caesar Constantius had Britain, Gaul, and perhaps also Spain (some authorities give this last to Maximian), and his residence was among the Treveri. His Augustus, Maximinian, kept for himself Raetia, Italy with its islands, Africa (and perhaps also Spain), and placed his court at Milan. The Caesar Galerius received the regions below the Danube, Illyria, Macedonia, Greece with Crete, and lived at Sirmium in Pannonia. His Augustus, Diocletian, retained the eastern regions, that is Thrace, the whole of Asia Minor with Syria and Palestine, and Egypt with Libya; his palace was at Nicomedia in Bithynia.

14. After the division of the Empire each dynast had a great deal to do in his own territory, since for five or six years afterward there was continual war along all the frontiers.

On the German frontier the barbarians were being urged on by Carausius who felt that his fictitious peace with the continent was nearly at an end (par. 9). Hordes of Alemanni broke into Gaul and Constantius met and defeated them time after time. Then came the campaign in Frisia — the coastlands between the mouths of the Scheldt and the Rhine. This campaign was very grueling because the terrain was marshy and broken by canals and, too, the dogged resistance of the fierce inhabitants led them to set ambushes for the Romans at every step. With equal tenacity, however, Constantius managed to make himself master of all Frisia and with the prisoners he had taken he attempted a repopulation of the deserted regions of Gaul.

Having secured his eastern flank, Constantius concentrated his forces on Gesoriacum, the fortress of Carausius and his bridgehead on the continent. Carausius' fleet was gathered in the port of this city, and Constantius tried to bottle it up by closing the entrance to the port. In this he was not successful and the fleet sailed for Britain. Nonetheless Constantius continued his work of blocking the entrance, since he saw that the city would not be able to hold out against a land siege if reinforcements could not come in by sea. At the same time, he prepared a strong fleet to attack Britain. At this moment Carausius was assassinated by an official, Allectus, who may have been the prefect of his praetorian guard and who now took the place of his victim. Gesoriacum was finally taken by storm. But before Constantius began operations against Britain he asked Maximian, who was carrying on a campaign in Africa (par. 10), to occupy Gaul so that he could not be attacked in the rear.

When Maximian arrived, Constantius divided his fleet into two squadrons which were to act independently and make landings in two different places. The first squadron, which was grouped at the mouth of the Seine, was commanded by a valiant admiral, Asclepiodatus; the second, based at Gesoriacum, was commanded by Constantius himself. The enemy fleet under Allectus formed up before the Isle of Vectis (Wight), more or less in the middle of the southern coast of Britain from where it could keep guard on both sections of the coast. When one of the usual channel fogs occurred, Asclepiodatus weighed anchor and, escaping the notice of enemy lookouts, managed to make a landing, although a tempest carried him rather more to the west than he had intended. He burned his boats on the shore and marched quickly toward London. Allectus was taken aback by a landing in the west when he had expected one in the east and, seeing all his plans go wrong, rushed in disorder to meet Asclepiodatus. Allectus was defeated and killed in the encounter. In the meantime, Constantius, although he was delayed and troubled by the storm, had landed on the southeastern corner of Britain. He advanced without encountering resistance. In fact, he was received with joy by the people who lamented the once all-powerful Roman dominion. In this way, the island returned whole-heartedly to the Empire.

15.   From Gaul, Maximian now returned in haste to Africa to finish the pacification of the western regions which he had almost completed. Here also the campaign was quick, thanks to the energy and single-mindedness of the Augustus; thus only a little while after the restoration of Britain to the Empire this part of Africa gave no cause for preoccupation to the Romans.

But there remained the opposite side of Africa — Alexandria with Egypt and the neighboring regions to the west and south (par. 10). Since the chief Augustus, Diocletian, considered these territories of particular importance, he kept their control in his own hands; he therefore directed a personal campaign which did not end until 298. Two cities were destroyed. Alexandria resisted a siege for eight months, and when the town was finally taken by storm it experienced Diocletian's full severity. Against Upper Egypt, he acted differently, inviting the peoples of the Nobatae, barbarians from Nubia, to fight against the Blemmyes who had invaded their country. The old Roman maxim — divide and rule — proved its value once again. The Nobatae expelled most of their invaders and received in compensation a permanent home around the first cataract of the Nile. They had the duty of keeping guard on those borders of their country which were also borders of the Empire. Egypt was now divided into three provinces which from north to south were Jovia, Herculea, and Thebais.

16.   Despite all these successes on the frontiers of the Empire there still remained the menace of Persia which was very serious (par. 10), and threatened not just the frontiers but the Empire itself.

For some time Diocletian had been worried by the growth of Manichaeism in Roman territories, especially in Egypt and neighboring lands. In general Rome had been tolerant toward foreign religious trends, though she did practice a prudent vigilance over them. This new religion, however, could hardly be tolerated, for not only did it teach a corrupt doctrine, but it took its origin from Persia, the eternal enemy of Rome. By means of active word-of-mouth and written propaganda it diffused a dangerous doctrine and also — it was commonly believed — disgusting rites and immoral habits. It was sufficient to consider the bloody disorders in Egypt in recent times; quite probably these had been provoked by secret Manichaean agitators who were working for Persia against Rome. Diocletian, therefore, decided to promote the internal health of the Empire by curing it of the disease of the Manichaeans.

When his war in Egypt was nearly over, probably in 296, Diocletian published an edict against the Manichaeans. This document has special value since it allows us to understand Diocletian's attitude toward matters which concerned both politics and religion. This question was to arise again in the case of the Christians. The edict (cf. *Codex Gregorian.*, xiv. 4) proposed to safeguard the ancient religion given by the gods from the corrupting touch of new sects coming from the Persians, the enemies of Rome. "Therefore," he says, "we command that the authors and leaders together with their abominable writings be punished severely by being burnt in flaming fires: Those, however, who are members of the sect and those who rebel against the gods are to be executed and we decree that their possessions be forfeited to the treasury. And if any well-known people of whatever dignity or excellence should have passed to this unspeakable, filthy and infamous sect or to the doctrine of the Persians, you (the governor) shall confiscate their possessions for the benefit of our treasury and send such criminals to the mines of Phoeno and Proconnesus. So that therefore this wicked evil may be uprooted from our most blessed time we expect that your devotion will urge you to uphold these commands with your own orders and statutes thereby bringing peace to Us. Given on the day before the Kalends of April at Alexandria."

17. Immediately after Diocletian had thus provided for the internal security of the Empire he began war against the Persians. Since he was still occupied in Egypt he put Galerius at the head of the expedition who was his own Caesar and expert in Persian affairs (par. 11). Diocletian had great faith in him, and Galerius accepted the difficult task quite happily, for up to now he had been occupied in secondary ventures along the frontier of the Danube while Constantius, the Caesar of Maximian, had made a great name for himself in his campaign in Gaul and Britain.

Unfortunately his impetuous daring led him to forget prudence — a virtue particularly required in this insidious war. After some secondary engagements of doubtful result, Galerius fell into precisely the same fatal error as Crassus, who in 53 B.C., in this very region, had lost his army and his life. Starting from Syria, Galerius, instead of crossing the mountains of Armenia and falling from there in all safety on the rear of the Persians, made his way directly across the Euphrates and penetrated into Mesopotamia, plunging farther and farther into the interminable and waterless plains on the other side of the Roman frontier. Here the enemy cavalry found themselves in their element. Rank after rank of deadly Persian bowmen swept down time after time on the Roman infantry which was already exhausted by long marches. Before a counterattack could be launched they disappeared on their fast horses. Before long the legions found themselves cut off; the faithful Tiridates who fought *pro domo sua* with the Romans saved himself with difficulty by swimming the Euphrates in full armor. As soon as the Romans tried to withdraw other grave losses were added to the initial defeat. A few survivors, led by Galerius, reached Antioch where Diocletian was waiting with reserve troops.

18.   The anger of the Augustus was terrible. Almost three centuries earlier after the defeat of Saltus Teutoburgensis, Octavianus Augustus had shouted frenziedly that Varus should give him back his destroyed legions; but Varus had died in the battle and could neither hear the shouts nor justify himself. Here, however, Galerius, the responsible one, was alive and in retreat and Diocletian was no less angry than Octavian had been.

Galerius asked for an audience, but this was refused by Diocletian. He was met by the Augustus riding in his carriage through the street and the defeated Caesar knelt on the ground and implored a hearing. But the Augustus did not stop or show by any sign that he had noticed him. To the wonder of the spectators Galerius followed him doggedly for an hour and the dust from the carriage covered his purple cloak. Finally, Diocletian did hear the humbled and degraded suppliant and, after long consideration, made a decision which was worthy of his intuition and full of psychological wisdom. He judged that a leader who had suffered so great a disaster now possessed a precious experience which would keep him from further imprudent action. He kept him in his command, and, ordering him to reorganize the army, he allowed him to take men from the legions who were guarding the Danube, and who had already been under his command.

This new expeditionary force of 25,000 men left, but followed another route. This time Galerius, keeping clear of the plains which still bore the mementos of his defeat, climbed the mountain paths of Armenia and then, turning on his right, came down along the bank of the Euphrates. This time he was very prudent and was favored also by fortune. He was almost in contact with the enemy before their suspicions were aroused. In a night attack he penetrated the enemy camp before the Persian cavalry had time to seize their arms and mount their horses. The Persians were slaughtered by the Roman legions; the sons, wives, and sisters of King Narse were found and captured in the royal tent. The King himself was wounded and barely managed to escape to safety in Media.

19. Imitating the celebrated gesture of Alexander the Great, Galerius ordered that the King's relatives should be respected. The distinguished prisoners of the royal family might prove to be valuable hostages in Roman hands. All treasure, however, came to the victor and the rest of the camp was sacked by the legionaries. Galerius advanced as far as Nisibis where he was joined by Diocletian with another army as reinforcement. With these troops, and after so devastating a victory, it was possible to think of occupying Persia and reducing it to a Roman province. But the prudent Diocletian discarded this idea immediately. When an embassy from Narse arrived to sue for peace he decided to impose hard conditions but to leave the monarchy of the King of Kings still on its feet.

Since Narse could not do otherwise he accepted the conditions. Five districts of the Upper Tigris were to pass to the Roman Empire whose boundary with Persia was fixed as the river Araxes; the faithful Tiridates got his Armenia back with the addition of some territories taken from Media. Thus Tiridates again took on his office as the alert sentinel of Rome toward the east. It was the year 297.

When the embassy of the King of Kings was presented to Galerius, one of the Persian chiefs gave a long discourse which began by praising the magnanimity of the conqueror who had respected the royal relatives of the conquered one. Galerius, still a plowman at heart and no diplomat, replied by recording the disaster suffered by the Romans not forty years before and by pointing out the bestial manner in which the Persians had treated the Emperor Valerian who had been taken prisoner by them. This memory, evoked by a ploughman diplomat and conqueror, had great influence on the outcome of the negotiations.

20. At this point if we wished to weigh the results of the institution of the tetrarchy — that is, from the year 293 (par. 11) — we should have to recognize that in the politico-military field the program ar-

ranged by Diocletian had been carried out extraordinarily well. No usurpers worthy of serious attention had challenged the imperial authority. That very Carausius who had forced his way into the company of the two Augusti, and whose presence had been tolerated by them, had finally been removed. The frontiers of the Empire were a great deal safer now than they had been only a few years before; Persia was in no condition to cause trouble for many years to come; Britain had returned to tranquil reliance on Rome; the barbarians across the Rhine and the Danube had lost some of their ferocity; the whole of North Africa was under efficient control.

Meanwhile magnificent public works and buildings needed for the new regime had been begun and in many cases were nearing completion. The four cities of the dynasts — Trier, Milan, Sirmium, and Nicomedia — were enlarged and worthily ornamented; the greatest care was lavished on Nicomedia, from which Diocletian ruled and which he destined to be another Rome. But even old Rome was not forgotten. Among the many works executed there, it is sufficient to recall what had the highest value for morale, the reconstruction of the Curia Iulia, the home of the Roman Senate, destroyed by the fire of 283. The largest and most grandiose work in Rome was the construction of the baths on the Viminal which had been begun by Maximian on his return from the campaigns in North Africa (par. 15), but which were called the Baths of Diocletian since they were built in honor of the latter. The work lasted from 298 to 306, and the vast building which resulted was worthy of Rome in every way. Even the ruins of the baths remaining today are, as everyone knows, among the greatest and the most impressive of the city and can be compared to the monuments of the Egypt of the Pharaohs.

Many centuries after Diocletian, a giant who was also a genius came to the ruins. His task was to put them in order and preserve them for posterity. Michelangelo found himself in his element among the colossal walls and giant columns and worked alongside his equals.

21. The industry of Constantius merits particular mention. Since this Caesar found that his distant territories were somewhat cut off from the vital center of the Empire, he worked fervently for the economic and cultural welfare of his people. He was refined and cultured himself, and he liked the company of learned men whom he used to consult even in political matters. Under him the local schools of rhetoric multiplied and the Gallo-Roman youth thronged their lecture halls. In the past one of the principal centers of culture had been the city of Augustodunum (Autun) but during the rising of the Bagauds it had been almost destroyed. Constantius rebuilt the city placing in the center a great edifice destined to be the school of rhetoric; his secretary, Eumenius, was put in charge of the school which was inaugurated in 297. A similar school was founded at Trier.

This material building did not hinder a serious attempt to solve long-standing and grave social questions in the rest of the Empire. Diocletian had found the Empire in the throes of monetary confusion, which had been created by past governments and which ruined commercial exchange; some coins were refused because they had no intrinsic value; others brought only half or a third of their nominal worth, and so on. Coins were now struck which were worth their face value, and which were intended gradually to take the place of the earlier coinage. This process was rather slow, however, and the difficulty continued. Years later, Constantine had to occupy himself with the same problem.

22. Then came the *edictum de pretiis*. This was a law which fixed the highest price of various goods and the highest wages which could be paid — a maximum which could never be exceeded. With the tetrarchy, State expenses were increased beyond measure since the four courts of the four dynasts had to be maintained together with their armies and a great crowd of clerks and officials in newly created posts. Taxes were overwhelming since, as the tax collectors were always increasing in number, they found great difficulty in discovering persons to pay the tax; "There were more tax collectors than taxpayers," said a witness of the times (Lactantius, *De Mortibus Persecutorum*, 7). Naturally in such conditions prices both of goods and of labor were reaching for the stars, especially since production was down in some regions. The government tried to standardize the duties and taxes which differed from region to region, in the course of which ancient privileges were suppressed and an entirely new fiscal partition of the Empire was introduced. But even this remedy, which in any case was hardly efficacious, brought with it an inevitable increase in the number of bureaucrats and therefore of expenses.

It was hoped that the *edictum de pretiis* would remedy the prohibitive height of prices. This edict had a military objective as well, for the troops which were continually being posted from one part of the Empire to another were finding the high prices a great burden since they had to buy their victuals on the public markets. The *edictum de pretiis*, which is preserved only in fairly large fragments, was for the whole of the Empire and contained detailed lists of goods and types of labor for all of which a maximum price was given. It was a very severe law, contravention of its orders being punished by death.

From our experience of modern times we could have told Diocletian what would happen. In those regions where the prices were lower than the maximum, they were raised immediately; where, on the other hand, current prices were actually higher than the maximum, goods quickly disappeared from the shops and were taken over by that intangible institution — the "black market." The good intentions which inspired the edict were totally frustrated by the inexperience on which it was based, and also by a certain military rigidity derived from its author. After a little while the edict was to all intents and purposes abandoned.

23. Provisions of a purely moral nature were not lacking. Besides the rescript published in Egypt against the Manichaeans (par. 16), Diocletian during his stay in Egypt caused all books of alchemy and magic to be burned. The authors say that they were Egyptian books and it is quite possible that they were actually written in Egypt. Diocletian, however, considered the origin of the doctrines rather than the authors. Anything to do with magic or occult knowledge came — according to the Romans — from Persia and Chaldea. Even in the time of the republic the Romans had said, "*Chaldaeos ne consulito.*" Since these teachings came from the same countries as Manichaeism, and since also Rome and Persia were eternal enemies, magic doctrine shared the flames with the works of Mani.

To this same period belongs a noble edict on marriage. Just as the first Augustus had taken care to restore the tarnished honor of matrimony, so now did Diocletian, basing his action on religious principles and maintaining that pious and chaste conduct would bring down the protection of the gods of Rome.

And it was this Emperor, fired with such clear pagan piety, who was to pass into history as the author of the most cruel persecution suffered by Christianity.

2. Religion

24. Toward the end of the third century after Christ the Roman Empire, so far as religion was concerned, resembled the crater of a volcano in eruption. There was a mixture of highly heterogeneous elements which combined in various ways to form a thousand different substances. The old form of the Latin Roman religion had been preserved especially in Italian regions, but this had been overlaid by many elements which had come from Greece. Greek divinities were identified with Roman and the names of the former used for the latter. Later still, Oriental gods were imported from Asia Minor and from other Semitic countries. Over all this mixture great influence was exerted by philosophical doctrines, especially in later years when people had begun to analyze and explain in a rational way the principles held by the various religions.

But now for three centuries Christianity had been in the field and its appearance had been very disturbing. Because of the enormous distance in morality between the pagan Greek or Roman religions and itself, Christianity had little appreciable influence on their natural evolution. To the pagan thinkers who were investigating the religious facts, however, Christianity seemed a very important phenomenon, greater than any in the past and worthy of a large place in their investigation. This did not mean that these thinkers became Christians or were powerless in face of its teaching. On the contrary, their enmity was constantly in evidence and they indulged in polemics, trying to demonstrate what was wanting in this new doctrine, and what good there was in the pagan religions. This very attitude, nevertheless, showed that they recognized implicitly the superiority of Christianity, for such polemics had not been resorted to in the face of other new religions.

25. This reaction to Christianity was not purely religious. In it was the note also of political expediency. All around the Empire crowded the threatening barbarian hordes, awaiting an opportunity to throw down the sacred institution which had been created and had grown up under the protection of traditional gods. Was it not therefore necessary, once and for all, to defend these gods desperately so that Rome could be saved from ruin? On the other hand, although the God Christ had never allowed himself to be allied with any of the usual gods, his followers were constantly growing in numbers despite the cruelest persecution, until the Christians now represented a more or less high percentage — according to the region — of the population of the Empire. Now, if the twenty or thirty or more millions of Christians living in the Empire at the end of the third century were to return to the worship of the old gods and stop weakening with their new doctrines the religion which had been handed down through the generations, how much more compact would the Empire be in itself and how much stronger would be its resistance against the barbarians!

26. This practical thesis was expounded in full precisely at the end of the third century by the Neoplatonist Porphyry, heir to the teachings of Plotinus, less subtle than he but more pragmatic and particularly interested in Christianity. His fifteen books "against the Christians," little of which is extant, did not pretend to be either a blind denial such as that of the ancient Celsus nor a collection of gratuitous assertions. Rather, he wished his work to be a calm and penetrating discussion of the basic principles of Christianity so as to show up their deficiencies and absurdities. Porphyry was obviously informed on Sacred Scripture and on the various ways in which the Christians interpreted it. He also recognized that Jesus was a most noble figure and that some of his opinions were worthy of being received by all men (this led some ancient writers, without any real proof, to see in Porphyry an apostate Christian). When he passed to criticism, however, he attacked the foundations of Christianity by historical or philosophical arguments.

This writing of Porphyry made a great impression on the Christians and he was answered by numerous writers, who quoted him freely, and thus made up to us, to some extent, for the loss of the actual fifteen books. The pagans were also greatly impressed, though in another way. Porphyry, however, never achieved what he had set out to do — to bring Christians and pagans into one religion which would show a united front against the barbarian menace. With all his philosophical acumen Porphyry failed to realize that such a fusion was absurd and that the new wine would not go into the old bottles.

27. Some restatement of the old pagan religion seemed necessary. When the Christians wanted to attack the current polytheism, it was easy for them to expose its absurdities and contradictions as Tertullian and Minucius Felix had already done. In fact, many of the arguments used by the Christians had been provided for them by earlier pagan philosophers. Because of this and for practical reasons, the whole of polytheistic teaching was being transformed. Already some fifty years before Diocletian, a kind of hierarchical confederation had unconsciously been made which collected the innumerable deities in one list and put them all under one supreme god. People were asking what all these gods and goddesses, so various and often so contradictory, did really add up to? Were they a great crowd of deities who ruled the universe, each one independent of the other? Or was there perhaps a *quid unum* which was common to all of them? If there was, then maybe they could all be reduced to such an all-embracing supreme principle? Such questions did not really lead to monotheism. Philosophers sought to fit all these deities into a system which was reasonable, compact, and harmonious. They were trying to build a solid pyramid with one apex only.

In this way, all the gods could most certainly remain and in fact there was room for others to be brought in; but all of them must become natural parts of the pyramid, sections of the sloping sides which supported the apex.

28.   There were many who received this solution gratefully, and added proof and example from nature itself. It was sufficient to raise the eyes to the sky and to consider the function of the sun in the material world. Did it not animate everything? — Was it not the great giver of light and life? Other founts of life and energy were to be found in nature, but these were all derived from the supreme source of the sun without which everything would fall into inertia, into darkness and death. These lesser sources were subordinate to the highest source and acted as so many mirrors reflecting more or less faithfully the greatest light and did not differ from it substantially.

The same thing was true, they said, in the world of the gods. There were many gods and goddesses, but they were all partial reflections of the highest god Sol and whatever could be predicated of them could in the ultimate analysis also be predicated of Sol.

The Emperor Aurelian had been an enthusiastic supporter of the cult of Sol. The son of a priestess of Sol, he had constructed in Rome, in 274, a sumptuous temple to *Deus Sol dominus imperii Romani*, uniting in this god the different sun gods of the Greeks and the Orientals (Helios, Baal) and placing them in the official Roman pantheon. He himself, as the emperor, was the representative of this god with the title *Deus et Dominus* and was shown on coins in the act of receiving a globe from Sol, to indicate his world-wide rule.

This linking up of the Emperor with the sun-god — often identified or confused with Apollo — went on for a long time; even Diocletian, when he killed Aper, called the god Sol as a witness of his own innocence (par. 2). In doing so he did not deny the Roman gods headed by Jupiter. Jupiter seemed more suited to political affairs and Diocletian himself later chose the name of Jupiter (par. 5), whereas the judicial business of the condemnation of Aper was better suited to Sol, the source of all light. The two gods, in any case, were very much alike and the greatest star in nature corresponded with the greatest god in the Roman pantheon.

29. This syncretic process culminating in the god Sol seemed to many pagan philosophers to be not only natural and spontaneous but even worthy of acceptance by Christianity. Had not the Evangelist called Christ "the true light which enlighteneth every man" (Jn. 1:9) which after all is the work of the Sun? Had not the Messias been called by the Hebrew writings "the sun of justice" (Mal. 4:2; cf. Lk. 1:78)?

There seemed to be, therefore, some common ground on which both Christians and pagans could meet. The Christians could continue to adore their Christ in peace since this god was no more than an emanation of the god Sol and before the latter the pagans were quite willing to prostrate themselves. Jupiter, Apollo, Mars, and all the others in the pagan pantheon could still be venerated since they were only other emanations of the sun-god. The adoration of both Christians and pagans was, in the sum, directed toward one object, the god Sol; both sides, therefore (said the philosophers), were in complete agreement.

30. It is superfluous to say that even if this suggestion seemed quite reasonable to the pagan syncretism of the day, it could not be considered by Christian monotheism for whom Christ was a "jealous" God; the same could be said of the God of the Old Testament (cf. the considerations of St. Augustine in De Consensu evangel., i. 12, 18). Given this intransigent "jealousy" of the God of the Christians toward every pagan divinity, there was nothing left but to watch the two currents flow separately and see which one of the two would dry up first. It was quite impossible that both should continue for long even if the unexpected should occur and there should not be violent shocks for one or the other as there had been in the past. Actually, it was the very nature of things that a steady progress of Christianity should dry up the founts of paganism and, from the opposite viewpoint, that the continued resistance of paganism should bring about the arrest and death of Christianity. For the present, one could only go on with the existing unstable balance of power.

It was the government of Diocletian, rather than his personal character, which finally upset this balance. During the early years of his rule he had no hostility toward religions which were not Roman and, in fact, regarded them with that ancient Roman tolerance which derived partly from theoretical skepticism and partly from practical prudence. Naturally when political expedience was involved he turned to legal repression. This had happened in the case of the Manichaeans, as we have already seen (par. 16). Christianity raised no political difficulty — or at least it did not seem to, and, in any case, Diocletian knew quite well the result of persecutions of Christians in the past by Septimius Severus, Maximinian, Decius, Valerian, and Aurelian; the persecuted sect, instead of disappearing, had increased in numbers and had given occasion to the aphorism of Tertullian that the blood of the martyrs was the seed of new Christians. This consideration and the desire not to disturb the peace of the Empire was going to have the greatest influence on Diocletian's mind on the eve of the new persecution.

31. Diocletian was a singular man. He was a soldier in upbringing and habit, but was not really inclined to violence and blood. He was courageous in war, but is frequently shown as hesitating and timorous when others were urging him to persecute the Christians. In his superstitious pagan mind he found something mysterious in that paradoxical sect which, struck down by deathblows, raised itself more alive than before and found victory in defeat. Perhaps this Christ was the last and most powerful of the emanations of the sun-god (par. 28) against which any hostility would be useless and even dangerous! Far better to avoid this peril. It would be much more prudent to allow the Christians the same consideration which was given to those who worshiped Jupiter, Mithras, Serapis, and other gods and allow them their freedom. He had found this had worked quite well for eighteen years (cf. Lactantius, *De mortibus persecut.*, 11) so why should he now try something else?

A glance into his court, and indeed into his own family, would show him every motive for not disturbing the Christians but rather for being pleased with them. His wife Prisca and his daughter,

Valeria, were certainly favorably inclined to Christianity and may perhaps have been catechumens (cf. Lactantius, *op. cit.*, 15). In the court, functionaries and officers who were openly Christians had been appointed by Diocletian himself and the most delicate office of chamberlain (*cubicularius*) or "eunuch" in which direct contact with the sacred majesty of the Augustus was allowed, had been held by Christians such as Gorgonius and Peter; the head of these dignitaries, Dorotheus, was a Christian (cf. Eusebius, *Hist. Eccl.*, viii, 1, 4; 6, 1–5). Besides this, various Christians had been appointed as governors of provinces and given important posts in the government by Diocletian personally, who had considered their conscience sufficiently to dispense them from the pagan sacrifices which would normally be required from them in their official capacities (cf. Eusebius, *op. cit.*, viii, 1–2). In the imperial city, Nicomedia itself, the Christians were numerous and their principal church was within sight of the imperial palace (cf. Lactantius, *De mortibus persec.*, 12).

Of all this Diocletian was perfectly aware and he gave due weight to facts which would seem to confirm him in his old method of tolerance. But against all this other forces were gradually breaking down his resistance and in time were to turn him into a persecutor of Christianity.

3. The Storm Gathers

32. In the tetrarchy the authority of Galerius was increasing greatly although he was still only a Caesar. Diocletian's faith in him, shaken by the sad result of his first campaign against the Persians, had been completely restored by his final victory (par. 19), and Galerius had by now become his right-hand man. His marriage with Valeria, Diocletian's daughter, bound the fortunate Caesar even more closely to the omnipotent Augustus and the latter came more and more under his influence and, in the end, saw everything with the eyes of Galerius.

It was precisely in the character of Galerius that all the motives could be found for a persecution of the Christians and for disposing of Diocletian's resistance to this action. The first motive was the Caesar's mentality which had conceived a profound hatred for Christianity under the influence of his mother, the Corybantic priestess. Other motives could be found in the frequent complaints of pagan priests and haruspices whose business had been damaged by the growth of

Christianity. Finally, to all this should be added the open encouragement of pagan polemic writers who, either by natural inclination or with the desire of gain and honor, put their hopes in Galerius. At first, the work of these intellectual auxiliaries had to be oral and private; but when not long afterwards, the persecution broke out, they began to circulate their writings to support and justify the campaign. It seems that among them we shall now find apostate Christians.

33. We have the vague mention of an anonymous pamphleteer who, after the first edict of persecution in 303, published three books against the Christians (cf. Lactantius, *Divin. instit.*, v. 2). In ancient times, students believed that the author was Porphyry (par. 26), but from the little we know this pamphleteer was very much inferior to Porphyry in intellectual and moral stature. His sole intent seems to have been to make money and to attract the attention of those in power. He, therefore, praised the wisdom of those who had decreed the persecution and exalted their virtues in terms of venal adulation. The part of his book devoted to argument seems to have been very small if it existed at all; it certainly contained an exhortation to the Christians to repent for their own sakes and to return to the traditional gods, abandoning the stupidities of a religion which had brought so much trouble to them. Such a writer, it would seem, would make no impression even on pagans.

34. Much more effective was the work of Hierocles. It is not certain that he was an apostate Christian. During the first campaign of Galerius against the Persians, he was governor of Palmyra on the edge of the deserts leading to Persia and, quite possibly, the two met there and exchanged ideas about Christianity. Also, possibly at this time, Hierocles was already collecting material for his later work.

Rejoicing in such protection, it is not surprising to find him promoted later from the governorship of Palmyra to the prefecture of Bithynia which contained Nicomedia, the seat of Diocletian. He succeeded the Prefect Flaccinus who had shown himself very severe against the Christians in the new persecution and probably Hierocles, to prove that he was not inferior to his predecessor, published his work on the occasion of his promotion to office. His book was entitled *A Friendly Discourse on Truth* (directed) *to the Christians* (Λόγος φιλαλήθης πρὸς τοὺς χριστιανούς). The work was not a fierce, death-dealing attack, but an attempt by friendly persuasion to invite Christians to conform to the official beliefs of the Empire. This method had been common from the time of Porphyry. Considerable knowledge of Christian doctrine is shown in the book which, according to Eusebius (cf. *Contra Hieroclen*, 1), was derived from earlier anti-Christian polemics rather than from the immediate consultation of Christian writings. This had been the method followed a couple of centuries earlier by Flavius Josephus in his *Contra Apionem* in regard to Judaism.

35. The way had largely been prepared for Hierocles in the well-known biography of Apollonius of Tyana written by Philostratus a century earlier. This biography — which was more of a novel — showed that the favorites of the Empress Julia Domna, the wife of Septimius Severus, favored the cult of the god Sol (par. 28). From this work Hierocles took the foundation of his own book, for it presented Apollonius as a kind of Christ, giving him similar qualities and attributes, and crediting him with miracles and discourses like those found in the canonical and apocryphal Gospels. Without difficulty Hierocles followed the same path presenting the two figures as parallel; at the same time he was careful to add to the picture of Christ some points taken from legends which contemporary Judaism had circulated to bring Christ into disrepute.

Hierocles' book was, no doubt, a cause of great alarm for the Christians who, at this very time, were undergoing the worst of the persecution. For its author it was a help in his career, since as a reward for his zeal he was made governor of Egypt (cf. *De Martyribus Palaest.*, v. 3, larger edition). Later, after the persecution was over, Eusebius of Caesarea took on himself the work of confuting him with his *Liber contra Hieroclen, animadversiones in Philostrati de Apollonio Tyanensi commentarios ob institutam cum illo ab Hierocle Christi comparationem adornatae.* As is evident from the title, Eusebius was more interested in Apollonius of Tyana than in Hierocles because he was disturbed by the artificial parallel made between Apollonius and Christ. In later times this distress was shared by other Christian writers who returned to the argument for apologetic reasons.

It was an exaggerated fear, however, and the polemic writings against Apollonius of Tyana had the undesired effect of spreading the fame of a mythical personage with whom the contemporary Neoplatonic philosophers did not bother themselves. After the victory of Christianity, Apollonius was completely forgotten by the pagans and did not come out of his obscurity until many centuries later when he was brought out into the light again at the Renaissance.

36. Encouraged by all these supporters of a persecution of the Christians, Galerius was ready to move to the attack. But against which sector of the enemy should he launch his first blow? It was important to choose a place where the enemy were most vulnerable and where the attacker had the greatest advantage. This sector was, without any doubt, the army.

At this time the Christians were numerous in the Roman armies, especially because the young men from the provinces tried to alleviate their impoverished condition by enrolling (par. 1). For the Christians, however, there was a grave question of conscience. Should a follower of Christ kill his neighbor? Could he swear loyalty to emperors hostile to Christ and use idolatrous and impious expressions in his army oath. This delicate question had been explicitly discussed more than a century before. Christians had been in the Roman armies from the earliest times (cf. Acts. 10:1 sqq.), but they had adopted a working compromise without any deep consideration of the matter. From the few references that we have, it would seem that the great majority of Christians held military service to be licit, while a few were either dubious or condemned it.

In 197, Tertullian with some exaggerated pride stated that Christians had filled all the various posts of the Empire where soldiers were stationed, including the Castella and the Castra Ipsa (cf. *Apologet.*, xxxvii, 4). Fifteen years later, he had become a Montanist and defended in his book *De Corona Militis* a Christian soldier who had not wished to receive a laurel crown in an investiture ceremony, although this laid him open to disciplinary action and the displeasure of his Christian colleagues. This idea was confirmed a little later in his writing — *De Idololatria* — where Tertullian declared that a Christian was not allowed to enroll as a soldier. The same ideas continued through the third century, and are found in Origen and Lactantius, even appearing in some of the *Acta Martyrum* which are historically accurate. Without doubt, such theories represented the conscience of a notable minority.

This attitude toward military service by Christians can also be connected with certain apocalyptic visions which saw the imminent collapse of the pagan empire; and are to be found in writers such as Commodianus, Arnobius, and Lactantius. Such visions were shared by a considerable minority of Christians.

37. All this was certainly known to Galerius and to those who were persuading him to persecute. They saw that the first attack must be directed against the Christianity which had crept into the army; thus the untrustworthy and perjured soldiers and the cunning traitors who were forecasting political disaster would be removed. Galerius would be regarded as the defender of the Empire and the patron *pro aris et focis* of the majestic Roman traditions. Action must be prudent and gradual, however, for there had been no recent legislation against the Christians, and in his desire for peace within the Empire the Augustus Diocletian did not approve of laws which would lead to bloodshed. On the other hand, normal military discipline revolved around the pagan religion and this would allow dispersed but general pressure to be applied, as it had been by Maximian in the affairs of the martyrs of Agaunum (par. 7).

There was, therefore, a first period of sporadic persecution of Christian soldiers before the great official persecution of 303. Eusebius refers to this period in two passages. The first (in *Hist. Eccl.*, viii, 1, 7) reads: "when (the Christians) were still holding their meetings . . . persecution began against those brethren who were in the army." In a later passage he says, "One could tell of thousands (of martyrs) who showed admirable zeal for the religion of God of the universe not only from the time of the general persecution but also before this when there was peace; for he (the enemy) did not declare war against all of us at once but attempted to shake first those who were in military stations; he thought that the rest would be conquered more easily if they were put down to begin with. It was given them to see very many ($\pi\lambda\epsilon i\sigma\tau\text{ous}$) soldiers prefer a private life rather than become renegades of the Maker of the Universe" (*op. cit.*, viii, 4, 1–2). In these two passages Galerius is not named as the author of the persecution in the army, but he is definitely named as such in a third passage which some manuscripts give as an appendix to the eighth book of Eusebius' work, and which probably comes from an earlier edition. Even from what Lactantius says of events a little before the general persecution (cf. *De mortibus persecut.*, 10–11), one gathers that it was Galerius who was the instigator of the persecution in the army and that Diocletian surrendered to his insistence only gradually and against his will.

38. The theory put forward by some modern students, that the pretext for the persecution was the refusal by Christians to perform the "adoration" of the Emperor required by court etiquette, has no real foundation (par. 13). This adoration ($\pi\rho\text{o}\sigma\kappa\acute{\nu}\nu\eta\sigma\iota\varsigma$), whatever may have been its original intention, had become part of a simple court ceremony

which could be interpreted as harmless by the Christian conscience. Indeed, the ceremony continued in the imperial court after Christianity had become the official religion.

The spread of persecution in the army had been connected with two different incidents. According to Lactantius (cf. *De mortibus persecut.*, 10), while Diocletian was in the East he was carrying out sacrifices of animals from whose entrails the haruspices were to foretell the future. Some Christians who were assisting at the sacrifices as court officials made the sign of the cross; the chief of the haruspices, who had been unable to foretell anything from the entrails, attributed this lapse to the presence of profane persons who were not pleasing to the gods. Diocletian became angry and ordered that the officials and everybody else present should immediately sacrifice to the gods under pain of flagellation. Orders were sent also to senior officers of the army that all soldiers should offer sacrifice or be expelled from the army. It seems that the matter ended there, for Lactantius himself adds that Diocletian "offended no further against the divine law and religion."

39. The story of Eusebius is a little different. "When he who was the commander of the soldiers (ὁ στρατοπεδάρχης ὅστις ποτὲ ἦν ἐκεῖνος) began the persecution in the army, he mustered and purged his forces by giving them the choice of obeying and thus keeping their rank or of disobeying and being deprived of it. Very many of them who were soldiers of the kingdom of Christ preferred without delay to confess him clearly rather than have apparent glory and well-being. Of these latter, however, it was rare that one or two should endure not only the loss of rank, but also the punishment of death, for he who directed this action was proceeding slowly and dared to shed the blood only of a few; it seems he feared the numbers of the faithful and did not wish to declare war on them all together" (*Hist. Eccl.*, viii, 4, 3–4).

The stories of Eusebius and Lactantius are not contradictory but complementary. Diocletian's act seems to have been an isolated one unless it was influenced by what Galerius had been doing in the meantime, for the chief Augustus was coming gradually under the influence of his Caesar. No dates are given to their relations by either author. According to the *Chronicle of Eusebius*, the "commander of the soldiers," not named by him in the text we have quoted, was Veturius, the *magister militiae*; but the year differs with the different manuscripts. It is assigned to the "year of Abraham," 2319, and the 270th Olympiad (cf. *Eusebii Chronicon*, Schoene edition, p. 187; *Die*

Chronik des Hieronymus, Helm edition, p. 277) and seems to fit best
with the year 301 of our era.

40. The activities of Veturius made few martyrs as Eusebius said
and these few may have owed their fate to particular circumstances
and not to the new laws which attempted to clear the army of Christians — at least in those divisions under the command of Galerius.
Very many, on the other hand, were expelled from the army and lost
their social position. Officers were punished by the *gradus deiectio* —
reduction to the ranks; private soldiers were given the *ignominiosa
missio*, that is, discharge with ignominy, which brought with it the
loss of the title of "veteran" and the advantages which went with it;
in both cases there came out men who had been cast off by society
and economically ruined. Despite all this, as Eusebius says, there
were very many (πλεῖστοι) who resisted.

But their number may have been greatly increased if we suppose that
the purge of the army carried out by Galerius, and referred to by
Eusebius, was quickly imitated in the territories governed by Maximian,
the other Augustus. The very character of Maximian, his jealousy of
the all-powerful Caesar Galerius, the general dispositions which pre-
dominated among the high dignitaries of the court of the first
Augustus of Nicomedia, all seem to make it correct to suppose that
Maximian also acted against the Christians of his armies if only to
put himself in line with what was happening elsewhere. We must,
however, confess that this suggestion is supported only by a few historical facts found in the *Acts of the Martyrs*.

41. It is difficult to learn very much about the period immediately
preceding the great official persecution from the insufficiently explored
Acts of the Martyrs and *Passions* (par. 75 ff.).

Putting aside those *Acts* which are obviously legendary or else so
touched up that it is difficult to find the inner core of truth, there is
no doubt about the historicity of the *Acts* of the conscript Maximilian
and of those of the centurian Marcellus and of Cassianus, all three of
whom were put to death in Africa — the territory of Maximian. It is
to be noted that the first two, Maximilian and Marcellus, were condemned on the plea of military discipline. Julius, Marcian, and Nicander
were also soldiers and, perhaps, Polycrates and Valentian and some
others who were all killed in the Moesia, that is, in the territories of
the Caesar Galerius; the *Acts* of this last group of martyrs contain good
historical material which, nonetheless, must be used with caution since

a secure chronological basis is often lacking. To give an idea of the
situation in which these soldier-martyrs found themselves, it will be
better to give a summary of the Acts of Maximilian and those of
Marcellus and Cassian.

42. Maximilian is a typical case of the conscientious objector. He was
not yet a soldier, but since he was the son of a veteran called Fabius
Victor he could be called on officially to enlist. At the age of 21 on
March 12, 295, he was called up, and together with his father he
reported at Theveste in Numidia before the proconsul Cassius Dio.
Although he was the son of a soldier, he was of the opinion of the
Montanist Tertullian and others (par. 36), who held that it was wrong
for a Christian to serve in the army. Either the son disagreed with
his father or more probably, the father had changed his opinion after
his service was finished. The Proconsul began the interrogation by
asking Maximilian his name.

"Why do you ask my name? I cannot be a soldier for I am a
Christian."

The Proconsul took no notice and ordered that he should be
inspected medically and measured to see if he was suitable as a recruit.

"I cannot be a soldier; I cannot do evil; I am a Christian."

The Proconsul repeated the order to measure him. It was done and
an assistant announced — "Five feet and ten inches."

"Mark him," continued the Proconsul. A conscript, when he had
been accepted, was stamped on the flesh with a red-hot iron with the
initial of the emperor, and a leaden seal carrying the imperial effigy
was hung around his neck.

Maximilian only replied, "I cannot be a soldier."

Marveling at his obstinate refusal, the Proconsul became angry.
"Be a soldier, or die."

"I cannot be a soldier. Cut off my head; I cannot be a soldier of
this world. I must serve only under my God."

"Who has given you these ideas?"

"My soul and he who has called me."

The Proconsul then turned to the boy's father: "Persuade your son,"
he ordered. But the father did not want to enter into the matter for,
almost certainly, he approved of his son's resolution.

He replied, "He has a mind of his own; he knows what he is doing."

The Proconsul turned once more to the son.

"You must be a soldier and accept the seal" (of the emperor).

"I will not accept it. I already have the seal of Christ, my God."

"I will send you straight to your Christ."

"Do it immediately. It will be my glory."

"Mark him," ordered the Proconsul. The assistants took hold of him but he fought back shouting:

"I will not receive the seal of the world. If you put it around my neck I will break it, for I put no value on it. I am a Christian; I cannot carry a leaden seal at my neck for I already carry the sacred seal of Christ."

The Proconsul continued to insist and urged that many of the soldiers were Christians.

"In the sacred company of our lords Diocletian and Maximian, Constantius and Maximum [i.e., Galerius] there are Christian soldiers and they are not afraid to fight."

"They do what they think is right. As far as I am concerned I am a Christian and cannot do evil."

"Do those who fight in our armies do evil therefore?"

"You know what they do."

Further persuasion and threats of death failed to move the conscript. The Proconsul then had his name canceled on the register and turning to him pronounced sentence:

"Since *indevoto animo* [with disloyal spirit] you have refused military service you will be punished as an example to others."

He then read the sentence from the book — "Maximilian, who has been found guilty of insubordination by not accepting military service, will be punished by the sword."

Maximilian replied, "*Deo gratias.*"

He was taken immediately to the place of execution and when he arrived there turned to the other Christians and said: "My dearest brethren, hasten with all your strength and desire to gain the vision of God and to merit a similar crown." Then smiling, he asked his father to give his new uniform as a conscript to the executioner. He was immediately beheaded. A matron called Pompeiana had the body transported on her own litter to Carthage where it was buried near the tomb of St. Cyprian. His father, Victor, returned home full of joy and thanking God for what had happened.

43. The martyrdom of Marcellus took place in Mauretania Tingitana at the extreme west of Mediterranean Africa. There, in a year which is doubtful but probably around 298, in the city of Tingis (Tangiers)

the birthday of Maximian was being celebrated. It was a good opportunity for bringing the hidden Christians into the open and presenting them with the alternative of adoring the gods or abandoning their military careers; this "screening" of the army had now made it obligatory for all soldiers to take part in the normal pagan functions on such occasions, whereas before little importance had been given to such participation (par. 31). Unlike Maximilian who had not yet been enrolled, Marcellus had been a soldier for many years and had become a centurion in the Trajan legion. (This legion was garrisoned in Egypt but Marcellus had probably been seconded for service in Mauretania.) In the midst of the adoration of the idols and the sacrificial banquets, Marcellus, instead of offering incense in the tripods, flung his belt to the ground before the legionary eagles exclaiming, "I am a soldier of Jesus Christ." He then threw away his staff of vine plant which was the insignia of a centurion declaring: "If to be a soldier means sacrificing to gods and emperors, behold I cast away my staff and belt and do not wish to serve." This was a serious act, both because of Marcellus' rank and because of its public nature. He was conducted to the prefect of the legion, Fortunatus, who put him under arrest and when the festivities were over sent him to Agricolanus, vicar of the prefects of the praetorian guard. The trial was not held until later, for the offense occurred at the beginning of August whereas the interrogation did not take place until October 30.

The trial, presided over by Agricolanus, began with the reading of the details of the offense sent in by Fortunatus.

"This soldier, throwing away his military belt declared himself a Christian and uttered many blasphemies against the gods and against Caesar. . . ."

When the charge had been read, Agricolanus turned to the accused: "Did you say the words reported by the Prefect in his letter?"

"I did."

"You serve as an ordinary centurion?"

"I do."

"What madness was it that made you refuse the military oath and speak in such a way?"

"Among those who fear the Lord there is no madness."

"Did you say all those things which are mentioned in this report?"

"I did."

"Did you throw away your arms?"

"I did. It is not right for a Christian who serves in the army of the Lord Christ to serve also in worldly armies (or troubles)."

The interrogation was thus ended and Agricolanus concluded by saying, "The conduct of Marcellus must be punished according to military law."

The sentence followed. "Marcellus who served as an ordinary centurion publicly refused to take the oath; said that it was foul and has uttered other words full of madness referred to in the report of the Prefect; we order that he be executed by the sword."

44. But this was not all, for the trial had a sequel. The secretary of the tribunal was a certain Cassian who was probably a Christian. The calm, serene replies of the accused disturbed the secretary and when he heard the sentence he was so moved that he flung down his tablet and pencil. He was immediately rebuked by Agricolanus for his action; he replied:

"You have pronounced an unjust sentence."

Marcellus was taken to execution; and as he passed in front of Agricolanus he said to him: *"Deus tibi bene faciat."* He was martyred on the same day, October 30.

Cassian was put in prison and remained there until December 3 when he was taken before the same Agricolanus, tried and executed.

Cassian was mentioned also by Prudentius (*Peristephanon, iv, 45*), but the story of his martyrdom was probably written later than that of Marcellus and by a different author who noticed the absence of any mention of the secretary in the story of the centurion and wished to remedy this.

45. No lawyer of the times would have regarded the sentences against Maximilian the conscript, Marcellus the centurion, or Cassian the secretary as illegal. A judge who gives sentence does not make the law but applies it. Undoubtedly the military laws under which these judgments were given were of great age. But the legal saying — *Summum ius, summa iniuria* — still had force. The real *iniuria* — the moral offense — had been committed by him who only a little before had made obligatory the participation of all soldiers in idolatrous ceremonies so that Christian soldiers could be discovered and punished. The obligation of such participation, which was quite reasonable in the days of a completely pagan republic, was an immoral stricture when the army was full of Christians, and this immorality was so obvious that enforcement of the obligation had been relaxed (par. 31). The reimposition of this old custom was a step backward, not forward, in the development of the law, for it took no account of the present situation and attempted a government with the uses and laws of some centuries before. The supreme author of this tragic anachronism was, without doubt, Galerius, the instigator of the persecution. But even he in the last months of his life realized his dreadful mistake and rather tardily attempted to put matters right (pars. 153–155).

4. The Storm Breaks

46. Galerius had now begun his persecution, but in his opinion it was going too slowly and the results were not very striking. The screening of the army had led to the expulsion of only some of the Christians, for no purge had been ordered in the territories of Constantius Chlorus, and there was little being done in the other regions. Besides this, those who had been expelled or degraded were generally very good soldiers and the worst effects of this injustice were felt by the Army and, ultimately, the Empire. The persecution must, therefore, dig deeper and put the ax to the root, taking the life from the tree of Christianity so completely that it could never live again.

Diocletian was opposed to doing this and Galerius knew it. The chief Augustus was extremely reluctant to pass laws which would entail wholesale bloodshed, and although he had issued some anti-Christian edicts, their effect was limited to his court and army, and the punishment of death was never envisaged (par. 38). Until Galerius could overcome this reluctance of Diocletian the extermination of Christianity was impossible. It was necessary, therefore, to work on his master, to bypass his authority when possible, and, finally, to persuade him to conquer his foolish sentiments.

On his return from the East, Diocletian passed the winter, 302–303, in his beloved Nicomedia; there Galerius joined him and immediately got to work on him. Their discussion was very secret and it was lengthened by a grim desire to prevail on the one side and a firm resolve not to give in on the other. During these weeks Lactantius was in Nicomedia and he describes what was going on in the following words:

"The rulers deliberated between themselves the whole of the winter and since no audiences were granted whatever, the general opinion was that some very important imperial matter was being discussed. The old man Diocletian fought back against the hatred (of Christians) in the heart of the other, making clear how great a disaster this disturbance of the world and shedding of blood would be. He insisted that it would be enough to ban this religion for officials in the court and for the Army. He did not manage, however, to break down the obstinacy of that furious man and finally decided to seek further advice from his friends. . . . A few magistrates and soldiers were therefore invited and their opinion asked in their order. Some were filled with hate and urged that the enemies of the gods and of the religion of the State should be destroyed, while others, although they did not share this hate, since they wished to please the Emperor or because they were afraid, advised the general persecution" (*De mortibus persecut.*, 11).

47. Diocletian was still undecided and after this consultation insisted on consulting the oracle of Apollo Didymoeus at Miletus. An haruspex was sent off and since the god Apollo was aware of the opinion of the all-powerful Galerius, the forthcoming oracle was hostile to the Christians (cf. Lactantius, *op. cit.*; Eusebius, *De Vita Constantini*, 11, 50–51). But even then Diocletian continued with his moderate policy; there was persecution indeed but no blood was shed. Galerius, however, wanted "all those who refused to sacrifice to be burnt alive" (Lactantius, *op. cit.*).

An edict was prepared reflecting the desires of Diocletian and, for the moment, Galerius was satisfied knowing that with this beginning other provisions would be issued more in accordance with his own wishes. The edict affected churches, writings, and the Christian people, but did not contain any penalty of death. Christians, even if they held important posts, were to be stripped of all their privileges and put to the torture. They were forbidden to defend themselves on any charge in the public courts or to make official complaints of injuries, adultery, or theft. If they were slaves, they lost the right of emancipation. The churches were to be demolished and the sacred books burned.

The edict was posted up in Nicomedia on February 24, but its execution began the day before. This was a day of good fortune and it could not be missed — the celebration in honor of the god Terminus who held sway over the boundaries of fields and properties and therefore was a good symbol of the end of Christianity, now shut in by the boundaries of death. Very early in the morning a strong force of troops with tribunes and officials of the Treasury attacked the church of Nicomedia; they broke down the doors and burst in where "they burned all the books of the scriptures they could find and, ranging over the whole of the building, ravaged and looted everything. Diocletian and Galerius were watching all this from a high window — for the church was in sight of the royal palace — and they discussed whether to set the church on fire or not, but Diocletian feared that so great a fire might spread to other buildings" (Lactantius, op. cit., 12). The praetorian guard came, therefore, and with picks and axes leveled the whole edifice in a few hours.

48. On the following day the edict was published giving legal backing to the events of the day before.

The edict had not been up for long when a Christian pulled it down and tore it in pieces. This was certainly a courageous deed — as Lactantius rightly observes — but it did not even serve to show what Christians thought about the new law for this was already general knowledge. The daring Christian — whose name remains unknown — was arrested and tortured over a slow fire; he was finally burned alive. He bore his sufferings with great courage. The heads of the Christian community, however, did not approve of what he had done. Remembering earlier persecutions, they urged the people to remain calm and either to hide or to seek safety in flight. They realized only too well how foolish and dangerous it would be to meet force with force and they feared that many of their people might not be ready to face the heroic death of a martyr.

A little later a curious thing happened. Part of the imperial palace was destroyed by fire. Eusebius cannot tell us the cause of the fire (cf. Hist. Eccl., viii, 6, 6); Constantine speaks of a "thunderbolt" and "heavenly fire" (Ad sanctorum coetum, 25); Lactantius has no hesitation in accusing Galerius of ordering his men to start the fire so that the Christians could be blamed for it (cf. De mortibus persecut., 14). If the usual judicial rule — that the unknown author of a crime must have some motive for his act (is fecit cui prodest) — is valid in this case, then Galerius cannot be exonerated. Whatever may have been the truth of the affair, he certainly made the best of it and accused the Christians of plotting with the palace servants to start the fire. The old Augustus was terror-stricken and accepted the explanation of his Caesar; he ordered a strict inquiry to be instituted with free use of rack and fire. Diocletian himself examined and gave judgment from the tribunal and ordered the same to be done by other magistrates. Nevertheless, "nothing was discovered for none of the servants of the Caesar were condemned (to the torture)" (cf. Lactantius, *ibid.*). These servants of Galerius probably knew quite a lot and were in danger of betraying their master if they were tortured; quite prudently, therefore, they were exempted from this.

Another very providential happening saved this inquiry from petering out; the imperial palace was on fire once more and, as before, no cause could be determined. Galerius, who meanwhile "had not ceased to inflame the madness of the unthinking old man [Diocletian]" (*ibid.*), made a great show of how frightened he himself was and, although it was the middle of winter, left the same day to find somewhere where he would be safe. This had the double advantage of making a vigorous impression on Diocletian and giving Galerius a perfectly reasonable excuse to remove his personal servants whose tongues might have wagged — especially under torture.

49. This time the plans of Galerius succeeded. Left alone in his palace, Diocletian was filled with terror and eyed everyone with the utmost suspicion. Wherever he went he saw plots and intrigue and everyone around him was viewed as a possible traitor. To defend himself, he fell back on cruelty and torture. His wife Prisca and Valeria his daughter, who were at least sympathetic toward the Christians (par. 31), were the first to be faced with the grim alternative of either sacrificing to the gods or dying; they chose the first and lived.

No surrender was given by Dorotheus and Gorgonius (par. 31), and they were executed. Peter, the trusted chamberlain, died a terrible death. It is described by Eusebius: "Since he had refused [to sacrifice] he was hung up naked and whipped on all parts of his body so that he might consent even though such surrender was against his will. The executioners were unable to shake his constancy and they then poured salt and vinegar over his torn body in many parts of which the bones were now protruding. Peter was still immovable in his decision and so they dragged a cooking stove under him and began to roast what was left of his body over a slow fire. They did this so that the torture would be even more prolonged and thus a chance given him to surrender. To enhance their chances still further, they roasted only a small part of him at a time giving him plenty of time to consider his position. Those who were torturing him were ordered to continue until he surrendered. He conquered these dreadful torments however and gave up his spirit without once being shaken in his fortitude. Such was the death of one of the imperial servants. He was indeed worthy of his name — Peter" (*Hist. Eccl.*, viii, 6, 2–4).

50. Once the cataracts were opened, the flood of persecution poured through the city and its territories. One of the first to suffer was Anthimus, Bishop of Nicomedia, who was beheaded (*ibid.*, viii, 6, 6). A great part of his flock followed the pastor; here also we can listen to contemporary testimony: "Priests and ministers were arrested and without any crime or confession were condemned and taken with all their families to execution. People of both sexes and of all ages were cast into fire; not one at a time but whole groups of them were bound together and burned; slaves were flung into the sea with a great stone tied to their necks. The persecution raged with no less violence over the other citizens. The magistrates were positioned in the various temples and everyone was forced to offer sacrifice. The prisons were full to overflowing while new kinds of torture were an hourly invention. Lest justice should be inadvertently administered to a Christian, altars were put up in the law courts and before the tribunals so that the participants in trials could offer sacrifice before their causes were discussed" (Lactantius, *De mortibus persecut.*, 15).

Those who had been executed were not forgotten by the law. By Roman law even criminals were allowed to be buried in tombs, but since in this case such burial places might become objects of veneration for their coreligionists, even the bodies of the high officials of the court who had recently been executed and buried, were exhumed and flung into the sea (cf. Eusebius, *Hist. Eccl.*, viii, 6, 7).

51. Diocletian did not confine his precautions to his own territories and those of his Caesar Galerius but sent letters to the other Augustus, Maximinian, and his Caesar, Constantius, ordering them to follow his example. Maximinian had already begun to persecute on his own authority (par. 40) and now merely intensified his drive against the Christians. Constantius, however, was a mild man and not given to pagan fanaticism (par. 11), and so under his rule affairs were quite different. He read the letters of Diocletian with the air of a junior officer receiving unpleasant orders from his colonel; he could not very well disobey openly but found means to avoid imposing the worst strictures. As Lactantius says: "Constantius did not wish to seem to be opposed to the orders of his superior and so allowed buildings to be destroyed which could be built again but did not destroy Chris-

tians who were the true temples of God" (*De mortibus persecut.*, 15).

Eusebius goes further than this and denies that Constantius pulled down churches (cf. *Hist. Eccl.*, viii, 13, 13; cf. Appendix 4), but here the imperial historian shows himself overkind or less informed for it seems that martyrs were not lacking even in Gaul; violence toward Christians and their churches, however, was probably isolated and sporadic arising from the enthusiasm of local governors, whom Constantius for the sake of good relations with his Augustus, would have notified of the edict of Nicomedia without pressing for its execution. It is fairly certain that no official searches for the Sacred Scriptures were made and no copies were destroyed.

52. The persecution, in full swing, was indirectly influenced by certain political events. Eusebius says rather briefly that very soon after the beginning of the persecution in Nicomedia, two attempts were made to usurp the imperial power, one in the region called Melitene, in Cappadocia, and the other in Syria (cf. *Hist. Eccl.*, viii, 6, 8).

The Melitene mentioned by Eusebius is Armenia Minor which stretched to the east of Cappadocia. No other contemporary writer speaks of a revolution there during this period. The revolt in Syria was led by Eugenius, a tribune who was in command of the soldiers working on the port of Seleucia. They were exhausted with their labors and urged Eugenius to take on the purple and proclaim himself emperor; a threat of instant death was needed before Eugenius agreed. His empire did not last very long. When he had taken rather unwilling residence in the imperial palace of Antioch, the people of the town, who did not approve of mutiny, rose up against him and his small bodyguard and killed them.

We have no ground for supposing that the revolt in Syria — much less so than that in Melitene — arose from the exasperation of Christians with the persecution. The quick and harsh reaction of Diocletian, in which all the magistrates of Antioch and Seleucia lost their heads, shows that the Emperor made no distinction of religion, for most of the victims were pagans. Diocletian, however, who was still suffering from fright after the double arson in the palace of Nicomedia, soon saw the hand of the Christians in these new troubles and decided to intensify the persecution.

In that same year, 303, two new edicts were published at Nicomedia, which brought fresh troubles on the Christians. The first ordered that all heads of churches should be imprisoned; the second allowed them their freedom if they would sacrifice to the gods and commanded that all kinds of tortures should be inflicted on those who refused (Eusebius, op. cit., viii, 6, 8–10).

These new edicts did not simply remain on the statute book but were rigorously applied. Eusebius, speaking about territories he knew well — Nicomedia, Syria, Phoenicia, and Egypt — said: "Everywhere numberless people were imprisoned; jails which had been built for murderers and violators of tombs were now so full of bishops, priests, deacons, lectors and exorcists that there was no longer room for common criminals. . . . No one can say how many suffered martyrdom in the various provinces. The persecution was especially severe in Africa and Mauretania, in the Thebaid and in Egypt. From this last place some moved on to other cities and became famous in their death" (ibid., viii, 6, 9–10).

53. If we are to be impartial, however, we must not just describe the highlights. There were thousands of heroes. There were also many weakhearted renegades.

Eusebius spoke of this only in passing, since his object was not to tell everything in detail but to show the splendors of Christianity without the miseries of the Christians. "We have decided not to mention those who failed the test of persecution nor those who made a total shipwreck of their salvation and of their own will were buried in the depth of the abyss" (ibid., viii, 2, 3).

Speaking of the heads of churches — that is the bishops — Eusebius says that very many ($\pi\lambda\epsilon\tilde{\iota}\sigma\tau o\iota$) conducted themselves heroically but that a large number of the others ($\mu\upsilon\rho\acute{\iota}o\iota$ $\delta'\check{\alpha}\lambda\lambda o\iota$), weakened by the spirit of sloth, surrendered at the first difficulty (cf. ibid., viii, 3–1).

These defections were to be expected psychologically and are not unexpected historically when their causes are inspected more fully; many Oriental Christian communities were in a sad condition of decadence. This also is noted briefly by Eusebius:

"As always happens when there is abundance of liberty our lives became indolent and careless; we envied one another and did harm to our brethren; any wretched excuse was sufficient to start a war of arms — as it were — with the spearthrust of words; leaders poured ill fame on other leaders; nation rose against nation; pretence and damned hypocrisy seemed to reach the limit of their evil height. . . . Like senseless people we did not trouble to make our God propitious and benevolent toward us but like certain atheists who consider that human affairs are neither guided nor watched over (by God) we piled wickedness on wickedness. Those who were supposed to be our pastors disdained the paths of divine piety and inflamed their hearts in contests one with another, only adding thus to the quarrels and threats, the rivalry, the envies and hates of the times. They filled their time in striving for position in no different a manner from the princes of this world" (*ibid.*, viii, 1, 7–8).

Eusebius refers elsewhere to the bad behavior of the bishops but in a rather vague way and thereby he annoys his modern reader. He says, for example, that certain pastors of souls having neglected their spiritual flocks were given by the justice of God to feed the camels and keep the horses of the imperial posthouses (cf. *De martyrib. Palaest.*, xii). From what one can gather from such sibylline words it seems that there were bishops who had been unworthy of their position before the persecution and who had fallen when it broke out; in this way they saved their necks but were despised by their judges as worthless renegades and were given the wretched jobs of camelkeepers, ostlers, and the like. Eusebius in the same place makes other references to various abuses which happened before and during the persecution — illegitimate ordinations, schisms, arbitrary innovations, and so on — but once more he restricts himself to the narration of worthy deeds and refuses to expose the full nakedness of such shame.

54. Clearly, these disorders in the churches and the negligence of their pastors were really graver than would appear from the reluctant admission of Eusebius. For once further information can be obtained from the disciplinary canons decreed by the council held at Elvira (Elliberis) near Granada in Spain about the year 300 just before the persecution began. We can discover quite a deal about the abuses current in the churches by the remedies proposed by this council for the Iberian peninsula.

Turning over the pages of the decrees we find that bishops, priests, and deacons are forbidden to leave their residences for the sake of commerce or to frequent public markets; clerics must not practice usury; no women must live in the houses of bishops or clerics except for a sister or a daughter who must be virgins consecrated to the Lord; idolatrous worship may not be offered by the baptized faithful; Christians are not allowed to place money *ad aleam id est tabulam*, that is, on games of chance; the Christian woman who has separated from her husband because of his adultery may not marry another;

the wife who in the absence of her husband has conceived in adultery and then committed infanticide is to be punished very severely for her double crime; young Christians guilty of fornication must do adequate penance before they marry; the daughters of Christians must not be given in marriage to pagan priests.

This list could be continued but what we have mentioned is sufficient to show how far from the Christian ideal both bishops and people had fallen. The cause of this cannot be other than the long peace which had been enjoyed by Christianity — the same easy circumstances which, according to Eusebius, had been the reason for slackness in the East. True, the canons of Elvira were intended to meet a situation in the extreme West, but in view of the information given us by Eusebius about the East, the difference between the two regions was probably very small. In fact, the West was probably in better heart, for the Spanish provisions seemed to be aiming for a severity which could not even be hoped for in the East.

We cannot be surprised, therefore, that under these conditions the number of waverers and apostates was large when a cruel persecution suddenly overwhelmed them.

55. The third edict of 303 was not the last. This dreadful year for the Christians was drawing to a close when on September 17 Diocletian entered on the twentieth year of his rule. To last for twenty years as emperor was an extraordinary achievement in those times when everyone could remember the dreadful years of the "thirty tyrants" (par. 1), and it was decided to mark the day with special celebrations — that is, by the "vicennials." Diocletian decided to combine these festivities with his own triumph and that of his colleague Maximian and further decreed that all this should take place at Rome. Some years before this, the Senate had traveled to Milan to pay their respects to Diocletian and to invite him to conduct his triumph in their city, but nothing had come of this for the chief Augustus had always disliked the city of the seven hills. Now he seems to have overcome his feelings and the solemn celebration was held on November 20 (cf. Lactantius, *De mortibus persecut.*, 17).

The military procession to the capitol was very impressive. Great enthusiasm was evoked by the trophies of Diocletian's victorious campaigns in all parts of the Empire; from Persia to Africa; from Egypt to the Rhine; from the Rhine to Britain. There were representations of territories and cities conquered by the armies of the two Augusti, and hard on these came important citizens of those countries now in the chains of slavery or else typical representatives of the races of different lands. Veterans of the principal campaigns marched on both sides of the procession which was closed by the two Augusti themselves clothed in purple and flashing their jewels in the clear Roman air. To the spectators they seemed like two divinities on a visit from Mount Olympus.

One of the two divinities was tired and unhappy. Diocletian was visibly out of sorts.

The inevitable games in the circus followed, presided over by Diocletian, but the Roman people did not think them as sumptuous as usual; the chief Augustus was indeed saving money. This economy did not please them since it was a tradition that no money should be spared in the entertainments of the circus, and their discontent was soon communicated to Diocletian who became more depressed than ever and soon found living in Rome unbearable. Probably because of his indifferent health, his depression began to show symptoms of madness and though only thirteen days lacked to his formal acceptance of the ninth consulate, on January 1, 304, he left without warning for Ravenna, although by now it was the depth of winter and very cold and wet (Lactantius, op. cit., 17). Although he made most of the journey in a litter, his health deteriorated and he contracted an incurable — but not serious — disease. In Ravenna he accepted his ninth consulate and then began his travels again. Very slowly, with many halts, he came down the coast of Dalmatia and at the end of the following summer he arrived at Nicomedia where he finally fell gravely ill.

56. Very solemn celebrations such as the vicennials usually included a general amnesty and according to the testimony of Eusebius (De Martyrib. Palaest, ii, 4) liberty was given on this occasion also "to all captives everywhere." The literal meaning of these words would mean that even the Christians who had been imprisoned for their faith were released. It may be, however, that Eusebius means that mercy was shown to prisoners who had been found guilty of common crimes and not to the Christians who in the eyes of the law were traitors who undermined the authority of the State — delinquents not yet sentenced and still perpetrating their crime. As it is, Eusebius mentions the amnesty and then immediately continues with a description of the imprisonment and martyrdom of the deacon Romanus.

Hence, even if the amnesty was applied to the Christians, it is certain that it did not last very long and the persecution was resumed with more ferocity than before.

Behind all this was Galerius, who had really begun the persecution in the first place. From the time of his departure from Ravenna, Diocletian had had little to do with the government of the empire because of his bad health and the length of his time on the road. For this reason, the direction of affairs passed into the hands of his Caesar Galerius, who needed no prompting to attempt to increase his own powers in the tetrarchy and the evidences of his hate for the Christians. The ferocious Caesar now became the most important ruler of the Empire *de facto* and it was not to be long before this post was his *de iure*.

His hand can be seen in the new edict of persecution issued in the spring of 304 for it was the expression of what he had obviously long wanted to do. This edict was even more severe than those of the year before and seemed to draw its inspiration from the bloody decrees of Decius. While the earlier edicts had dealt only with certain categories of persons, this law of 304 was directed against all Christians without distinction. Any Christian, whatever his age, sex, or position, was now obliged to offer sacrifice to the gods. The infamous sect of the Christians which threatened the Empire and despised the gods must now be seen no more and die; in the whole of the Roman Empire there was to be no person who had not sacrificed to its gods.

The execution of the edict began immediately in all the provinces of the Empire except in those ruled by Constantius where, as before (par. 51), little or no attention was paid to the now fashionable terror and bloodshed. While the Empire was busy killing its own citizens with Galerius as butcher-in-chief, the latter did not forget his personal aspirations. He had destined himself to be the first among the dynasts of the tetrarchy.

5. Changes in the Tetrarchy

57. When Diocletian finally got to Nicomedia he was only a shadow of his real self; he was sick in body and in mind. During the autumn he grew worse. In December he was carried to the inauguration of the grandiose circus which he had built to add to the beauties of the

city, but the ceremonial of the formal opening was too much for him and he was taken back to his palace a dying man. News went around that he was actually dead and, despite frequent official denials, many believed that the news was being kept back to avoid trouble in the army and to allow Galerius time to get to Nicomedia whither he had been called. Suspicions did not finally clear until the beginning of March, 305, when the old Augustus once more appeared in public. He had been so changed by the year of sickness that he was recognized with difficulty. Diocletian was still a very sick man. Lactantius says that he was "so weak that at times he was really insane, and at other times was master of his senses" (De mortibus persecut., 17).

A man in such a condition would not put up much of a fight against his eager Caesar whose only interest in his master was the way in which he could take his place. Galerius paid him a visit and, having congratulated him on his recovery, began to lead the conversation toward a possible abdication. Here again Lactantius (op. cit., 18) gives us some interesting details. Galerius apparently had already informed the other Augustus, Maximian, that in the event of Diocletian's abdication he would be expected to do the same, adding that Maximian would probably prefer this to civil war. He spoke gently to Diocletian pointing out that he was getting on in years, had lost his physical powers, and was really incapable of keeping the reins of government in his own hands; he ended his talk with a suggestion that the Augustus could do with a well-merited rest.

The Augustus objected that to put away his high dignity would not only be indecorous, but also dangerous since after so long a rule there were many who hated him and would seek their revenge. In an attempt to conciliate the ambition of his Caesar, he showed himself willing to concede the title of Augustus to him and, therefore, also to Constantius, the other Caesar. But Galerius was not simply looking for titles and insisted that the distinction between Augusti and Caesars should be retained according to the system which had already been set up. He added that whereas two people could usually manage to agree, this would become impossible if there were four dynasts with equal powers. The old Augustus was not to be persuaded in this way and so Galerius changed tactics and began to threaten; he would soon find a way of not remaining the least important of all despite his having spent fifteen years fighting the barbarians in Illyria and along the Danube while others were governing rich and tranquil territories at their ease. Diocletian was horrified at such threats, especially as they confirmed letters he had received recently from Maximian, telling him that Galerius was building up his army with the intention of forcing the abdication of the two Augusti. The old man was weak and wandering; he burst into tears and agreed to everything.

58. Arrangements for the take-over of power were made with every secrecy. Diocletian and Maximian were to abdicate at the same time and their places — according to the constitutional rules of the tetrarchy (par. 12) — would be taken by their respective Caesars, Galerius and Constantius. But when it came to choosing the new Caesars, Galerius already had candidates for both places. By the rules, the office of Caesar should have been given to Maxentius, the son of Maximian and son-in-law of Galerius, and to Constantine, the son of Constantius; but for different reasons neither of these young men was acceptable to Galerius who wanted members of his own gang for Caesars. He, therefore, forced through the nomination of Severus, a general who was much attached to him and even more to wine and debauchery; and of his own nephew, a certain Daia or Daza, a great beast of a barbarian who had lately begun calling himself Maximin so as to have something Roman about him. Severus was to be the Caesar of Constantius, and Maximin Daia, that of Galerius. Diocletian was horrified at these nominations and complained to Galerius: "You have not proposed men worthy of governing the state." Galerius reassured him: "I know them better than you do." Diocletian's eyes filled with tears and he replied, "You will soon know more when you have taken supreme power. I have labored long and done all I could to keep the Empire together during my office. If things go wrong now, the fault will be all yours."

These words were a kind of prophecy. The old Augustus, at the point of relinquishing the power which later he was to refuse to take on again, feared for the stability of the building he had erected with such loving care. Despite his mistakes — and the greatest of those was that he had been persuaded against his will to persecute the Christians — Diocletian had restored the Empire to its old unity with a loyal and sincere heart; now the whole edifice was rocking on its foundations and he was fearful of the future. What was to happen shows that this was no empty fear, even though things could not have turned out any other way, for his construction lacked a really solid foundation and would have stayed up only in the very unlikely case that all the subjects of the Empire were as loyal and sincere as Diocletian himself.

59. The change-over took place at the beginning of May, until which time the affair remained secret. Very much against his will, Maximian abdicated in Milan and Constantius became the new Augustus of the West. The abdication of Diocletian took place on the same day with a certain solemnity on a little hill three miles from the city of Nicomedia; on this same hill nineteen years before Maximian had received the purple from the hands of Diocletian (par. 5). Among the soldiers and their officers present at the ceremony was Constantine (par. 11), the son of Constantius, who resided in the court of the chief Augustus as a kind of hostage. This pleased the troops, who liked him for his bravery and nobility of manner. He was also appreciated by Diocletian who had elected him a tribune of the first order.

The old Augustus spoke briefly with tears in his eyes to the soldiers and announced that since he felt old and weary, he was now passing the burden of the Empire to stronger shoulders and that he would also elect new Caesars; the latter statement caused great excitement along the lines of troops and everybody looked at Constantine, expecting that he would be chosen as the Caesar of his father. To the general amazement, Severus and Daia were named as the new Caesars. Galerius moved smartly forward, bringing Daia with him and, in the sight of all, removed the garment of a private citizen from his Caesar's shoulders. In his turn, Diocletian took off his purple robe, threw it over the shoulders of Daia and, now as a common citizen, drove off in his coach to Salona, the town of his boyhood (305). There he built a magnificent villa and having cultivated the affairs of the Empire with loving care, now in his retirement, he transferred this care to growing cabbages.

Galerius had won, and to all intents and purposes he was now the master of the Empire. The new Caesars were his own men and the other Augustus, Constantius, did not give him much cause for worry for he lived a long way away in Britain and, in any case, had no grand ambitions. Constantius was in poor health and the kind fates would soon be at work with the shears, so that Galerius could put one of his own gang in his place.

60. Things did not work out quite so smoothly as Galerius had expected, for neither Constantine, the son of Constantius, nor

Maxentius, the son of Maximian, were particularly satisfied by the new arrangements which excluded them so completely.

After a little while, the illness of Constantius suddenly grew worse and he wrote to Galerius asking him to send Constantine to Britain so that he could see him for the last time. This put Galerius in a difficult position for he not only regarded the young man as a valuable hostage but saw in him the possibility of a dangerous rival. He had indeed tried on various occasions to dispose of him. Lactantius tells us (cf. *De mortibus persecut.*, 24) that with the excuse of providing exercise and diversion, Galerius had urged Constantine to pit himself against wild beasts in the public circus; and other historians speak of the singular feats of bravery and endurance performed by Constantine in military campaigns. There can be no doubt that Galerius would have liked to see the last of his young guest provided he did not go to live with his father. He therefore resorted to various stratagems to prevent his departure but a rapid turn for the worse in Constantius — and perhaps a certain sagacity in Constantine — made it impossible for Galerius to stop him. In a very short time Constantine was at his father's bedside (Lactantius, *ibid.*).

On July 25, 306, Constantius died at Eboracum (York). He left his wife, Theodora (par. 11), and, besides Constantine, six other children, three girls and three boys; the last, Julius Constantius, Dalmatius, and Hannibalianus, were still children. On his deathbed Constantius recommended his eldest son to the army where the gifted young man already enjoyed cordial sympathy. When the matter of succession arose, Constantine did not show himself eager but played the careful diplomat. He called a council of high-ranking officers to sound their opinions. They urged him to take on the purple left by his father and though this undoubtedly fitted in well with what he himself wanted, it would not have been legal, for by the rule of succession established by the tetrarchy, the Caesar should succeed the Augustus and Severus was the Caesar. Constantine put these difficulties to the meeting and sent the officers home without making any decision.

On the day of the funeral the dead father and living son were associated in the acclamations of the people, especially as the latter saw the features of the father in the son and were in admiration of his broader muscles. The soldiers, almost it seemed in obedience to some secret order, acclaimed him vigorously, the German auxiliaries under the command of Crocus shouted themselves hoarse; in the midst of all the shouting and huzzas, the bereaved son followed his father's coffin apparently thinking of nothing else. After the funeral he had to give in to the wishes of all, if only not to run the risk of being killed by the soldiers, as had happened before in the case of reluctant nominees (par. 52). Constantine now could maintain that he had been elected against his will and had accepted only to avoid disturbance and sedition. The army gave him the title of Augustus.

As a matter of practical wisdom, Constantine sent Galerius his effigy crowned with a laurel wreath to inform him of his election and to seek his recognition as an Augustus.

Galerius' first impulse was to burn the statue with its wreath and bearers, but he could not help noticing that his soldiers were already very discontented at the election of the two Caesars, Severus and Maximin Daia, and that they would be quite likely to side with Constantine in the event of war. So he was forced to disguise his anger and to content himself with the appointment of Severus as Augustus with Constantine as his Caesar. Constantine showed himself very diplomatic once more; he was not bothered over mere names. The question of what he should call himself could be settled at a more suitable time.

61. Like Constantine, Maxentius had been forgotten and he was very anxious to put this right when he saw that Constantine had got substantially what he wanted. A magnificent opportunity was put in his way by new and very severe fiscal provisions made by Galerius to fill the empty coffers of the Empire. Until now Rome had been exempted from such taxation but the new provisions applied to the whole of the Empire and were enforced rigidly and without exception. When the news got around that agents of the imperial treasury were on their way to Rome to make a census, the people of the city became angry and restive.

This was Maxentius' opportunity — he could put himself forward as the protector of the people and they would all support him. He won over Lucianus who supervised the distribution of victuals in the city and arranged a conspiracy for his own advancement, among members of the praetorian guard. In the streets the people began the riot and Abellius, the underprefect of the praetorians who was faithful to Severus, put up what resistance he could. He was murdered by some of his own men who were in the plot with Maxentius, and with the support of the rest of the praetorian guard Maxentius was proclaimed emperor immediately on October 27, 306. He quickly made it clear that so far as he was concerned the tetrarchy ceased to exist. The Roman Senate, which had allowed nominations of Augusti and Caesars to pass over its sleepy head, suddenly came to life once more and confirmed the proclamation of Maxentius with rather dusty pomp.

The assent of the Conscript Fathers was little help to Maxentius, if he could not offer some legal front to the tetrarchy. He decided to turn to his father Maximian who, after his unwilling abdication, had retired to a sumptuous villa of Lucania. There had been grave quarrels between father and son but in the present situation they could help each other; they both wanted power, and if they stood together one or other of them would get it. The son offered the purple officially to his father, and Maximian grasped at it, calling himself *bis Augustus* (Augustus for the second time). This intervention of Diocletian's old colleague was very valuable not only because by it Maxentius acknowledged the existence of the tetrarchy once more but also because Maximian still enjoyed great authority among the veterans. This influence was soon found useful.

62. Severus had been sent off with all speed by Galerius and he advanced on Rome by forced marches with an army formed mainly of Maximian's veterans. His object was to dispose of the usurper Maxentius and occupy Rome. The outcome was laughable. When the army reached the walls of the city, all the veterans deserted and joined the defenders — some out of respect for Maximian; and others out of love for the gold Maxentius had paid them. None would fight against their old leader and his bribe-dispensing son. Severus was left with only a few soldiers and he hurried off to shut himself up in Ravenna. Even there things went badly for him; by means of secret agents Maximian got him to believe that what soldiers he had left were plotting to betray him and hand him over to his enemies, and that he had better forestall them and give himself up on his own accord. This Severus finally did and was at first treated well by Maximian; when it became evident, however, that Galerius was going to take a personal hand in the affair, Severus committed suicide in February, 307. Thus departed one of the two official Augusti of the tetrarchy.

Galerius, the remaining Augustus, was furious at the turn events had taken and with a strong force of Illyrian troops moved off to finish the affair once and for all in person, to punish the traitors and save the threatened tetrarchy. The outcome of the campaign was as laughable as that of Severus. Galerius advanced into Italy avoiding strong points to save time and men and got as far as Terni before realizing that he had walked into a trap. The lands he had passed through were hostile and his lines of communication with bases in the East were almost nonexistent. Besides this, his Illyrian troops were deserting in greater numbers the nearer they approached the cause of their desertion — Maxentius' money. Galerius tried to treat with the enemy, but his message was dismissed in contempt. His soldiers began to desert in companies; he lost his nerve and, to avoid Severus' fate, began to retreat. During this retreat he allowed every excess to his men, both to retain their loyalty and to leave no supplies for a pursuing army. "That part of Italy where this wicked army passed was completely ruined. They stole everything, seduced the women and violated young girls; they forced fathers and husbands to hand over their daughters and wives and their property. Like the barbarians, they drove before them flocks and herds as booty." Such is the description of Lactantius (cf. De mortibus, 27).

63.   Meanwhile, Maximian was looking to his own affairs. He had never really trusted his son and he paid a visit to Constantine in Gaul on the pretext of giving him his daughter Fausta in marriage. While there he signed an alliance with his proposed son-in-law. In his own territories Constantine was bent on strengthening his position. Along the Rhine he had beaten back the Franks and the Alemanni and to celebrate the victory he held for several days the so-called "Frankish Games" where the principal spectacle was a meal made by wild beasts in the public circus of hundreds of gladiators who had been forcibly enrolled from barbarian prisoners. He kept a watchful neutrality in relation to the various dynasts of the tetrarchy. The Augusti, the Caesars, and the usurpers were fighting among themselves, making themselves weaker and Constantine relatively stronger.

Keeping in mind both this and the political authority still enjoyed by the onetime colleague of Diocletian, Constantine agreed to the treaty Maximian offered him. In order to marry Fausta, Constantine had to abandon a certain Minervina, the mother of his eldest son, Crispus. The marriage was celebrated with great solemnity and, after signing the treaty, the bridegroom received from his father-in-law the title of Augustus which had been denied him by Galerius (par. 60). Everything was now in legal order, for this nomination was from the man who had been Augustus when Galerius was only a Caesar. After this satisfactory settlement of affairs for both sides, Maximian returned to Rome.

Feeling that he was now in a stronger position he began to undermine, as far as he could, the authority of his son Maxentius. The old antipathy between father and son, forgotten for a time in the rush of events, now showed itself once more and increased daily. Jealousy hastened its growth, for both army and people preferred the son. Although he was dissolute in his habits Maxentius had labored hard to give Rome back some of her ancient glory. Without persecuting the Christians he reinstated some of the ancient local cults of paganism, restored buildings in the Forum and along the Via Sacra, and by the side of this famous road constructed the basilica whose remains are still admired (and serve excellently as a stage for symphonic concerts). Maximian was greatly angered by the popularity of his son and finally, at a public audience, he came to blows with him and tore off his purple garment. Maxentius managed to get away with the help of his faithful soldiers whose services he had retained by all kinds of bribery. The army were making plans to revenge the insult, when Maximian, seeing his danger, fled from Rome. Since Maxentius was now free of his father and since the Augustus Severus had conveniently died, he proclaimed himself Augustus on the anniversary of his nomination by the soldiers on October 27, 307.

64. With the increase in numbers of dynasts in the tetrarchy, confusion also increased. Hardly two years had passed since the abdication of Diocletian and there were already four Augusti — Galerius, Maximian, Constantine, Maxentius — and one Caesar (Maximin) all more or less hostile to one another. It became clear that it was Diocletian who had held the tetrarchy together and instinctively, like bewildered orphans, some of the dynasts called on him to act as father once more. A meeting was held at Carnuntum in Pannonia attended by Galerius, Maximian, and Diocletian.

Diocletian had been won over by the persistent pleas of Galerius and had agreed for the present to leave his retreat at Salona. But he would have nothing to do with the suggestion that he should take on his old post as Augustus to re-establish the tetrarchy in its old strength. He advised, however, that an intimate friend of Galerius, called Licinius, should be made Augustus in place of the dead Severus, and that Constantine and Maximin should be given the title of "Sons of Augusti." Maxentius as a rebel and usurper was left out altogether. Maximian had to give up the purple and as a small compensation was designated consul for the following year. With these decisions the meeting of Carnuntum closed on November 11, 308. As a result of these arrangements there was now another Augustus, Licinius, who ruled over Pannonia and nominally over Italy (this country was really dominated by Maxentius) but pretensions and rivalries were as plentiful as before.

Maxentius, who had been ignored at Carnuntum, also had his troubles. Rome depended on Africa for its supplies and now rebellion broke out there under a Phrygian general called Alexander; he proclaimed himself emperor and offered stout resistance to Maxentius (par. 156).

65. The restless Maximian was hardly content with second place and soon began to look for ways in which he could restore himself to his original position as Augustus. Quite naturally he turned to treachery. While he was thinking out ways and means he returned to Constantine, his son-in-law, by whom he was treated with respect and trust.

Constantine had to leave for the northeastern frontiers to hold off an invasion of the Franks; while he was away, Maximian attempted, by means of gifts paid for out of the imperial treasury, to win over the soldiers who had been left as a garrison. He was not very successful for the army was very devoted to Constantine and did not believe Maximian's rumors of Constantine's defeat on the borders. Constantine soon heard of this treachery, and breaking off his campaign returned with all his army before Maximian was ready for him. The latter, taken aback by the speed of Constantine's return, retired hurriedly to Arelate (Arles). Constantine was not satisfied and hurried on to Cabillonum (Châlons-sur-Saône) where he had already arranged transport for his army down the Saône and Rhone, and thus arrived before Arelate. Maximian equaled Constantine's speed by the haste in which he left Arelate and shut himself up in Massilia (Marseilles). Constantine soon arrived there too but found that he had to fall back on a siege of the town, for his army had no means of scaling the powerful walls.

Constantine now decided that in the absence of ladders he would scale the walls by psychology. The soldiers serving under Maximian were really in favor of Constantine and the latter spoke frequently with the men on the walls pointing out the foolishness and injustice of their conduct and exhorting them to be wise once more. The father-in-law also appeared on the parapets and Constantine invited him to reflect how completely unprovoked his treachery had been. While Maximian replied only with abuse, Constantine's words had an effect on the soldiers; they repented of their desertion and came out of the city gates as one man, acclaiming their old commander and assuring him of their future loyalty. Maximian was handed over to Constantine, who kept him with honor in his court but saw that his movements were carefully watched.

66.   The claws of Maximian were not all blunted as yet. Immediately after the affair at Massilia, Constantine returned to fight the barbarians on the Rhine. On his way he stopped at Augustodunum (Autun) which had been highly esteemed by his father (par. 21) but which, with the surrounding country, had fallen into the utmost poverty through the cruel taxation policy of Galerius (par. 61). There he held a meeting of the principal people of the city to find some way of permanently improving the conditions of the region. After this had been settled satisfactorily he offered sacrifice in the temple of Apollo (Sol) so that the god would look kindly on his approaching campaign and then set off for the Rhine. Maximian took advantage of his absence, and this time tried to draw Fausta, Constantine's wife, into his plans.

According to Lactantius (cf. De mortibus persecut., 30), Maximian, who promised his daughter a more likable husband, thought he had persuaded her to help him against Constantine who once again had suddenly appeared back from the frontier. All she had to do was to leave his bedroom door open and entice some of the guards away; Maximian would see to the rest. Fausta, however, informed her husband of the plan and between them they concerted a scheme which would bring Maximian's plotting out into the open. Fausta followed Maximian's suggestions, but a eunuch of little value took Constantine's place in her bed. In the middle of the night, Maximian passing through the depleted guard approached the bed and killed what he thought was his son-in-law. When he rushed out noisily proclaiming his success, Constantine with a body of soldiers took him prisoner. The body of the eunuch was brought out and the self-proclaimed murderer was allowed to choose the manner in which he would like to die. It appears he chose the gallows. It was February in the year 310.

67.   This was the official story of the end of Maximian which is given

by Lactantius and repeated in other records. How far it is really true and how much was fabricated to conceal the facts is not known. Quite a few of these carefully arranged stories circulated later in the court of Constantine; they cover such important matters as the disappearance of his son Crispus, and also that of the lady who played so great a part in the story we have related — his wife, Fausta.

After his death, Constantine decreed the *damnatio memoriae* of Maximian; this brought with it the destruction of anything which might recall the criminal, of statues, paintings, and inscriptions. But since Maximian had been the first colleague of Diocletian, the latter also appeared on many of the monuments scheduled for destruction and so Diocletian became involved in this condemnation. After his return to Salona, although he was still in retirement, he followed with understandable interest the fortunes of the Empire and his "tetrarchy" and when he heard that his own statues, pictures, and inscriptions were being destroyed he was distressed that, unlike any other emperors, he was forced to see in life the destruction of his own monuments. When this disgrace was added to the loss of Maximian — the only one who had remained faithful to him — the solitary of Salona seemed to lose his mind; he wept and raved, tossed on his couch and rolled on the floor, implored justice and the release of death (cf. Lactantius, *De mortibus persecut.*, 42). But the unfortunate old man was denied the peace of death for some years yet (par. 194).

II. THE GREAT PERSECUTION

1. *Historical Sources*

68. While the events of the preceding chapter were taking place the persecution had become even more oppressive. The three edicts of 303 (pars. 47, 52) had been supported and their application made wider and more cruel by the edict of 304 (par. 56), which decreed the punishment of death for all Christians without distinction. In practice — except for the territories of Constantius which had now passed to his son, Constantine, by whom the persecution was not really enforced (par. 51) — the carrying out of the edicts was backed by a severity which was more or less ruthless according to the character of the local governors.

The short accounts by Eusebius and Lactantius, which we have already seen, refer either to the purge in the army (par. 37 ff.) or to the effect of the first edicts (pars. 47 ff., 56). To know more we shall have to visit the different regions of the Empire and see what has been happening in them; in this long journey we must be guided by trustworthy historical documents. Many stories of what happened during this persecution have indeed come down to us through the centuries, but great trust cannot always be put in their veracity. They sound very much like the stories put out by the Roman *ciceroni* who until the end of the past century used to take foreign visitors around their city and give vibrant descriptions of the slaughter of the early Christians which were unhistorical and highly imaginative. We must, therefore, make a careful examination of the documents which have come down to us and separate those which are at least substantially historical from those which have little or no value.

Apart from secondary sources which give us some information on isolated incidents in the Great Persecution, the principal historical sources are Eusebius of Caesarea, Lactantius, and the *Acts* or *Passions of the Martyrs*. We shall deal with these sources in this chapter.

69. We can assume *a priori* that an upheaval such as a great persecution would have led to many written accounts, put down either at the time or shortly after it. A Christian venerated by his brethren for his sanctity or honored for his learning by the pagans suffers martyrdom. Important officials in the civil government or members of illustrious families well known for their liberality and goodness shed their blood under the cruel edicts; and it would be only natural that their sad death should be celebrated by Christians with some account of their end to keep their memory alive among their friends and fellow Christians.

Very often, indeed, the nucleus of these short accounts already existed in the word-for-word transcription of the interrogation which the martyr underwent before the pagan judge. According to Roman procedure, this transcription was deposited in the archives of the court where it would not have been difficult to obtain a copy either by knowing the right people or by greasing the palm of some favorable civil servant. At the beginning of one *Passion* we read that the unknown author got a copy of the interrogation for two hundred silver pence (cf. *Acta SS. Tarachi, Probi et Andronici*, preface; cf. however par. 133). On other occasions the trial could be given with substantial fidelity from the information obtained from those who actually assisted at it.

When the public confession which the martyr had made of Christ had been obtained in one way or another, other information could be added by the author — the tortures to which he was subjected, his manner of death and burial, how he came to be arrested in the first place, the length or the cruelty of his imprisonment, and so on. The narration which resulted from all this was of interest not only to the relatives and friends of the martyr, but also to the Christian community or "church" to which he belonged. These communities kept such accounts with great care and much pride, and gave them their official approval. In some of the African churches the public liturgy included reading from some such *Acts* or *Passions* after the reading of Sacred Scripture; the result was that since these *Acts* of the martyrs of Africa were supervised by the church authorities from the beginning they have a much greater historical value than *Acts* written in other parts of the Empire.

70. Clearly, the authors of these writings had not only to be animated by a deep interest in their subject, but to be persons of culture and ability. Speaking in general, the ideal would have been that each church or group of churches should have chosen a suitable writer and given him the task of drawing up the *Acts* of his own region. During the heat of the persecution, however, this would have been impossible and when the persecution was over, other interests — not all spiritual and otherworldly — grew large and damped down the old enthusiasm for the fallen heroes.

There were some willing scribes, however, among whom first place must be given to Eusebius of Caesarea. When he was explaining the scope of his work he first mentioned the martyrs of Egypt and the Thebaid and then continued as follows: "To put down in writing the battles of those who in all parts of the world have fought their way by piety toward divine things and to give an accurate account of the several incidents in their struggle is not my task but that of those who were actual witnesses of the events. In regard to those, however, at whose side I stood I shall write another book which will describe their courage even to another generation" (*Hist. Eccl.*, viii, 13, 7).

Eusebius kept this promise in his *Historia Ecclesiastica* by his next work — *The Martyrs of Palestine* — where he fulfills excellently his self-imposed role as historian of the persecution.

The program suggested here by Eusebius was as serious as it was honest. Everybody should, in the interest of his own region, write down what he had seen with his own eyes and in this way historically accurate stories would be available. The union of all these particular narratives into a general history of the persecution would provide something which was impossible for any single author. Unfortunately, though the program was carried out by Eusebius for his own area, no volunteers came forward anywhere else.

EUSEBIUS

71. Eusebius, Bishop of Caesarea, was born in Palestine about the year 265 and passed the first forty years of his life in that peace which the Church enjoyed toward the end of the third century. He liked study, especially of history, and found copious material for his researches in the very well-stocked library of Caesarea which had been started by Origen and of which Pamphilus was the curator. Of the latter he became the disciple and collaborator as well as a spiritual son;

Eusebius joined his name to his master's and called himself Eusebius of Pamphilus.

He was buried in such studies when the great persecution broke out. He was present when the churches were destroyed, at the burning of the Sacred Scriptures, at single and collective martyrdoms in Palestine and Phoenicia, in Egypt and the Thebaid. When Pamphilus was imprisoned at Caesarea in November, 307, Eusebius was by his side and collaborated with his imprisoned master in his *Apologia of Origen* which was cut short by the execution of Pamphilus on February 16, 310 (pars. 120–122).

To save himself from the persecution, Eusebius now took refuge in Phoenicia at Tyre and in Egypt in the Thebaid. Though the persecution was raging in these places, Eusebius himself was not known so well there. He somehow managed to escape any grave ill-treatment and when the persecution was over his enemies accused him of apostatizing to save his life. This was without doubt a calumny invented by his theological opponents, for his election as bishop of Caesarea in 313, or just after, could never have taken place had he been an apostate. He was highly esteemed by Constantine for his erudition and he took part in the Council of Nicaea, allying himself with the opponents of the term "consubstantial." When the word was accepted and canonized by the Council Eusebius gave in and with some distaste accepted the decision. Later, however, he maintained close relations with the enemies of the definitions of Nicaea, accepted and protected Arius before and after his condemnation by the same Council, and opposed Arius' great opponent, Athanasius. In doctrine Eusebius was not a complete follower of Arius but believed a rather similar theory; he represented a current of belief between heresy and orthodoxy which has been called "semi-arianism."

He entered more and more into the good graces of Constantine who was now all-powerful in the Empire and became a kind of court prelate. He gained the confidence of the Emperor who gave him personal accounts of various events in his life. This must have been very gratifying for Eusebius but unfortunately it tended to affect his judgment and appreciation of historical values.

72. A most diligent and indefatigable collector of manuscripts, Eusebius wrote a great deal. Of his works which have come down to us, those which concern themselves with the great persecution are the last three books (VIII, IX, X) of the *Historia Ecclesiastica* written from

312 onward, the *Martyrs of Palestine* written about 313 (which is extant also in a shorter form), and *The Life of Constantine* in four books. This last was completed about 339.

We need not spend time here on the first seven books of the *Historia* for it is well known what precious treasures they are of the deeds and writings of the first three centuries of Christianity. Without such a collection our knowledge of those three centuries would be insignificant. The last three books, which were added a little at a time from about 312–324, tell the story of the great persecution and were written in accordance with the program and intention previously mentioned (par. 70). In them, Eusebius speaks of events in Palestine and neighboring regions (Phoenicia and Egypt) but gives only a few isolated references to more distant lands. The narration of *The Martyrs of Palestine* is conducted with the same criteria but at greater length; the people spoken of were friends of the author and he was an eyewitness of the events described. The authenticity of these two works leaves nothing to be desired.

73. The *Life of Constantine* is quite another matter. It is not really a biography in the modern sense of the word but a panegyric which shows all the good points of its subject and omits everything which might be to its detriment. It was a common literary form of the times called an *encomium*, ἐγκώμιον, and *The Life of Constantine* was regarded as such by the ancient Greek writers such as Socrates the Scholastic and Photius. Obviously writings of this kind, although they tell nothing but the truth, give a very false impression; in them the position taken by the author leaves many details of his subject in shadow; and though he displays isolated features with all exactness, the general picture is not a true one for the highlights are exaggerated by the surrounding darkness. But custom allowed works of this kind and Eusebius followed the custom. After all, in modern times the same kind of thing is taken for granted for inscriptions on tombs where it is allowed to say good — but no evil — about the deceased.

In any case Eusebius could have justified himself with an example of the highest authority — Sacred Scripture itself. The biblical books of Chronicles (Paralipomenon), in telling the story of King David, leave out his adultery and consequent act of murder although these two crimes had already been described in detail in the books of Samuel. But since the Chronicles are intended to be an *encomium* of the great King of Israel these two offenses are left out because they would have cast a shadow over the shining figure of their hero. Constantine, who gave peace to the Church, is for Eusebius a new David; at times he compares him to Moses (*De vita Constant.*, i, 20). Eusebius, therefore, has no place in his work to mention that Constantine executed both his son, Crispus, and his wife, Fausta, and he manages to talk about the Council of Nicaea and the Synod of Tyre without referring to the heretic Arius or the orthodox Athanasius. This last omission is clearly attributable to the author's semi-Arian propensities.

In conclusion, even if the reader accepts the documents in the *Life of Constantine* as genuine and the statements in it as true, he must remember that the moral figure shown in the book is false because of omissions and dissimulations expressly intended by Eusebius.

Besides this, many objections have been raised against the authenticity of the documents transcribed in this work — about 15 letters or edicts of Constantine. Doubts on certain of them were aired by Baronius and by Tillemont but a skeptical approach to all of them was popular in the last twenty years of the nineteenth century. Many students of different schools, however, defended their authenticity — among them Harnack who in 1904 considered the matter as settled. In more recent years other students have again rejected them, at least in part, although their defenders are still in a majority.

LACTANTIUS

74. After Eusebius, the historian who offers the greatest abundance of material on the great persecution is Lactantius. L. Caecilius Firmianus Lactantius was born in Africa about 250 and studied under the rhetorician Arnobius. He began teaching in Africa but was then called to Nicomedia by Diocletian who liked to bring illustrious masters to his capital. In the Greek world of Nicomedia the teacher of Latin rhetoric did not find his fortune; indeed, instead of the expected honors and life of ease he found only oblivion and poverty. He began to write and became a convert to Christianity at about the same time as his master Arnobius in Africa. As a Christian he still continued to teach until after the persecution broke out, but was forced to leave this work on the abdication of Diocletian in 305. He left the capital and did not return until after the Edict of Tolerance promulgated by Galerius in 311. Later, about 317, he went to the court of Con-

stantine at Trier where he had been called to take over the education of his son, Crispus. We know no more about his life after this — he probably died at Trier at an advanced age.

The work of Lactantius which concerns itself with the great persecution is the *De mortibus persecutorum* written in 314 or soon after, certainly before the persecution of Licinius in 321. The general thesis of the book is that those who persecute Christianity always suffer a wretched end as a punishment from God. Earlier persecutors from Nero to Aurelian are dismissed briefly in the first six chapters, while from the seventh chapter to the fifty-second he treats in detail the acts of Severus, Maximian, Galerius, Diocletian, and Maximin Daia. Licinius is not mentioned.

The book is written with deep feeling and passion, which explains why its style is so different from that of the author's other works, such as the seven books of *Divinarum institutionum* where the treatment is logical and philosophical. In *De mortibus persecutorum* the immediate impression is that the tragic events are described by one who actually saw them and who throughout was in continual danger of death. In the past some students have pointed to the difference in style as a proof that the book is not from the pen of Lactantius; but the passionate and agitated manner of writing seems to confirm his authorship, for it would be surprising if one who had been so tragic a witness could write in a calm and composed style. Every now and then, indeed, the professional teacher of rhetoric appears in classical references and quotations and especially in certain dialogues which according to the custom of other historians of the time are carefully dramatized. The substantial content of these conversations was certainly known to Lactantius during his stay at Nicomedia and when later he was a member of the court of Constantine at Trier.

Even though he differs in small matters from other historians and the conversations he reports make no pretense at verbal fidelity, Lactantius can be regarded as a first-class historical source in whom complete trust may be placed.

ACTS AND PASSIONS OF THE MARTYRS

75. The historical and psychological circumstances which led to the composition of the first *Acts* or *Passions* of the martyrs have been described in paragraph 69. Unfortunately those old stories, simple, clear, and without the slightest touch of rhetorical decoration, which give the plain facts without any comment even pious or seemingly justified, were too beautiful in their simplicity to be properly appreciated by later generations when the heroic age was quickly passing into ancient history. These foolish people were not content with a story of the heroic sacrifice of life for an ideal but looked for wonders and magic, for childish miracles; foolish students did not look at the massive eloquence of a silent martyr, but wanted turgid oratory and a wordy exposition of some doctrine or pious thought. Such expositions could just as easily be heretical as orthodox and opponents of Christianity were able to put into the mouth of a martyr speeches which assisted their own heterodox teachings. In the apocryphal gospels heretical ideas are based on supposed teachings and deeds of Christ, and if this happened to him we cannot be surprised that the same should be inflicted on his martyrs.

These two muddy streams (of amplification and bias) polluted very many Acts of martyrs and only a little later there began to flow yet another — that of fantastic invention rising in the first place from curiosity. Where a martyr had been venerated in a certain place from time immemorial it was but natural that people should want to know the particulars of his death, especially if they possessed his tomb as well. To satisfy this natural desire the best procedure, of course, would have been to search out reliable information on the matter and to draw up a trustworthy story of the martyrdom. Very often, however, such information could not be found. Sometimes it was not even sought — invention was less trouble. The passion of some unknown martyr came to be based on the facts of some other Passion or on no facts at all, while the resulting narration was accepted as true; sometimes it was substantially so, but more often than not it was completely fictitious. These three streams mixing one with the other finally reached the clear waters of the authentic Acts and having fouled some of the clear water with their own muddy inventions created around the Acts a great stagnant pool of useless and unreliable stories.

76. Attempting some kind of classification of these sources, it is possible to have in regard to any one martyr the following:

1. A verbal transcript of his interrogation with or without a few descriptive details of his imprisonment, tortures, manner of death, and so on.

2. A *Passion* composed by an eyewitness or by a writer who has gathered his information from eyewitnesses. Such a writer often speaks in the name of a whole Christian community, hence his narrative is guaranteed by that community.

3. Narratives put together a good while after the events they describe but based on documents of some value; such narratives usually have additions and explanatory passages of various kinds.

4. Narratives which have some elements of truth but which are otherwise quite fictitious in plot and character. Examples of this species in profane letters are novels such as *I Promessi Sposi* and *Quo Vadis* which represent some historical scenes and persons but where plot and everything else has been supplied by the imagination of the author.

5. Completely imaginary stories made up by the author either from his own fancy or from pagan, Greek, Latin, or even Buddhist tales.

Only stories under the first three headings can be even considered by the historian. In fact, the third kind — the later *Passions* — requires careful examination before it is possible to learn which parts are acceptable and trustworthy and which are without foundation, imaginary, and plainly untrue. Little or no information can be obtained from the fourth kind — none whatsoever from the fifth.

77. The fact that a certain *Passion* contains little or no historical truth is no proof that the martyr was not an historical personage. The actual existence of the martyr can be proved from archaeological sources or other ancient testimonies, though these are usually not very informative and give little more than the name and fact of martyrdom. As we have noted it was precisely to provide the missing information that the later *Passions* were written. Their authority varies greatly. Even when the whole Passion is obviously imaginary, the martyr's existence is not denied. This is true even if the fact that he lived and suffered is proved by ancient — albeit uninformative — sources. The fact that there were martyrs at Agaunum (pars. 7–8) about whom little is known is an example of this.

Though it is rather off the point, we must concede here that among the vast congeries of these writings true literary masterpieces are often to be found. Renan was exaggerating somewhat when he said that the cell of a scholar condemned to imprisonment could be changed to a pleasant retreat if he had in it the immense collection of the *Acta Sanctorum* which contains precisely these *Acts* and *Passions*. Though an exaggeration, this statement is based on reality — always, of course, from the point of view of a literary scholar. For an historian, the situation is quite different.

78. Another difficulty which lies in the path of the historian wishing to make use of the *Acts* and *Passions* of the martyrs is that these narratives often give no geographical or chronological references. Even in the optimistic hypothesis that the *Passion* of a certain martyr is substantially accurate, the document will frequently make no reference to the time or place of the events recorded. The martyr may have suffered in the last great persecution or in one of the earlier ones; his city or province may have been anywhere in the Roman world. Open contradictions are not wanting between old records; for example, according to her *Passion*, the Sicilian martyr Agatha suffered under Decius while other narratives say she was executed during the persecution of Diocletian; according to the best documents her native land was Catania, but there are later assertions that she came from Palermo (par. 149). Modern students will attempt to solve this contradiction between documents with ingenious conjectures, but this often leads to worse confusion. According to a recent theory, for example, in the case of the Roman martyr Agnes, two persons of the same name can be distinguished; there is no foundation for this hypothesis and it has been generally rejected; because of it, however, there is no reason to doubt the actual existence of St. Agnes (par. 148).

The story of the last persecution suffers most from chronological and geographical vagueness in its records. The four principal persecutors — Diocletian, Maximian, Galerius, and Maximin (without mentioning Licinius) — had their own regions of jurisdiction. But, unfortunately, they are frequently not named or else they are confused one with another so that there is no way in which the year or the place of a martyr's death can be discovered.

2. During the Storm

THE *TRADITORES*

79. The first edict ordered the churches and the Sacred Scriptures to be destroyed (par. 47). For the persecutor it was a clever move to attack the Christians through their sacred books for it became a matter of honor to save their books even at the cost of their lives. The edict

commanded them to surrender (*tradere*) them to the authorities. Any person who obeyed this order was "one who surrendered" (*traditor*); he was favored by the persecutor and hated by the Christians who called him precisely what he was — a *traditor* — traitor. Though Christians generally did their utmost to save the Sacred Scriptures there were many *traditores* among them. The resulting destruction of the Scriptures was not complete but it was very extensive — this is shown by the fact that none of the great uncial codices of Scripture which exist in modern times dates any farther back than the fourth century. This century with its hecatombs of manuscripts marks a real break in the transmission of the text. Daring Christians hid the sacred rolls or carried them on their persons to distant places. When the persecution broke out in Thessalonica, some women made it their special work to preserve the Scriptures (par. 136), carrying on in some way the ancient office of the deaconess Phebe who brought from Corinth to Rome the original of the Epistle of St. Paul to the Romans (16:1-2). Under the edict the libraries and archives of many local churches and those of Rome were destroyed. In the sequestration, the political authorities were sometimes not particularly thorough and obviously rather ashamed of themselves, but more frequently a hatred of Christians urged them to implacable efficiency. The written accounts of such searches and confiscations were kept by those involved for a long time and those referring to the Church at Rome were used during the violent disputes of the later Donatist controversy. Good fortune has preserved for us the account of what happened to the Christians in Cirta (Constantine) in Numidia where all the members of the clergy from the bishop to the lowest cleric were *traditores*. This is what happened.

80. On May 19, 303, Munatius Felix, the "curator" of Cirta — in charge of public order — arrived before the meeting house of the Christians and said to the Bishop Paul: "Bring out the writings of your law and any other religious objects you may have; thus will you obey the precept and command of the Emperor." The Bishop Paul said: "The lectors have them; we will give you what we have here." Felix said: "Show me the lectors or send for them." The Bishop Paul said: "You know them all." Felix said: "We shall see later those lectors brought in by my men; meanwhile hand over whatever you have." The Bishop Paul sat down as did also the priests, Montanus and Victor, etc.; the deacons, Mars, Aelius; the subdeacons, Marcoclius,

Catullinus, Silvanus, etc.; the fossores (gravediggers), Januarius, Merac-
lus, etc., and the following inventory was drawn up: two gold chalices,
six silver ones, six silver cruets, etc. Felix said to the fossores Marcoclius,
Silvanus, and Carosus: "Bring here whatever you have." They replied:
"We have brought out everything." Felix said: "Your reply has been
recorded." They then went into the library where the shelves were
found to be empty. Here Silvanus handed over a *capitulata* (box) of
silver and a lamp of the same metal which he said that he had found
behind a chest. One of the officers, Victor, said to Silvanus: "If you
had not found it you would have been put to death." Felix said to
Silvanus: "Look more carefully in case there are more." Silvanus
replied: "There is nothing else. We have brought out everything."
Felix said: "Bring whatever writings you possess in obedience to the
imperial command." Catullinus then handed him a very large codex.
Felix said to Marcoclius and Silvanus: "Why have you handed us
but one codex? Bring the rest." They replied: "We have no others
for we are subdeacons: it is the lectors who have the codices." Felix
then said: "Point out to us these lectors." Marcoclius and Catullinus
replied: "We do not know where they live." Felix said to Catullinus
and Marcoclius: "If you do not know where they live you can tell us
their names." Catullinus and Marcoclius replied: "We are not traitors
(*proditores*). If you wish to execute us we are here." Felix said,
"Arrest them."

At this point some explanation is necessary. The reply of the two
subdeacons — the only bit of courage in this story of abject servility —
uses the term "traitors" in the sense of "spies."

The next council of Arles, A.D. 314 (par. 241), in its discussion on
Christians who had surrendered during the persecution, distinguished
three classes of "traitors": those who had handed over the Sacred
Scriptures, those who had surrendered the sacred vessels, and those
who had revealed the names of the Christians who had such things
in their possession (Canon 13). Clearly the two subdeacons used the
word in this last sense — they did not wish to sink so low as to be
spies and informers on their brethren although they had already handed
over their books and sacred vessels. The subdeacon Silvanus appears
later in the same town, Cirta, as its Donatist bishop (par. 246). We
now continue with the story.

81. When Felix had arrived at the house of Eugenius the lector, he
said: "Hand over the writings that you have in obedience to the

official command." He brought four codices. Felix said to Silvanus and Carosus: "Show me where the other lectors live." They replied: "The bishop has already said that the chancellors Eudoxius and Junius know them all. They will show you their houses." Eudoxius and Junius said: "We will show you them, excellency." When they arrived at the house of Felix the mosaic worker, five more codices were surrendered; at their arrival at the house of Projectus they were given five large codices and two small ones. When they got to the house of Victor the grammarian, Felix said to him: "Surrender the codices in your possession in obedience to the official command." Victor offered him two codices and four bundles of quinions (gatherings of five leaves). Felix said to Victor: "Bring out the rest for you have more." The grammarian Victor replied: "If I had had any more I would have given them to you." When he got to the house of Euticius of Caesarea, Felix said to him: "Surrender the codices in your possession in obedience to the official command." Euticius said: "I have none." Felix said: "Your reply has been recorded." When he arrived at the house of Coddeo, his wife brought six codices. Felix said: "Look around and see if there are any more and bring them also." The woman replied: "I have no others." Felix said to Bovus, a municipal slave: "Go into the house and search." The public slave then said: "I have searched but have found none." Felix said to Victorinus, Silvanus, and Carosus: "If you have not done your whole duty you will be held responsible."

The sequestration had been very successful for the pagan authorities. They had seized about thirty-five volumes large and small of which the greater part were certainly Sacred Scripture. They were all burned. To think that such manuscripts were of earlier date or at least the same as those which were used later by Jerome and Augustine for their biblical studies! What value they would have today if they had been preserved for modern students of textual criticism! But as always, fanaticism could see its way only by the light of such bonfires.

82. The Christians remembered this destruction of the Sacred Scriptures for a long time. Augustine speaks of it as the "persecution by the surrender of books" (persecutio tradendorum codicum) or the "days of the surrender" (dies traditionis). He distinguished them from the "days of incense burning" (dies thurificationis) when the Christians were commanded to offer incense to idols.

In the "days of the surrendering" not all the Christians were as pusillanimous as those of Cirta. There were many martyrs and among them were representatives of the extreme right — the fanatics. The latter were inspired by Montanism which was popular in Northern Africa and had even won over Tertullian. These fanatics presented themselves to the police and boasted that they possessed copies of the Sacred Scriptures but that they would rather suffer death than hand them over. And, in fact, many of them did die but the ecclesiastical authorities — remembering without doubt that our Lord had warned the devil not to tempt God (cf. Mt. 4:7) — did not consider their death as a martyrdom but rather as a natural punishment for fanatical provocation. This was the opinion of Mensurius, bishop of Carthage, and the Council of Elvira decreed about the same time in its Canon 60 — referring to the Gospels and the practice of the Apostles — that the title of martyr should not be given to anyone who suffered for throwing down idols.

83.　This Mensurius was a man of good judgment who knew how to square the requirements of his conscience with the difficulties of life. He even knew how to get rid of unwelcome visitors. One day the police arrived at his house to confiscate his books and without any delay he ushered them into the library. The officers were not theologians and so did not notice that he had replaced his own books with shelf after shelf of heretical works. They worked very hard to load this great library on to a cart and they handed in their booty at the proconsul's office (very pleased with themselves and boasting of their great haul). Rather later in some way or another, some well-known pagans of Carthage got to know or suspect what Mensurius had done and told the proconsul. But Anulinus, the proconsul, showed that he did not lack good judgment either for he would neither listen to their complaints nor order another search of the Bishop's house. After all, he might find what his own officers had missed.

As usual there were fanatics who accused Mensurius of equivocation and of giving scandal to the faithful (par. 232). But he had not surrendered the Sacred Scriptures and no Christian should have indulged in scandal before finding out what the Bishop had actually done. In any case, it is certain that such tricks were frequently played in other places. In Africa, Donatus the bishop of Calama gave in medical treatises (codices medicinales); at Aptonga where Felix (pars. 233, 234) was the bishop nothing was found in his house but some personal letters. At Aquae Tibilitanae the bishop Marinus surrendered his archives but managed to save the Scriptures.

84. There were some who did not wish to use such stratagems and simply refused to surrender the Scriptures — they were executed. Such was the end of Felix, bishop of Tibiuca in proconsular Africa, whose trial lasted for a long time and ended with his decapitation (not in Italy as is asserted by a later addition to his *Passion*).

Some bishops, however, were real *traditores*. Purpurius of Limata, a violent man of bad reputation, was one (pars. 232, 235); Donatus of Mascula, Victor of Rusicade in Numidia were others. The last of these burned a codex of the Gospels with his own hands when ordered to do so by the magistrate and explained to his people afterward that it was after all only a worn copy. The conduct of Secundus, bishop of Tigisi, was very much discussed at the beginning of the Donatist schism. He was commanded to surrender the Scriptures but — according to what he wrote to Mensurius, perhaps to embarrass him — he flatly refused to do so without resorting to any tricks of substitution. There were some who did not believe the Bishop of Tigisi (par. 232).

In certain parts of Africa no great significance was attached to the surrender of sacred books; it was considered that since they were only material objects they could sooner or later be replaced (par. 138).

THE *CONFESSORES*

85. After the "days of the surrender" came the "days of incense burning" (par. 82). These were begun by the second and third edicts of 303 and continued by the even crueler one of 304 (pars. 52, 56). Scriptures were burned, churches destroyed, and bishops killed; the Christians could not meet for services and all they could do was to wait for the time when they would be called upon to offer incense to the idols under pain of death. At Nicomedia the reign of terror had begun right from the beginning of the persecution, not because of the first edict of 303 which was comparatively mild, but because of Diocletian's excitement at the incendiarism in his palace. In other places, the persecution gradually became more and more harsh and extreme severity became the law with the edict of 304 — we must except always the territories ruled over by Constantius and then later

by Constantine. Life and Christianity were not compatible — one or the other had to be sacrificed. There seemed little safety in flight when the Roman Empire extended over almost the whole world.

Many did abandon everything and turned fugitives. Some went into the deserts, some to the mountains or to the forests, some even left the Empire and found a more civilized home among the barbarians. St. Basil and his younger brother Gregory of Nyssa, both of Caesarea in Cappadocia, had as their paternal grandmother a certain Macrina who had been born in Neocaesarea in Pontus. When the great persecution broke out she fled with her husband and other Christians into the forest of Pontus where they spent a most unpleasant seven years. It must have been a great trial for Macrina and her husband, for until then they had lived a life of ease and comfort. Others sought safety in the deserts of the Thebaid and of Arabia where they wandered until the Roman authorities or death caught up with them. Among the barbarians who gave a kind reception to fugitives (cf. *De Vita Constant.*, ii, 53), a special place should be given to the people on the other side of the Euphrates. During the persecution of Maximin Christians fled in great numbers toward the five districts of the Upper Tigris which bordered on Armenia Minor. These had passed to the Roman Empire after the victory of Galerius over the Persians (par. 19), but local governors still ruled the land. Here the Christians had increased greatly in numbers (cf. Eusebius, *Hist. Eccl.*, ix, 8, 2) and were not molested in any way. The Armenian Christians received with open arms their brethren who fled from Roman persecution. This annoyed Maximin and later led to war (par. 184).

86. Probably parties of Christian fugitives found their way to the border of Persia; some possibly found refuge in Persia itself where Christianity had already arrived by the middle of the second century. At the end of that century we have reason to believe that Abgar IX, king of Edessa, was a Christian. In his city was a church where lay the bones which tradition says were those of the Apostle Thomas. Many bishops came to the Council of Nicaea from Roman territories which bordered on Persia; and a little afterward, catechetical schools were founded at Edessa and at Nisibis where Ephraem taught. All this shows that the fleeing Christians were given as warm a welcome in Persia as their brethren had received from the Armenian Christians.

Those who did not leave the Empire and did not hide themselves defended themselves and their faith as best they could. Some resorted to trickery of varying degrees of courage to deceive the police. The simplest method was to buy a witnessed document (*libellus*) which testified that they had duly offered incense to the idols. The officials, however, did not often allow these documents to be sold. Another way was for the Christian to send a pagan slave or friend to offer the incense for him, but this worked only when the magistrates affected short sight or a bad memory. Many of these magistrates were most severe and, either to cut a good figure before their superiors or out of native zeal, were even more oppressive than the already oppressive edicts (cf. Lactantius, *Divin. institution*, v, 11).

There was a little town in Phrygia where the whole population including the "curator" and the municipal magistrates were all Christians. Everyone refused to offer incense and they fled to the shelter of their church. This made it simpler for the Roman officers to dispose of them — they burned the church with the Christians, men, women, and children inside (cf. Lactantius, *op. cit.* Eusebius, *Hist. Eccl.*, viii, 11, 1–2). Such methods, as Eusebius quite rightly observes, could be expected during war but did not seem an essential part of the ordinary administration of justice. Since the story of Eusebius continues without any break it would seem that among this multitude of martyrs was found a certain Adauctus of Italian origin who had held a high position in the administration of the privy purse of the Emperor and was then attached to the Treasury. This last office did not prevent his sharing the flames with the rest of the Christians in the church.

During the persecution of Maximin it was the custom to go along the streets calling the people out of their houses according to a prepared list and then to put out search parties for those who did not answer the call. When the roll call was finished everyone was taken off to the nearest pagan temple to offer incense. Such wholesale methods are still favored by tyrants.

87. Some magistrates were more interested in making apostates than in destruction and death. They are mentioned by Lactantius as being apparently milder and more persuasive. They put their victims to the torture but in small doses over a long period in the hope that this painful repetition would sap the moral strength of the patient and lead him to surrender; they cared for the wounds and bruises of one day so that the pain of their opening again the following day would be more excruciating. One of these magistrates boasted that in many years of office he had not executed a single Christian, but had always

aimed at breaking down the constancy of his victims. A governor of Bithynia was filled with happiness when one day he saw signs of weakening in a Christian who had been receiving measured treatment for two years. Sometimes magistrates claimed a victory where there had been none; sometimes the intervention of relatives and friends of the victim made what would in other circumstances have been an amusing scene. The accused proclaimed his Christian faith in a loud voice while his friends shouted him down asserting that the magistrate must not listen to him and assuring the bystanders that he had already offered sacrifice or was willing to do so. In order to gain another victory the magistrate would listen to those who shouted the loudest and write down the accused as an apostate. Scuffles sometimes took place between the Christian and his friends. The latter, to save him from the death to which his obstinacy would condemn him, would carry him bodily to the altar; sometimes they would gag him to avoid any contradiction; having tied his hands they would put some incense in his palm and hold it over the tripod; in the scuffle some of the incense would fall into it and behold the poor man had sacrificed. It was quite useless to attempt to explain things to magistrates later for retractions were not accepted. Here is a description of such a scene by Eusebius:

"A certain Christian who had been forced bodily to offer impure and filthy sacrifices was then dismissed as if he had really sacrificed although this had not been the case. Another one who had not been anywhere near or touched anything impure was said to have sacrificed. Since he heard calumny in silence, he was allowed to go away. Yet another was taken up half dead and flung to one side as if he were a corpse. Another lying on the ground was dragged by his feet for a long distance and was counted among those who had sacrificed. One made a great commotion and shouted out in a loud voice that he refused to sacrifice and another proclaimed himself a Christian, boasting in his confession of the life-giving name; another asserted with vigor that he had not sacrificed and would never do so. These also were struck on the mouth frequently by soldiers who gathered to torment them, and reduced to silence, bleeding on their mouths and faces, they were violently thrown out" (*Hist. Eccl.*, viii, 3, 2–4: cf. *De Mart. Palaest.*, i, 4).

88. As time went on the Christians for the most part showed no signs of giving in and since even the pagans began to be heartily sick of the continual slaughter, the penalty of death was frequently com-

muted to that of forced labor in the mines. In this way at any rate, the Christians would help the treasury. There were copper mines at Phoeno in Palestine (to the south of the Dead Sea) and others in Cyprus. Porphyry was quarried in the Thebaid alongside the Red Sea and marble at Sirmium in Pannonia (par. 144) and in Cilicia. By sending the condemned Christians to mines and quarries instead of killing them off, the treasury found a ready made labor force for this exhausting work. These Christians were called "miner (mining) confessors" (confessores metallici) by the Church because they were condemned to the mines (ad metalla) where they worked in groups under the direction of engineers (Philosophi).

Their life of bestial labor was of a horrifying severity which is difficult to conceive in our time and was no less than martyrdom extended to months and years. The mines were always in desolate country and the prisoners got nothing more than the bare necessities of life. Christians sentenced to the mines were mutilated in various ways. The tendon of their left foot was usually cauterized so that any escape they made would have to be a slow one; their right eye was cut out with a knife and the wound burned with a hot iron; some youngsters were castrated (cf. Eusebius, De Mart. Palaest., vii, 3–4, etc.; Hist. Eccl., viii, 12, 10, etc.). The substitution of forced labor for the death penalty — a supposedly lenient policy — became quite usual after some years of persecution, perhaps even before the year 307.

From that time long files of "mining confessors" could be seen on their weary journey northward or southward — transferred from the mines of the Thebaid to those of Palestine or of Cilicia or of somewhere else. These human skeletons trudged under the burning sun for hundreds of miles through the desert under the watchful eyes of their guards. Many fell exhausted along the route and served to feed the jackals — only a comparatively small number reached their destination. Wives and children, even those of tender age, went with them and in these long journeys were expected to keep up with them (cf. De Mart. Palaest., viii, 1).

89. But even under these terrible conditions the "mining confessors" did not lose their spirit and kept up their religious practices as far as they could. In the marble quarries of Pannonia Christianity made proselytes, especially through the efforts of Bishop Cyril of Antioch who had been condemned to forced labor already in 303. Though they did their work without complaint, the deported Christians are recorded

not to have answered the call of the superintendent of the works for men to carve idols for temples (par. 144).

More than this happened in the copper mines of Phoeno where there were very many Christians who had come originally from Palestine and Egypt. Also a large group had been transported to Phoeno from Gaza in Palestine where all the Christians had been surprised at one of their meetings when they were listening to the Sacred Scriptures (cf. *De Mart. Palaest.*, viii, 4). Periodically, other groups of condemned Christians arrived from Egypt. The large number of workers in the mines led to the putting up of all kinds of sheds and huts and the Christians profited by this by adding another shed for a church. The clergy who served the Church were numerous and included bishops, priests, and lectors. The superintendent of the mine got to know about this, but surprisingly allowed the building to be used provided the day's work was finished. Among the bishops were the Egyptians Nilus and Peleus; and another active bishop was Meletius who later was to take a large part in the religious affairs of Egypt (par. 95). Eusebius also highly praised Silvanus, who was first a priest at Gaza and then consecrated bishop by Meletius. He did an immense amount of work among the prisoners at Phoeno, and was finally beheaded — the last martyr of Palestine (cf. *Mist. Eccl.* viii, 13, 5; *De Mart. Palaest.*, vii, 3; xiii, 4–5).

90.   But the most marvelous figure at Phoeno was the lector John. He was totally blind, but in accordance with the regulations he had not only been lamed in the left leg, but his useless right eye had been burned out with a hot iron. Like others in the East, especially the blind, John had a prodigious memory. He could recite from memory whole books of Sacred Scripture both of the New and Old Testaments in such a way that it seemed that he was reading them from the text. Eusebius was an eyewitness of this:

"I was much struck the first time I saw this man standing erect in the midst of a great crowd at a meeting and reading part of the Sacred Scriptures. While I could only hear his voice, I imagined that he was one reading to the people as was customary in meetings but when I got nearer I saw the situation. Those who had the use of their eyes crowded around him in a circle and he using only the eyes of his mind, spoke simply and like a prophet far better than those who are whole in body" (*De Mart. Palaest.*, xiii, 8).

Finally a governor came to inspect the mines at Phoeno, and the conditions of the prisoners seemed too easy to him. Maximin himself was informed and gave new orders which were carried out immediately. The Christians were transferred elsewhere; some to Cyprus, some to Lebanon, and some to other places in Palestine. Four of the most important among them were burned alive, among whom were the bishops Nilus and Peleus. Thirty-nine others who were too weak to work and had been spending their time in prayer and pious exercises were beheaded on the same day. Among these were the lector, John, and the bishop, Silvanus (cf. De Mart. Palaest., xiii, 10).

91. The lot of the "mining confessors" was followed with affectionate anxiety by those Christians who were still at large and they tried to convey secretly material help and words of comfort. This was especially done by the Christians who lived near the mines, but help came from a distance as well. It had always been the custom of the Roman Church from ancient times to help persecuted brethren in distant lands as Eusebius points out (cf. Hist. Eccl., iv, 23, 9); and this is proved by a letter of Dionysius of Corinth to Pope Soter toward the year 170 (cf. ibid., iv, 10).

The Christian who visited the mines was in great danger of discovery and arrest. With freemen working alongside the prisoners, a visiting Christian could pretend that he had come to see one of them. He had to keep his wits about him, however, for the smallest slip might be his downfall; or perhaps carried away by the pitiful sights of suffering fellow Christians he might openly announce his faith. In such cases there was a new prisoner for the guards who patrolled the mines and even the roads leading to them.

In December, 308, a party of brave Christians left Egypt to carry assistance to their brethren confined in the mines of Cilicia. They journeyed along the seacoast and got as far as Ascalon where they were arrested by the guards at the gates of the city. They were lamed and blinded in one eye and continued on their journey to Cilicia to join their fellows in forced labor. Three of them who showed some resistance were put in chains and executed at Ascalon. One called Ares was burned alive and the other two, Promus and Elias, were beheaded (cf. De Mart. Palaest., x, 1).

92. Little more than a year later, in February, 310, a similar affair occurred. Five Egyptian Christians who had been keeping company with prisoners on their way to the mines of Cilicia were arrested at the port of Caesarea on their return. When they were interrogated

they openly acknowledged themselves to be Christians, and explained the reason for their travels. Their names were Elias, Jeremias, Isaias, Samuel, and Daniel; they had taken these names from the Old Testament when they had become Christians in place of the names of Egyptian divinities given them by their parents. They were taken before the Governor and their interrogation, which was prolonged by theological disputations and excruciating tortures, ended with their decapitation (cf. *ibid.*, xi, 6–13; par. 20).

A piece of curious information is given us by Eusebius on this occasion. Even before the death of these five Egyptians a young ascete, called Apselamos (Semitic, *Ab-salam*), was burned alive in a small town of Palestine near Eleutheropolis (modern Bet-gibrin to the southwest of Jerusalem). "He gave proof of his faith in the Christ of God. . . . On the same pyre died a certain Asclepius possibly a bishop in the heresy of Marcion (who died) as he believed through desire of piety but not (through piety) according to true knowledge" (*De Mart. Palaest.*, x, 3). In these words Eusebius showed how careful he is to distinguish the orthodox martyr from the Marcion heretic. This Marcion heretic, however, is the only Palestinian bishop whose martyrdom is related by Eusebius (except for Silvanus of Gaza who became a bishop during the persecutions; cf. pars. 89–90). It would be strange if among the twenty or so bishops of Palestine none was martyred. On the other hand, it would be more unlikely that if there were any martyrs among them, Eusebius would not have mentioned them especially, as he recalls a priest Pamphilus, three deacons, a subdeacon, and two lectors.

THE *LAPSI*

93. A catastrophic event like the great persecution was bound to have repercussions on the internal discipline of the Church, just as had happened in earlier persecutions. During a short respite in the persecution granted by Maximin in 305, the urgent question arose of the Church's attitude to those of the faithful who had "fallen." These *lapsi* were numerous (pars. 53, 80, 84), and all were not equally to blame. What should be done if they wished to be reconciled to the Church? Were they all to be refused, or should they be given a second chance? If they were to be readmitted should there be any discriminations made or conditions laid down?

Rigorism, which had been very powerful when the same questions had been asked after the Decian persecution, flourished once more and gave rise to many contrasting policies in various churches. However, from the beginning there had been a document which not only had official value, but was admirably compounded of psychological experience, firm prudence, and mercy. In 306 Peter the bishop of Alexandria, probably in his "festal" letter for Easter of that year, issued a series of penal canons regarding the treatment of *lapsi* who asked for reconciliation. The inspiration of these rules can be found in the directions given some fifty years before, immediately after the persecution of Decius, by Cornelius of Rome, by Cyprian of Carthage, and by Dionysius of Alexandria. To evaluate the true historical importance of these new plans not only must we take into account the various stratagems which were used by the *lapsi* to escape the executioner (par. 86), but also the common human weakness which is present in all periods. The legislator must take into consideration this human weakness and strengthen it with the principles of Christian redemption. **94.** Here are some examples —

Canon 1. Christians who, after denunciation, imprisonment, and torture, have surrendered to the violence of torment and have been penitents for three years, shall do penance with fasts, vigils, and prayer for forty more days.

Canon 2. Christians who were not put to the torture, but were overcome by the sufferings of imprisonment shall add one year to the period of penance already completed. If they were assisted in prison by the charity of the brethren they must restore in abundance what they received.

Canons 3–4. Christians who apostatized immediately without having suffered either torture or imprisonment shall add four years of penance to those they have already done.

Canon 5. Christians who bought false certificates which said they had sacrificed or sent pagan friends to sacrifice in their place shall add six months' penance.

Canons 6–7. Christians who sent their Christian slaves to sacrifice instead of going themselves shall do penance for three years, and the slaves for one year.

Canon 8. Christians who after apostasy have then suffered torture or imprisonment shall be held to no disciplinary penance, but shall be received with joy both at the receiving of the Body and Blood and at the sermon.

Canons 9–10. Christians who offered themselves spontaneously to the judges, forgetting the counsels of our Lord and the examples given by the Apostles Peter, Paul, James and by Stephen, acted in ill-considered zeal and in ignorance; if they came out victorious from the trial they are to be admitted to Communion and shall keep their ecclesiastical positions if they had any. On the other hand, the clergy who acted thus and then surrendered will lose their position even if they refused to apostatize later in the persecution.

Canon 11. Those Christians are censured who, when they were witnesses at the trial and torture of the martyrs, revealed themselves spontaneously as Christians even if they did it through emulation or to assist the patience of the martyr in his torment. Further approval is given to prayers made for those who surrendered through fear or under torture.

Canons 12–13. Those who avoided persecution by means of bribery are also censured. No action is to be taken against those who fled from their persecutors, even if other Christians were taken in their place for this was what Paul did at Ephesus, Peter at Jerusalem, and the Child Jesus at Bethlehem when others suffered for them.

Canon 14. Those Christians who had their mouths forced open so that they would drink the wine of the libations, or whose hands were burned to make them drop incense into the sacrificial fire, are innocent and should be given all honor as confessors.

95.   These dispositions with their measured mercy did not satisfy the rigorists of North Africa where severity was a local disease. The spiritual sons of the Montanist Tertullian found that the sanctions in these Canons against the lapsi were not fierce enough; they also felt that the Church should wait until the persecution was really over (and not start arranging affairs during what was obviously only a respite under Maximin) before the matter of the lapsi should be considered at length. A representative of this rigorous movement was Meletius, whom we have already found among the deported Christians at Phoeno (par. 89); but at this time he had not been arrested. He was the bishop of Lycopolis in Upper Egypt, but since he was imperious in character he often extended his activities to matters which were the business of others, and he was often found where he was not wanted.

The Canons of Peter of Alexandria afforded a good opportunity for interference, and he immediately accused their author of laxism. What annoyed Meletius most in these Canons was the open recognition of the fact that a Christian could save himself by flight. This canon became in his hands a personal weapon against Peter for, when the lull in the persecution ceased and Christians were being hunted once more, Peter and his vicars took to hiding again. "Inde irae." The fiery Meletius considered Peter to have forfeited his see by his flight and substituted two of his own men as his vicars. He won over to his side some of the faithful of Alexandria who had suffered severely during the persecution, and other important people among whom was a certain Arius, who was perhaps the future heresiarch. Peter followed the adventures of this reforming intruder from hiding, and had Meletius deposed by a synod of bishops which warned the faithful to beware of him. Meanwhile, Meletius traveled through Egypt holding ordinations in those churches where the bishops were imprisoned, and generally behaving as the supreme moderator of the Egyptian Church. Four Egyptian bishops who were in prison, among whom was Phileas of Thmuis (pars. 114–119), wrote in protest but without any result. Meletius widened and deepened his schism.

Before long Meletius became involved with the law, and in 308–309 he was arrested and sent to Phoeno. Even there he continued to diffuse his rigorist theories and make disciples. When the persecution ended in 311, the prisoners at Phoeno were released and Meletius came back to Egypt. Peter of Alexandria had not been so fortunate for he had been killed in the persecution (par. 113). Despite all this Meletius continued to oppose the followers of Peter and to organize his schism. He called his followers the "church of the martyrs." All others, even if they had given their lives for the faith, as the bishop Peter had done, were nothing but traitors and lapsi.

The church of Meletius extended over more or less the whole of Egypt and the Council of Nicaea gave part of its time to a consideration of the schism; the provisions made by the Council did little to satisfy the Meletians (par. 266). After the death of Meletius, about 326, his followers became more closely connected with the Arians especially in their fight against the champion of orthodoxy, Athanasius. By the end of the fourth century the schism had lost its force and during the fifth century little traces of it are to be found except among monks.

96. The discussion on the lapsi had grave consequences also in Rome.

The See of Peter was held by Pope Marcellinus when the persecution broke out. He had succeeded Pope Gaius in 296. Before the persecution the Church in Rome had had a long period of peace and prosperity. The atmosphere of general security had allowed the Christians there to forget the measures which had been adopted both during and after the persecution of Decius and Valerian for the protection of the city's Christian cemeteries from pagan profanation. Under Marcellinus the tempest suddenly broke. It began as usual with the confiscation of all Church possessions and continued with the imprisonment of the leaders of the clergy. Eusebius says (*Hist. Eccl.*, vii, 32, 1) that Pope Marcellinus was also "engulfed by the persecution" (κατείληφεν). This seems to have had no other interpretation than that he died and this would have been on October 24, 304. There are, however, some doubts about the end of this Pope. All through the grueling controversy which followed the persecution he was the favorite target of the Donatists who accused him of surrendering the Sacred Scriptures. Such accusations, according to Augustine, were never proved. Two documents go further than this, though they are of later date and without authority on this point. They are the biography of Marcellinus in the *Liber Pontificalis*, and the acts of the false synod of Sinuessa. They present Marcellinus as a *lapsus*, since they accuse him of offering incense to idols. This was not condoned by his later martyrdom. All this seems an echo of the argument set out by the Donatists. In the Catholic and Roman catalogue known as the *Depositio Episcoporum* Marcellinus appears on January 16, but according to the *Liber Pontificalis* this is the date of Pope Marcellus (who is not mentioned in the *Depositio*). No reference to Marcellinus is found in the *Depositio Martyrum* or in the *Hieronymian martyrology*. Should this omission be attributed to *damnatio memoriae* — a punishment for his fall? This is a modern theory but there is no proof for it. In fact, there is no evidence that the custom of *damnatio memoriae* existed in Western churches. It seems that the sepulcher of Marcellinus in the cemetery of Priscilla was venerated in antiquity and this would confirm the reference to his martyrdom given by Eusebius and later authors.

97.   After the death of Marcellinus the Chair of Peter remained vacant for four years — a long time. The length of this break was mostly due to the persecution, but also in part to the critical internal condition of the Roman Church. After the abdication of Diocletian and Maximian the persecution gradually decreased, and was almost nonexistent

after the second proclamation of Maxentius (par. 63). Under the government of the latter the Roman Christians, although they did not get back their confiscated property, were not disturbed at their meetings. There was an opportunity, therefore, for them to reorganize their scattered communities. Just as in Alexandria and Carthage, the Christians in Rome were troubled with the problem of the *lapsi*. This led to internal division and was certainly one of the causes of the long break before another pope was elected.

Finally, toward the middle of 308, a successor to Marcellinus was elected in the person of the priest Marcellus. We do not know exactly what happened for the documents are vague. The fact that in some lists only one pope is given, sometimes called Marcellinus and sometimes Marcellus, makes it very difficult to separate the two men historically especially since things are already confused owing to their similarity in name. According to Monnsen's questionable theory there was only one pope called Marcellinus, and Marcellus was merely in charge of the Roman Church during the vacancy as he was the senior priest in the community.

After his election Marcellus found the Roman Church in confusion; restoration and reorganization were needed everywhere and above every other problem loomed that of the *lapsi*. In the matter of reorganization the *Liber Pontificalis* attributes to Marcellus the division of the city into twenty-five *tituli* (very much like parishes) for the preparation of catechumens, the guidance of the penitents, and the care of the cemeteries. The *lapsi* were confident in their numbers and claimed that they could be reconciled without the usual penance. This is the opposite of what had happened in Rome after the persecution of Decius, when Novatian had promoted a schism of fairly rigorous tendency. Now, however, if the preceding pope, Marcellinus, had really been wanting in courage, the *lapsi* could quote his case to their own advantage.

98. Marcellus resisted and demanded that penance should be done. According to his epitaph written by Pope Damasus there were fierce and violent quarrels (*hinc furor hinc odium*), and plotting and assassinations were not wanting (*seditio caedes*). One of the ringleaders of the dissidents was an anonymous apostate who had renounced his faith even before the persecution (*Christum qui in pace negavit*). All this did not please Maxentius who had every reason to keep Rome calm and tranquil; he accepted the accusations of Marcellus' enemies and

held the Pope responsible for the disorders; he was sent into exile and died shortly afterward.

In his place Eusebius was elected in 309 or 310. But even this did not heal the wounds in the Christian community, for those who did not believe in penance for the *lapsi* elected as antipope a certain Heraclius. There were plots and murders once more as is testified by Damasus in his epitaph for Eusebius (*scinditur in partes populus . . . seditio caedes bellum . . .*). Maxentius intervened once more, and after four months cleared the ground altogether by sending both Eusebius and Heraclius into exile. The former died in exile in Sicily not long afterward.

There was now a fairly long gap before Miltiades was elected on July 2, 311.

By this time Galerius had published his Edict of Toleration. Maxentius did not wish to appear less generous than Galerius toward the Christians, and so he restored to Miltiades the Church property which had been confiscated at the beginning of the persecution. From this time there was no trace of schism on the matter of the *lapsi* in the Roman Church.

3. *"Flower From Flower"*

Salvete, flores martyrum!   *. . . and now*
    (Prudentius)   *singing and choosing flower from flower
    with which the whole way was blazoned.*
    (Purgatory, 28, 40–42)

99. So far we have only given a general view of the persecution — as from a mountain peak. Now let us go down into the plains and explore in more detail some of the country according to our plan in paragraph 70. For guides we have appropriate documents. These, however, as we have already seen, are often uncertain and would lead us completely astray. Especially unreliable are the *Acts* or *Passions* of martyrs (par. 75 ff.). A complete history of the great persecution will be possible only when these *Acts* and *Passions* have been thoroughly investigated and what is certain or at least very probable separated from its clinging errors. This work will take some centuries, and meanwhile it is only possible to present an incomplete history by using those documents whose authenticity is not in serious doubt. Keeping in mind, therefore, the general conditions already explained we will examine a few isolated episodes of the great persecution which will help us to have some idea of the full picture.

Starting from the extreme west coast of Mediterranean Africa we shall travel along this coast to Egypt; from here we shall go north to Palestine and Syria, then pass into Asia Minor, and then cross over into Europe — going through Macedonia, Thrace, Illyricum, Rhaetia — and passing through the West come back once more to our starting point.

MAURETANIA, NUMIDIA, PROCONSULAR AFRICA

100. Fabius, the Standard-Bearer. In 303 or 304 Fabius, the official standard-bearer of the governor of Mauretania, was martyred at Cartenna in Mauretania Caesariensis.

The *Passion of Fabius* was written between the fourth and fifth centuries about the time of Augustine, and has an appendix which endeavors to show that the Christians of Cartenna had a right to possess his body. The story of the martyrdom, however, is based on a precise record of the facts which is almost completely free from later additions.

The edict of persecution had just been issued, and the governor ordered the assembly of the provincial *concilium* to put it into execution. Fabius, who should have taken part in this *concilium* in his official position, refused to come and declared himself a Christian. He was imprisoned and subjected to interrogations, but firmly refused to obey the imperial edict. He was beheaded and buried at Cartenna on July 31.

101. Crispina, a Matron. Going toward the east from Cartenna we leave Mauretania for Theveste (Tebessa) in Numidia. This was the city of the conscript Maximilian (par. 42). Also martyred in this town was Crispina, a noble matron born at Thagora (modern Taoura). We know about Crispina not only from her *Acts*, but also from the sermons of Augustine. She seems to have been a well-known figure among the African Christians (St. Augustine says of her *hanc . . . numquid est qui in Africa ignoret?*), and her veneration seems to have spread quickly to other places. She is even to be found on the mosaics of Ravenna. Some of the information given by Augustine is not found in the *Acts* which are extant; either he took them from another account of her martyrdom or else from other sources, possibly oral ones. The *Acts* which we have date back to the end of the fourth century and reproduce in substance the official transcription in the government archives apart from some additions of suspect origin. It is not impossible that these additions are from the pen of a Donatist; and it may be that the fuller relation used by Augustine, which is now lost, was that common among the Catholics, while the one that we have is a Donatist version.

Crispina was not only noble and rich, but also cultured and good looking; *femina dives et delicata* Augustine calls her, and in another place he says she was *nobilis genere, abundans deliciis.* When offering incense was made obligatory by imperial decree she did not hesitate to flatly refuse. She was imprisoned and then brought with hands bound before Anulinus, the proconsul.

"Do you know what is commanded by the sacred edict?"

"I do not know this edict."

"It commands you to sacrifice to our gods for the safety of our rulers in obedience to the law given by the pious Augusti Diocletian, etc."

"I shall never offer this sacrifice. I offer sacrifice to one God only and his Son our Lord Jesus Christ who was born and suffered."

"Abandon this superstition and bow your head before our gods."

"I venerate my God every day and I know no other gods but him."

"You are being very obstinate and difficult. You will soon find out to your cost the force of our laws."

"Whatever happens to me I will suffer it willingly for my faith."

"You will lose your head if you do not obey the orders of our lords the emperors to whom you owe obedience. They have power over all Africa and you know it."

The accused replied to this and the Proconsul answered. The conversation now becomes colored by theological dispute and quotations from the Bible and perhaps this is a later addition. To make her more amenable the Proconsul ordered that her beautiful hair should be cut off. Crispina said, "Let your gods speak and then I will believe them. If I had sought my safety I would not be standing before your tribunal."

The give and take of the interrogation went on and finally the Proconsul became impatient and sentenced her to death by beheading.

"*Christo laudes ago*," said Crispina who rejoiced to hear her condemnation ("*gaudebat . . . cum damnabatur*," says Augustine). She was beheaded on December 5, 304. Over her tomb at Theveste at the beginning of the fifth century a basilica was built. The ruins found there today are possibly the remains of this basilica.

102. Saturninus, Dativus, and Companions. Going on toward the east one leaves Numidia for proconsular Africa. There, not far from Carthage, was a little town called Abitina, which had close connections with that ancient city. If one can believe the accusations of the Donatists, Fundanus the bishop of Abitina had given very bad example at the beginning of the persecution; for he had been a *traditor*, obeying the command to surrender the Sacred Scriptures. The first edict, which ordered the destruction of churches, had implicitly prohibited meetings of the faithful, but a large number of the Christians of Abitina with those from Carthage still continued to meet for the celebration of the *dominicum* — the Eucharistic rite. It seems that Fundanus, after his act of treachery, did not attend these meetings either because he was not welcome or else because he was still an unrepentant *traditor*; and so the services were conducted by Saturninus, a priest of advanced age. But the police were on the lookout and soon located the place where these meetings were held, and one day took about fifty Christians by surprise. Besides Saturninus, there were his four children — one called Saturninus after his father; another named Felix who were both lectors; Maria who was a virgin consecrated to God; and, finally, Hilarianus who was still a boy. In addition there were twenty-six other men among whom was Dativus, a decurion, and seventeen or eighteen women, among whom was Victoria a virgin who had come from Carthage with some other women especially for the service. In all there were thirty men besides the women. They were all arrested, underwent a preliminary interrogation at Abitina, and were then taken in chains before the proconsul Anulinus at Carthage. They were interrogated here on February 12, 304.

The *Passion* of these martyrs which has come down to us was written in the fourth century, but incorporated the primitive *Acts* which were a word-for-word transcription of the interrogation. These *Acts* were adopted by the Donatists in their conference at Carthage in 411, and were accepted as authentic also by the Catholics. The later writer of the *Passion*, however, was a Donatist and took the opportunity to scatter comments here and there which reflect the principles of his sect. In addition, the *Passion* was given a Donatist introduction and appendix. It would seem that at the time of Augustine a *Passion* was in circulation which was different from the one we have now, and which contains information which is not in the present one.

103.   The first to be interrogated was the decurion Dativus, who confessed immediately that he had taken part in a meeting of Christians. When he was asked if he was the responsible leader (*auctor*) of the meeting it seems that he refused to answer. He was then tortured. He was stretched on the rack and the executioners were tearing his flesh with iron hooks, when another accused, called Telicus, to draw down the anger of the judge on himself, cried out: "We are all Christians and have all taken part in the meeting." Then it was Telicus' turn to receive the blows and undergo the torture, during which he praised God and begged him to preserve his servants. He was asked the question to which Dativus had refused to give an answer — who had been the leader of the meeting — and pointed to Saturninus and said: "The priest Saturninus and all."

This answer cannot be easily justified. However, there certainly was no treachery, for Saturninus had been arrested and was present at the trial. If it was not extracted merely by the horrors of his tortures, then perhaps it was to please the old priest who wished to show clearly that he was a worthy leader of these aspirants for martyrdom. The torture of Telicus was continued, interrupted now and then only by exhortations to give in from the proconsul Anulinus. The latter was the first to tire and ordered that Telicus should be taken back to prison. During this the tortured Dativus had remained on the rack assisting at the torments of his brother in the faith. When executioners once more approached him he began to cry in a loud voice that he was a Christian and had taken part in the meeting.

104.   At that moment Fortunatianus, the pagan brother of Victoria, one of the accused, appeared. He was a lawyer and had come in an attempt to save his sister despite her efforts to the contrary. He began with a lie, for he affirmed that Dativus, who was still on the rack, had seduced his sister Victoria and had taken her with two other Christian women from Carthage to Abitina. This was immediately denied by Victoria who cried: "I was not at Abitina with him and I can prove this by (the testimony of) other citizens. I came here of my own free will. I was at the meeting and took part in the *dominicum* because I am a Christian." The lawyer continued to abuse Dativus despite

this denial; but the latter replied from the rack to all his accusations, although the executioners were very busy tearing him so cruelly that his bowels were exposed.

After a brief suspension, the interrogation was resumed when another accuser presented himself. He was a certain Pompeianus who was greeted by the martyr with the words: "What do you want here, devil." (The Greek διάβολος means "adversary," "accuser," "calumniator," just as the Hebrew "Satan": cf. Job 1:6 ff.; Mt. 16:23). When the torturers began once more to tear Dativus with the iron hooks he exclaimed: "I pray thee, Christ, let me not be confounded. . . . I pray thee Christ, give me the power to endure." Meanwhile the priest Saturninus was brought up, and the Proconsul reproved him for having held the meeting. The priest replied: "We were celebrating the dominicum in secret." "Why?" demanded the Proconsul. "Because the dominicum must not be interrupted" was the reply. The Proconsul then accused Dativus of giving bad example to the other citizens, but Dativus replied stoutly: "I am a Christian." Two interrogations at the same time became rather confusing and so the Proconsul ordered Dativus to be removed from the rack and taken back to prison; the priest was then put on the rack and became the principal object of the energies of the torturers.

Saturninus, already soaked with the blood of the other martyr, took on himself the responsibility for the meeting; but a lector called Emeritus, who was among the accused and longed for martyrdom, broke in and stated that he was responsible for the meeting for it was held in his house. For the moment the Proconsul continued to question the priest, and the torment was so dreadful that they laid bare the bones of the old man. Saturninus prayed: "I beg thee, Christ, to hear me! I thank thee, God; let me be beheaded! I pray thee, Christ, have pity! Son of God, help me!" When the Proconsul asked him why he had broken the imperial edict, the priest replied: "The law commands thus. The law teaches thus." He was then carried back to prison and placed with the other two who had been tortured.

105. Now it was Emeritus' turn. The Proconsul asked him why he had allowed Christians in his house. Emeritus replied: "They are my brethren; they came to celebrate the dominicum without which we cannot live." He was extended on the rack, and since the executioner was tired a fresh one was called. The torture began, accompanied by the prayers of the martyr and the remorseless words of the interrogation.

The martyr prayed: "Lord Christ, give me the strength to bear these sufferings." The inquisitor demanded: "Why did you receive them? Should you not have preferred the edict of the emperors to the will of your brethren?" Emeritus answered: "God is greater than the emperors." Then he added: "Christ, I suffer for thy name; may I not be confounded." Knowing that he was a lector, the Proconsul hoped that at least he could have a haul of the Sacred Scriptures, and demanded: "Have you the Scriptures in your house?" The reply was: "I have them, but in my heart." Hope of breaking down the martyr was wearing thin, and in any case the Proconsul was becoming as tired as the first executioner through the nervous tension of the interrogation. Nevertheless, he had one more try, this time with the accused who were waiting their turn for interrogation: "I hope that you have resolved to be obedient so that your lives may be saved." But one of them called Felix stepped forward and spoke in the name of all: "We are Christians and we must observe the law of the Lord to the last drop of our blood."

To the disgust of the Proconsul, he had to continue the hearing. He replied to Felix: "I did not ask you if you were a Christian, but if you had taken part in the meeting, and if you have in your possession the Scriptures." This was based on a subtle juridical distinction. The imperial edicts as yet did not punish people for being Christians, but for meeting together, and for possessing the Scriptures. Felix replied: "We celebrated the *dominicum* solemnly and listened to the reading of the Scriptures of the Lord." For this reply Felix underwent a flogging so cruel that he died under the lash. As far as we know he was the first of this group to give his life for Christ.

106. Then came another Felix who ended the same way as his namesake, except that he did not die in the court, but later in prison. After him there was a lector, Ampelius, then Rogatianus and Quintus, next Maximian, and finally another Felix, who may have been the son of the priest Saturninus. They all declared their Christian faith, and apart from Rogatianus — who for some reason was not tortured — were all flogged and taken back to prison.

Then came Saturninus, another son of the priest. The Proconsul demanded if he had taken part in the meeting and he replied that he was a Christian. The Proconsul replied as he had done to Felix that he had not asked this but if he had attended a Christian meeting. The reply was: "Yes, I have taken part in the *dominicum* because Christ is my Saviour." Then the Proconsul placed him on the rack which was bathed with the blood of his father and demanded several times if he had taken part in the meeting and if he had the Scriptures in his possession. The martyr replied always that he was a Christian and kept the Scriptures in his heart. He was torn with iron hooks so that his blood mingled with that of his father. The Proconsul finally had him taken back to prison.

The Proconsul was completely worn out. He saw that there was no hope of getting retractation from the accused and therefore made a statement which can be taken as a common interrogation: "You have seen what happens to obstinate people. If you do not obey you will be treated in the same way. If anyone wants to save himself let him speak up." They all replied together, "We are Christians." It was obviously quite useless after this to prolong the interrogation and so the Proconsul sent them all back to prison to await their execution.

107. The women among the accused had not as yet been interrogated apart from the spontaneous intervention of Victoria in protest at her brother Fortunatianus' attempt to save her. Fortunatianus had not yet lost all hope and had remained in the court attempting to show that his sister was crazy and not responsible for what she said or did. He had some good points to make in his argument. The young woman was noble and beautiful, but despite this did not wish to be married; her parents had arranged a very advantageous union but a little before the wedding she had made a secret escape through one of the windows of her house with every danger of killing herself. (This is perhaps a Donatist addition; cf. par. 109.) Was not this a clear sign that she was not right in her head? Fortunatianus informed the Proconsul of all this suggesting that the latter should entrust a poor crazy sister to her brother who would accept the duty of caring for her and guarding her. The Proconsul, who by now was worn out and bored with the whole affair, would have been quite happy to grant the request; to save appearances, however, it was necessary that he should make a rapid interrogation of the accused.

The other women were passed over and Victoria was questioned privately in the presence of her brother, for whom her answers provided no consolation. She affirmed that she was a Christian, that she was and always had been quite sane. The Proconsul disregarded such mad statements and asked her whether she would like to go away in peace with her brother. But Victoria replied: "I do not wish to go with him for I am a Christian and my brother is he who observes the commandments of God." The Proconsul found himself heading rapidly down a blind alley and perhaps remembered the aphorism of Horace that the person who insisted on saving one who refused to be helped was a murderer. He had brought death to so many that day that he felt he could not now kill off a young and beautiful girl. He sent her back to prison with her chosen brothers to await execution.

108. The tribunal was now becoming quite empty. There was only the youngest son of the priest Saturninus, Hilarian, a boy of tender years. The Proconsul tried to help him by suggesting that perhaps he had gone with his father and brothers to the meeting without knowing what the meeting was all about. The reply was quite clear: "I am a Christian. Of my own free will I took part in the meeting in company with my father and brothers." There was nothing to be got from this youngster either, it would seem. The Proconsul then thought that he might get somewhere by frightening the boy and said: "I have ordered my men to cut off your hair, your nose and ears before I send you away." Hilarian was not frightened and said cheerfully: "Do what you like. I am a Christian." The Proconsul then gave up the unequal struggle and commanded him to be taken to prison to join the rest. The boy replied: "*Deo gratias.*"

What happened to them all in the end is not known, for the end of the trial is not preserved. The Donatist interpolator of the *Acts*, or some other editor after him, wrote an appendix which is full of Donatist sentiment. This damns it as history for modern critics. One can presume that the Christians either died in prison from their dreadful wounds or were executed at a time convenient to the pro-consul Anulinus. It is possible that some of them escaped with their lives — for example Rogatianus who was not flogged — but we have no proof either way.

109. **Maxima, Donatilla, and Secunda.** Also in proconsular Africa we come across an episode which brings together great courage and the vilest cowardice, a bright spot on a dead black canvas. In the city of Thumbarbo (Lucernaria) we once again find the proconsul Anulinus executing the imperial edicts.

After the publication of the edicts the Proconsul, in July of 304, took a personal interest in enforcing them in a place near Thumbarbo called *Possessio Cephalitana* which was probably the private property of the Emperor. The population of the place was gathered; the Christians were notified that the Emperor required them to sacrifice to the gods, and that any who refused would be punished in various ways. The Proconsul's announcement was like an earthquake. All the Christians gave in at once — including priests, deacons, and the other clergy — and everybody offered the pagan sacrifice. It was one of those general apostasies which happened in other places and which we have already seen in Cirta in the matter of handing over the Sacred Scriptures (pars. 80–81). Two young girls, however, did not give in. They were Maxima, who was only fourteen years of age, and Donatilla; they were both fervent in their faith and were living an ascetic life in retirement. They did not turn up at the general roll call and this would probably have gone unnoticed except that a peasant woman denounced them. They were searched out and taken to the tribunal where in their first examination they replied not only with firmness, but even with a certain unexpected argumentiveness and pride. (Such replies may, however, be interpolations of Donatist inspiration.)

The *Passion* that we have today was composed in the fifth century, but is obviously an enlargement of an earlier narration which was concerned only with Maxima and Donatilla. In the longer version, however, Secunda was also introduced perhaps because in the liturgical cycle she is commemorated on the same day, July 30. The section referring to Secunda seems to be the work of a Donatist editor and contains various interpolations. The general framework of the story corresponds quite well to the historical circumstances and customs of the time, and seems to be worthy of belief at least in substance.

As Maxima and Donatilla were being taken through the city they were seen by Secunda from her house. Secunda was twelve years old, but in the warm airs of Africa this meant that she was already of marriageable age, and indeed because her family was rich she had been asked for several times. Her Christian faith had made her choose the state of a virgin, and now the possibility of martyrdom urged her to a public confession of her faith. When she saw her two sisters being conducted to their sufferings, Secunda jumped down from a high window and took her place beside Maxima and Donatilla, begging them not to leave her behind. The two women showed good sense by reminding Secunda that she was the only daughter of her father who was now in old age, and that great courage was needed to expose oneself to the danger of being sentenced to death. But Secunda, confident in the help of Christ, insisted on going with them. Her wish was granted. The next day at Thumbarbo the Proconsul began the trial and invited the three accused to sacrifice. In the morning Maxima and Donatilla once more gave sharp replies to the commands and threats of the Proconsul. What Secunda may have said is not written down. Seeing that his efforts were in vain the Proconsul condemned all three accused to be thrown to the wild beasts in the arena. Later, after more difficulties with Christians, he commuted this to beheading. They replied: "Deo gratias," and were executed.

Above all other difficulties, the hardest fact to explain in this story is that Secunda flung herself down from the balcony of her house, which was very high, but was still able to pick herself up and run along beside the other two martyrs. This jump must be due to the Donatist principles of the interpolator, for the Donatists considered suicide for religious reasons to be licit, especially if the death were procured by launching oneself out into the open air (Franchi de'Cavalieri; cf. par. 107). A little later another editor, this time a Catholic one, disposed of the attempted suicide and allowed Secunda to go to her martyrdom with her feet firmly on the ground. The consideration of this one episode is sufficient to show the discrepancies and incongruities of the story as we have it in its present form.

EGYPT AND THE THEBAID

110. Leaving proconsular Africa and passing through Libya and Cyrenaica, we come to the valley of the Nile which besides Egypt proper extends over the Thebaid to the south. Our examination of this last region of the African continent will be longer for we have the good fortune to possess an excellent guide. Eusebius gives eyewitness accounts of what happened, or else quotes authentic documents. The persecution in Egypt was conducted with particular ferocity — here is what Eusebius says:

"There thousands and thousands of people, men with their wives and children, who despised temporal life according to the teaching of our Saviour, suffered all kinds of death. Some after bearing the iron hooks, the racks, the whips and other torments innumerable and terrible to hear were finally consigned to the flames; others were drowned in the sea. Still others bravely offered their heads to the executioner, died under torture, or expired from hunger. Some were crucified in the manner used for criminals, and others even more cruelly were fixed to the cross with their head down and left to die of hunger" (*Hist. Eccl.*, viii, 8).

On this matter we have the story of another eyewitness, Phileas of Thmuis, who in a letter which is noted by Eusebius (cf. *ibid.*, viii, 10, 4–10) describes what he saw in Alexandria.

"What words would be sufficient to describe the bravery and courage of these Christians in their peculiar torments? For indeed, liberty to persecute was given to anybody; some they beat with clubs; some with rods; some with straps and some with cords. The methods of persecution differed, but were always as cruel as possible. Some with their hands tied behind their backs were hung from a post and by means of winches their limbs were pulled in all directions; while they were still hanging the executioners in obedience to orders used their tools on their bodies — not just on their sides as with assassins, but over all their parts, their belly, their legs and faces. Others were hung by one hand from a doorway and suffered the greatest torment from the stretching of their joints and limbs. Others were bound in pairs, face to face, to columns in such a way that their feet were off the ground; the cords were thus tightened by the weight of their bodies.

"These tortures were continued not only while they were being subjected to the remorseless interrogation of the governor, but sometimes almost for a whole day. When others were being interrogated officers were left sitting beside earlier victims in the hope that one of them might show signs of giving in. If this should be noticed, they would order without pity [here the text is broken; perhaps the original said, 'that the whips and ropes should be increased']. Those who died under the torture were cut down and flung on the ground . . . [some lines of the text here are uncertain]. Some, after these tortures, were put into the stocks with their legs stretched to the fourth hole (the widest allowed for on the Roman stocks) so that they had to lie on the stocks and were not able . . . [text doubtful; possibly 'to rest the wounds given by the blows over all their body']. Others were flung to the ground and fainted from the extremes of torture, giving thereby a dreadful display of the treatment they had received by the various marks and mutilations on their bodies. In such conditions some died, putting their torturers to shame with their constancy. Some were taken back to prison and lay half dead until, in a few days, they died from their injuries. Others were able to obtain treatment for their wounds, and in course of time, and after long imprisonment, became even more courageous. Indeed, when they were again commanded to choose between touching the unclean sacrifice — and thus be free from more torture and obtain wicked liberty — or refusing to sacrifice and being condemned to death, without any hesitation they went to their death with all happiness."

111. To be moved by such suffering, one need not be a Christian. It was sufficient to have a human heart, even if a pagan breast did cover it. For this reason quite a few pagans tried in various ways to protect and save the persecuted Christians. The Egyptian Athanasius, who was a baby at this time, says that he heard his parents speak of pagans who, when the persecution broke out, hid Christians who were being sought by the police. Their pagan hosts allowed their goods to be confiscated and went to prison rather than betray them. They sheltered the Christians who fled to their house and braved all danger to protect them (cf. *Historia arianorum ad monachos*, 64).

While giving due regard to such sentiments among the pagans we must remember that their conduct may have been motivated by hostility to the imperial government. The government did not enjoy much favor among the Egyptian people, for they remembered all too well their bloody repression by Diocletian in his campaign of 298 (par. 15). They revenged themselves by sheltering those who were now sought by that government.

Athanasius (cf. *Vita Antonii*, 46) gives us a curious, if not surprising, bit of information. The famous ascete Anthony who already had considerable fame as a leader of hermits and who was then living in the district of Memphis followed with anxiety the events of the persecution from his cell in the desert. One day he could no longer bear to help his fellow Christians by long-distance methods, and set off for Alexandria to help and comfort the imprisoned and those condemned to hard labor in the mines. This was in 311, in the persecution of Maximin. Later he returned to his desert, but the physical solitude did not separate him from his brethren in feelings and prayer.

112. Coming down from Alexandria toward the south we find that the persecution was even more bloody in the lands around Thebes. Here again we must listen to the story of Eusebius who was a witness of what he relates: "It is beyond power of words to describe the outrages and torments suffered by the martyrs of the Thebaid. They were scraped with shells instead of iron hooks all over their bodies until

they died. Women were tied by one leg and hauled up into the air by winches; they were left hanging upside down completely naked and presented the worst and most cruelly inhuman spectacle of all. Some died tied to trees and stumps. Strong trees were bent together by winches until they met at the top; a leg of the martyr was fixed to each tree and then the trees were allowed to spring back to their former position. This torture had been discovered to tear the sinews of the limbs of those who suffered it. And all these deeds were practiced not for a few days or for a short time, but for years. Sometimes ten were killed at the same time, sometimes twenty or more; at other times not less than thirty and sometimes nearly sixty. Once in the space of one day a good hundred men with women and children were all executed after having endured various prolonged tortures.

"We ourselves were witness of the great crowd who in the space of one day endured beheading or the punishment of fire; the orgy went on so long that the murderous blade became blunt and killed by its weight. The executioners themselves became exhausted and took turns at their work. We also saw the most marvelous inspiration, a force which was truly divine, and the readiness of those who had faith in the Christ of God. Immediately, when sentence had been pronounced on one group, another party came before the tribunal from the opposite side acknowledging themselves Christians and remaining unmoved before dangers and torments of all kinds. Indeed, they reasoned bravely and clearly concerning the service of God of the Universe; and lighthearted and happy, they received with joy the final sentence of death. They sang hymns and offered thanksgiving to the God of all until their last breath" (*Hist. Eccl.*, viii, 9, 1–5).

113. Peter of Alexandria. In the paragraphs on the Egyptian schism of Meletius we have mentioned Peter the bishop of Alexandria and referred to his martyrdom (pars. 93–95). He was bishop of the Egyptian capital from 300 to 311, and in an atmosphere thick with the doctrines of Origen he showed himself as unfavorable to them as Alexander and Athanasius, his successors in the see. As a shepherd of souls and a promoter of ecclesiastical discipline, he fixed for the *lapsi* those sensible rules which so raised the hackles of Meletius.

When the persecution of Maximin recommenced, Peter once more hid himself and from his hiding place continued to govern his diocese and oppose the schism of Meletius. This time Peter was unfortunate. His refuge was discovered and he was beheaded without trial, by direct order of Maximin (cf. *Hist. Eccl.*, ix, 6, 2; vii, 32, 31; viii, 13, 7).

114. Phileas and Philoromus. A letter describing the massacres of Christians which Phileas, bishop of Thmuis, a city to the east of Alexandria, had witnessed has already been mentioned (par. 110). Now we must regard him, not as a witness, but as a victim. The documents associate him with Philoromus. Both men occupied high places in society. Philoromus was head of the financial administration of Egypt (*procurator summarum Aegypti*), a very important office with powers over a large army of functionaries and fiscal agents. Before becoming bishop, Phileas had served honorably in public affairs, had studied philosophy deeply, was young, noble, and very rich. He had a wife and children and it seems certain that they were pagan; this shows that he had married before becoming a Christian for he would not have married a pagan after his conversion.

Both Eusebius (cf. *Hist. Eccl.*, viii, 9, 7–8; 10, 1–11) and the *Acts* which we have link the stories of Philoromus and Phileas. The *Acts* appears to have been composed at the end of the fourth century and has as a basis the official interrogation or other equivalent documents; some short additions have been made to this original record. Jerome (*De viris illustr.*, 78) seems to have known the *Acts* which is attributed by Rufinus (*Hist. Eccl.*, viii, 10) to a certain Gregory. Besides their trustworthy edition by the Bollandists and by Ruinart, there is another of little value by Combefis.

We do not know the circumstances of the capture of Phileas and Philoromus. They were in prison at Alexandria before their trial; and Philoromus appeared only after the trial had begun. Phileas had opposed the schism of Meletius (par. 95) and had written to the Christians of Thmuis praising the martyrs of Egypt; the moment had now come for him to prove his words by deeds.

115. On the tribunal the judge was Culcianus, prefect of Egypt. The hall was filled with important people — friends, admirers, and relatives of the accused including his wife and children. They had all come with the firm purpose of saving him and had been working on the judge before the trial. Culcianus, for his part, was quite ready to listen to such pleas for he did not wish to make enemies of people so well placed in society and — what was perhaps more important — in finance.

Phileas was conducted to his place and Culcianus began:

"Are you now able to see yourself more clearly and to free your mind of this madness which has seized on it?"

"I have never been mad and am quite sane now."

"Very well then, sacrifice to the gods."

"I will not sacrifice."

"Why?"

"Because the Scripture says that he will be uprooted who sacrifices to the gods except to God alone [*soli Deo*]."

"All right then, sacrifice to the God Sol [*deo Soli*]." The judge was playing on the sense of the two Latin words; for the god *Sol*, see par. 28.

"I will not sacrifice, for God does not wish such immolations. He says that he does not want holocausts of lambs, or bulls or offerings of flour."

At this point a lawyer intervened with desperate sarcasm: "Is this a question of flour? You are treating for your life."

The intervention of this lawyer, like other incidents of the kind that we shall see later, was unusual. Lawyers did not commonly defend those who had been accused of being Christians; such an action would be very dangerous (cf. Tertullian, *Apologet.*, ii, 2–3). The martyr Victoria was defended by the lawyer Fortunatianus (par. 104) but he was her brother. The same situation occurs in this trial, for later among the lawyers a brother of the accused appeared. Given the position of the relatives of Phileas and the benevolent disposition of the judge, it is easy to understand how the lawyers of Alexandria were anxious to help their colleague. They did not help much anyway for the trial soon became more and more a personal discussion between the judge and his prisoner.

116. Calcianus took no notice of the interruption and asked Phileas:

"What kind of sacrifices does your God like?"

"Purity of heart, sincere faith, and truth."

"Well then, sacrifice!"

"I will not sacrifice. I do not know how to."

"Didn't Paul sacrifice?"

"No."

"Moses sacrificed anyway."

"The Jews were commanded to sacrifice to one God only in Jerusalem. They sin now when they celebrate their feasts in other places."

"Enough of this double talk. Sacrifice."

"I will not stain my soul."

"Can we throw away our soul?"

"Both soul and body."

"This body perhaps?"

"This body."

"The body will rise again?"

"Yes."

"Surely Paul denied Jesus Christ?"

"No."

"But he was a persecutor. Was he not uneducated and a Syrian who only spoke his native tongue?"

"He was a Hebrew, spoke Greek, and was the wisest of men."

"You will be saying soon that he was wiser than Plato."

"Not only wiser than Plato but than all the philosophers. In fact he argued with and convinced very wise men. If you like, I will explain his teaching to you."

"The gods forbid. Sacrifice!"

"I will not sacrifice."

"Because of your conscience?"

"Yes."

"Then what about your duty to your wife and children?"

"My duty to God is more important. The Scripture indeed says, 'Thou shalt love the Lord God who has made you.' "

"Which god?"

"The God," replied Phileas lifting his hands to heaven, "who made the sky and land, the sea and everything which is in them. He is the Creator and Author of all things visible and invisible, the Unspeakable one who alone exists and remains for ever and ever, Amen."

The lawyers broke in: "Why do you defy the Governor?"

"I am answering his questions."

Culcianus cried: "Save your tongue then and sacrifice."

"I will not sacrifice. I prefer to save my soul. Not only Christians save their souls but even pagans. I give you the example of Socrates. When he was taken to his death although his wife and children were there he did not try to avoid his sentence but willingly accepted death. And he was an old man."

117. After some theological argument about Christ, Culcianus returned to the direct attack:

"You must remember the consideration I have shown you. I could have humiliated you in your own city but out of regard for you I have not done so."

"I am grateful for this kindness and would beg you to add another favor to it."

"What do you want?"

"Use your authority [temeritate, or better — auctoritate tua utere] and follow your instructions."

"You wish to die without reason?"

"Not without reason; it will be for God and his truth." The judge realized that he was fast becoming a tool of the prisoner and changed the subject:

"Was Paul God?"

"No."

"Who was he then?"

"A man like you. But the Spirit of God was in him and by this Spirit he did wonders and miracles." Culcianus tried an unexpected shot: "I will pardon you for your brother's sake." This move did not spring from the current disputation but from the pressure put on the judge before the trial by the friends and relations of the accused. The reply of Phileas was:

"Give me the favor I ask. Use your authority and execute the orders you have received."

"If I thought you were in poverty and had been driven by starvation to this madness I would not pardon you. But because you have great possessions, and have responsibilities, if not to yourself, certainly to almost all our province, I will spare you and persuade you to sacrifice."

"And I will not sacrifice to save my life."

118. There was no way out. By now the judge was in a muddle and looked toward the relatives and friends of the accused as if to say that he had done all he could and that if he had not been able to keep the promises he had made to them in private it was certainly not his fault. The lawyers then intervened with a rather pitiful lie. They maintained that there was no need for the accused to sacrifice a second time for he had already made private sacrifice in the phrontisterion (a place set aside for thought and meditation). Phileas denied this flatly.

At this moment Culcianus thought he might find some assistance in the piteous condition of Phileas' relations, especially his wife, who was distressed and tearful. "That unfortunate woman your wife is looking at you [tibi intendit]." The poor lady was a pagan and hoped only for the collapse of her husband's principles and was gazing into his face hoping to see signs of what she wanted. But Phileas replied: "The Saviour of all our souls is Jesus Christ whom I serve in these chains. He who has called me to share his glory is powerful enough to call her also."

The lawyers who were looking for an opening pretended to understand that these words referred to the trial and exclaimed to the judge: "Phileas asks for adjournment."

The benevolent Culcianus replied immediately:

"I allow the court to adjourn so that the accused may consider his position."

Just as immediate was the retort of the defendant:

"I have given much thought to my situation and I am determined to suffer for Christ."

At this the pretense of a trial collapsed. An extraordinary scene of sincere emotion began with the lawyers, the officials of the court, the "curator" who was the first magistrate of the city, Phileas' relatives and friends surrounding the accused, clasping him around the knees, and begging him to have pity on his wife and children. But Phileas was immovable and, as the story has it, he seemed a mighty rock battered by the waves in vain. His mind was raised to heaven and he saw only God. His relatives and friends were now the martyrs and the apostles.

119. At this point, according to the *Acts* we have now, Philoromus comes on the scene. He had been present at least during the last attempts of the lawyers and perhaps had already been questioned by the judge. Of this interrogation, however, no trace has remained in the *Acts* which have probably been shortened so as to leave the whole field to Phileas. Referring to what had happened at the hearing he exclaimed in a loud voice in the hall:

"Why do you try uselessly the constancy of this man? Why do you wish to make unfaithful one who is faithful to God? Why do you want to force him to deny God just to satisfy man? Do you not realize that his eyes do not see your tears, that his ears do not hear your words? He who contemplates heavenly glory is not moved by earthly tears."

Inevitably, all those present were furious at these words and turning to the judge demanded that he should be sentenced to death for them and, to finish the sorry affair, that this sentence should also be given to Phileas. The judge had also reached the limit of his endurance and condemned both men without delay to be beheaded.

Not everybody had as yet lost all hope. The two condemned men had already left the judgment hall and were on their way to the place of execution when a lawyer cried out to the judge:

"Phileas appeals [abolitionem, or better — appellationem petit]."

The lawyer who had cried out was the brother of Phileas and this explains his desire to snatch up the smallest straw of hope. The judge hurriedly called back Phileas and asked him:

"Quid appellasti? [What appeal do you make?]"

The reply of Phileas removed all hope.

"I have not appealed; anything but that! Take no notice of that unfortunate man. For my own part I am very grateful to the emperors and to you, my judge, for allowing me to become a coheir with Jesus Christ."

When Phileas arrived at the place of execution he gave a brief exhortation to the Christians who were there and then both he and Philoromus were beheaded.

Their martyrdom probably took place in 306.

PALESTINE, PHOENICIA, AND SYRIA

120. Leaving Egypt we now go up to Palestine, Phoenicia, and Syria. We will take Eusebius as our guide. He lacks details found in the Acts and the Passions but has the advantage of having actually seen the events and of being a close friend of some of the people involved.

Pamphilus and Companions. The master from whom Eusebius took his surname, Pamphilus (par. 71), fell at the height of the persecution. He was one of the great scholars of the early Christian centuries; even Jerome had such veneration for him that when he came into possession of Origen's commentaries on the minor prophets, copied by Pamphilus, it seemed, Jerome says, that he now possessed the treasures of Coresus and on those pages, filled with his writing, he seemed to see traces of the martyr's blood (cf. De viris illustr., 75).

He was born at Berytus (Beirut) in Phoenicia and from his youth he gave himself to asceticism, distributed all his possessions to the poor, and became a priest at Caesarea in Palestine. He became a great student working at the library at Caesarea which had been founded by Origen. Pamphilus added to it considerably and gave funds for a scriptorium for the copying of the Bible. Eusebius was much attached to him and wrote his life in three books which are now, unfortunately, lost. In November, 307, Pamphilus was imprisoned by the governor of Palestine, Urbanus, who first tried out his learning and then after he had refused to sacrifice, had him tortured and his sides torn with iron hooks. After this, he was sent back to prison. He remained there for a couple of years, and with the assistance of Eusebius wrote the five books of the *Apologia of Origen* (par. 71), to which Eusebius later added a sixth book. In prison he had as companions Valens, an aged deacon of the church of Aelia Capitolina (Jerusalem), who was learned in Sacred Scripture; Paul who had come originally from Jabne (now Jebna), and bore on his arms the scars of the red-hot irons with which he had been tortured earlier for his Christian faith; and some others.

The occasion for their martyrdom was offered by the passage through Caesarea of the five Egyptian Christians returning from the mines of whom we have already spoken (par. 92). When these Christians were taken before the tribunal of the new governor, Firmilian, who had succeeded Urbanus, Pamphilus and his companions in prison were brought out once more. When the Egyptian Christians had been beheaded, Firmilian demanded of the group with Pamphilus that they would now obey the imperial edicts. They all refused and received the same sentence as the Egyptians.

121. The condemned men were taken to their execution. At that moment there appeared from the crowd, standing around, a young man not yet eighteen years old clothed in the simple cloak of a philosopher who asked in a loud voice that burial should be allowed for the bodies of the martyrs. This was Porphyrius, a slave of the house of Pamphilus, who had been considered by his master more as a son and who had become an excellent scribe in his school. The judge asked him if he was a Christian and when he confessed that he was — he was perhaps only a catechumen — had him tortured and lacerated so cruelly that his bones and inner organs were laid bare. No cry of pain escaped the lips of the martyr. Seeing his obstinacy the judge condemned him to be burned at a slow fire. Eusebius remarks that thus the last arrival at the contest came first to the crown, preceding even his master Pamphilus. He went quite calmly to the stake planted in the midst of the bundles of wood and spoke cheerfully to his friends about him. They bound him to the stake and after the fire had been lighted at some distance around him, he blew the flames to both sides of him to

hurry on his own holocaust. He did not speak. Only when the flames reached him he called on the help of Jesus, the Son of God, and during this invocation he died.

Eusebius, who tells us these particulars, probably had Porphyrius as his companion in the *scriptorium* of Caesarea when he was copying the Bible under the guidance of Pamphilus. In some Greek codices of the Bible which have come down to us we find at the end annotations like these: "Compared with a very ancient copy which had been collated by the hand of the holy martyr Pamphilus." In its turn this "very ancient copy" contained the following annotation which has been reproduced faithfully in the copy which has come down to us: "Corrected according to the hexapla of Origen. Antonius collated, I, Pamphilus, corrected." In another place we find the note: "Pamphilus and Eusebius corrected." Or else "I . . . wrote; collated in the library of Caesarea with the copy written by the hand of the holy Pamphilus." The name of Porphyrius does not seem to appear in any of the codices which we have; perhaps, however, the martyred copyist was too young to have his name in the colophons of the codices on which he had worked.

122.   But the tragedy was not yet ended. It had an unexpected development. While Porphyrius was being martyred, Pamphilus and the other condemned Christians were waiting for their own execution. A young man ran up to Pamphilus to tell him of the glorious death of his slave; this messenger, in his joy at the news he brought, kissed one of the condemned men.

Obviously this young man was a Christian. He was called Seleucus and had been born in Cappadocia. He had at one time been in the army, where he had reached a high position by meritorious and brave services; at the time of the purge in the army (par. 37 ff.) he had been flogged and had then left the service. If his tall, athletic build showed him to be a soldier, his gentle countenance displayed delicate and kindly feeling. In fact, when he left the army he had dedicated himself to works of charity, giving help to abandoned orphans, looking after the sick, giving protection to widows and outcasts.

His happy face among the sour executioners and those condemned to death and especially the kiss annoyed the soldiers who were on guard, so they seized him and took him to the Governor. The Governor was even more annoyed than the guards and he condemned him to be beheaded with those who were already waiting their turn. The

Empire had already lost a brave soldier and now the people lost their protector.

But the tragedy did not end with this fresh victim. Immediately someone else followed Seleucus' example. He annoyed the Governor even more, for he came from his own household. He was called Theodulus and was advanced in years and a great-grandfather. The Governor liked him especially for his loyalty and exemplary conduct. He was possibly a Christian or perhaps the goodness of his heart urged him to behave like one. He committed this new crime of kissing one of the martyrs. The Governor was more furious than ever and instead of condemning him to the usual beheading he had him crucified.

Meanwhile Pamphilus and his two companions were executed. There were therefore eleven victims: Pamphilus with Valens and Paul, the five Egyptians, Porphyrius, Seleucus, and Theodulus.

123.   Eusebius, however, in his story felt that this number of eleven was not right. The number twelve must be arrived at for this was the number of the Apostles. And so it was to be. A certain Julian came back to Caesarea after a journey. He was a fervent Christian who, like Seleucus, had originally come from Cappadocia. As soon as he learned what was happening in the city, he ran to the place of execution to assist at the triumph of his brothers in the faith. He arrived to find their triumph complete and their bodies stretched on the ground. Full of happiness he embraced them and kissed them all. Quite naturally he was arrested and conducted before the Governor. The latter, who by now was very angry indeed, did not crucify him as he had Theodulus but returned to the punishment inflicted on Porphyrius, condemning the new rebel to be burned at a slow fire. When Julian heard the sentence his happiness knew no bounds and he danced for joy, thanking God in a loud voice for having considered him worthy of taking his place with the other heroes. He was taken off to the place of execution.

By order of the Governor, the bodies of the martyrs remained exposed for four days and nights. The soldiers on guard were to capture or at least keep off the Christians who should try to approach their brethren living or dead, but had orders not to molest birds, dogs, or other beasts who might come to feed on the bodies. Although on other occasions the Governor had succeeded in engineering this final disgrace, for once the whole time that the bodies remained exposed they were untouched by the animals (par. 126). When his anger had died down the guards were withdrawn and Christians came and gave the bodies an honorable burial. The slaughter took place on February 16, 310.

124. Apphianus, Edesius, Procopius.   Eusebius gives individual treatment to many other martyrs of these regions, but in one way the most interesting are the cases of those who showed a more or less aggressive front before the pagan magistrates.

A typical case of this was Apphianus who lived for a long time with Eusebius. He came of a rich pagan family in Lycia and had been sent to pursue his studies at Berytus where he read law and probably became a Christian. In that city of luxury he maintained austere habits although he was not yet twenty years of age. When he returned home he soon saw that it was going to be difficult to live there according to his new faith, and so he moved to Caesarea in Palestine where he made a special study of Holy Scripture. In 306 Maximin gave a new impulse to the failing persecution and the public criers moved up and down the streets of the city calling the people out to sacrifice to the gods. One day they passed before the house where Apphianus lived with Eusebius, and without telling anybody, the former set off for the house of Urbanus, the governor (par. 120). He managed to evade the guards and got into the household where he found Urbanus in the act of making a libation to idols. He pounced on him and snatched at his arm to prevent him. Urbanus was then made to listen to an energetic exhortation to put away his idols in favor of the one true God. It is hardly necessary to add that the intruder was quickly arrested and suffered various terrible tortures. Finally, he was flung half dead into the sea in February, 306.

Apphianus, however, had a brother, Edesius, who was quite worthy of him and was even more direct and energetic in his methods. He was also more learned than his brother and went about in the cloak of a philosopher. He had already experienced prison and forced labor in the mines in Palestine when he moved to Alexandria. He happened to be present one day in the tribunal when the judge was unburdening himself of some of his hatred of the Christians, attacking respectable men, and sending venerable matrons and virgins, consecrated to God, to the brothels. At this Edesius could contain himself no longer and went up to the judge and not only told him what he thought of him but added deeds — he punched and kicked him. It is quite superfluous also here to add that this daring deed was immediately rewarded with the most excruciating torments. Like his brother he was finally cast into the sea.

Procopius was not handy with his fists, but was an old ascete who showed himself subtle and clever. He was a lector in the Christian community of Scythopolis near the Jordan. He was arrested and taken before the governor, Flavian, at Caesarea. When he was commanded to sacrifice to the gods Procopius replied that he knew only one God and would only sacrifice to him in the way he had commanded. Flavian was not in the mood for theological discussion and quickly introduced a political flavor by ordering him to offer the sacred libations to the four emperors. Procopius, however, had no intention of leaving theology and only replied with a verse of Homer: "A many faced rule is not good; let there be one ruler and one king" (*Iliad*, ii, 204). This was quite enough, however, to make Procopius a political rebel and he was quickly beheaded. The first martyr of Palestine, he fell at the very beginning of the persecution in June of 303.

125. Daring Women. In Palestine the women shared the energetic daring of their Christian menfolk. They resisted the judges in their own way. Among the Christians captured at Gaza while reading Scripture (par. 89) and sent to the mines was a woman of outstanding courage. She had made a vow of virginity and the judge threatened to send her to a brothel. She sprang up like a lioness and quite soundly denounced the "tyrant," the emperor, who saw fit to entrust the government of his provinces to idiots like the one sitting there on the judgment seat. She was flogged and then strung up and her sides were torn with iron hooks.

While this torture was going on, another woman called Valentina, a native of Caesarea and a vowed virgin, raised her voice from the crowd. She was only a little thing and not much to look at, but had plenty of spirit. "How long," she called to the judge, "are you going to torture my sister so cruelly?" She was arrested and when she was conducted into the middle of the hall "she enlisted," says Eusebius, "under the mighty name of the Saviour." That is, she put on her arms for the coming battle. At first the judge, with pleasant talk, tried to persuade her to sacrifice but when this had no effect she was dragged bodily to the altar. When she finally arrived there, instead of offering the ritual incense she dealt a number of well-directed kicks and pushed over the altar with everything on it and the tripod with the fire. The judge was furious and after this new rebel had been tortured he condemned her to be burned alive with her sister. It was July of 308.

Trouble was also caused by three Christians, Anthony, Zebinas, and Germanus, who agreed without any direct provocation to face up to the Governor of Palestine while he was performing a public sacrifice. On November 13, 308, they approached the Governor in the middle of the ceremony shouting to him to stop since there was only one true God. They were arrested and declared themselves Christians. Without the usual preliminary tortures the Governor had them beheaded immediately.

On the same day a virgin of Scythopolis, Ennathas, was martyred. She had given no provocation, but had caught the eye of a certain military tribune, Maxys, whose vast muscles were only equaled by his amorous propensities. Without any command from his superiors he stripped the woman to the waist and caused her to be publicly whipped. After this she was taken to the tribunal and under some charge or other was condemned to be burned alive.

126. Other Martyrs. The governor of that time was Firmilian whom we have already met in the martyrdoms of Pamphilus and companions (par. 120). What he had done then was his usual custom: he ordered that the bodies of the martyrs should be left unburied so that they could be devoured by the beasts of the plains and the birds. This was quite against the Roman law and custom, which did not persecute the condemned person after his death and respected his body. With the abundance of Firmilian's victims spread over the plains, the surroundings of Caesarea became a charnel house and while the guards of the Governor stopped the Christians from taking away the bodies, the wild animals had all they could eat. Eusebius was a witness of this: "All around the city were scattered bowels and human bones . . . very close to the gates there was a sight which passed all words and any tragic theme, for human flesh was not being devoured just in one place but was flung about in all directions. Some said that they had seen, even inside the gates of the town, whole human members, pieces of flesh and lengths of bowel" (De Mart. Palaest., ix, 10–11).

127. Directly to the north of Palestine extended Phoenicia which had Tyre for its capital. Eusebius speaks as a personal witness for what happened in this country.

We must speak first of individual executions, specifically those of Ulpian and Theodosia. The young Ulpian received the usual flogging and torture and then was condemned to a kind of death anciently reserved for parricides, but not used for a long time. The condemned man was shut up in a sack made of the fresh skin of an ox with a live dog and a poisonous viper. The whole package was then thrown into the sea. This punishment had been discontinued since it had been judged too frightful even for parricides. Since the judges were dealing with Christians, however, it was reintroduced for the latter were far more execrable than parricides. Ulpian died at Tyre in 306.

The virgin Theodosia was also born at Tyre, but died in Caesarea. She was hardly eighteen. She had gone to visit some Christians who were waiting for judgment (this may have been her reason for coming to Caesarea, for there may have been some of her relatives among them), and went to them not only to wish them well but also to ask them "to remember her with the Lord" or as the longer version says "to remember her when they had obtained what they were aiming for" (*De Mart. Palaest.*, vii, 1). It is a clear attestation of what those Christians thought about the intercession of martyrs after their death. Her desire was fulfilled more quickly than she expected. She was arrested immediately by the soldiers for revolutionary conversation and taken to the Governor. She was put to the torture and her sides and breasts were torn to the bone. She was still alive at the end and smiling, so she was thrown into the sea. This was the year 307, perhaps on Easter Sunday.

Toward the end of the persecution, perhaps in 311, Silvanus, the bishop of Emesa in Upper Phoenicia in Syria, was martyred. He was very old, and he remained at the head of his flock for forty years, having been made a bishop in the time of Aurelian. He was fed to wild beasts with two of his clerics.

128. The Massacre at Tyre. Without referring to other individual martyrs in Phoenicia it will be sufficient to listen to the relation which Eusebius gives of the massacre of Christians exposed to wild beasts in Tyre. The majority of these Christians were Egyptians.

"We assisted personally as such happenings . . . the devourers (wild beasts) of men did not dare for a long time either to touch or even to approach the bodies of the friends of God although they sprang accurately enough on the outsiders (the pagans) who were urging them on with pointed sticks. It was only the holy athletes who were untouched although they stood still and naked and beckoned to the beasts with their hands, as they had been told to do. And if one of the animals sprang towards them, it seemed to be pushed back by divine power and at once went away from them. This went on for a long time and produced no little wonder among the spectators, for when the first beast had retired in this way, a second and third did the same. All were dumbstruck by the fearless constancy of these saints and the unbreakable resolution of those young bodies. You would see a young man of not yet twenty years of age who stood without movement although unbound with his hands outstretched in the form of a cross. He prayed for long with untroubled and tranquil mind to the Divinity, neither moving nor going away from his place while bears and leopards, breathing rage and threats of horrible death, were almost touching him. But in some way, I know not how, by a divine and hidden force their mouths were closed and they finally ran away from him. Such was one case. Others you would have seen, there were five in all, exposed to an infuriated bull who tossed in the air the other outsiders (the pagans) who were urging him to the martyrs, and wounded them so seriously that they were picked up half dead. When the bull rushed against the holy ones (the Christians) with all fury and menace he suddenly stopped and could approach no nearer but pawed the ground and tossed his horns here and there breathing anger and fear towards those who were goading him with hot irons. He had been stayed by Divine Providence and could inflict no harm on the martyrs. Other beasts were set against them without success. Finally after all these terrible and varied trials they were all slaughtered with the sword and instead of being buried in the earth or in sepulchres they were all flung on the waves of the sea" (*Hist. Eccl.*, viii, 7, 2–6).

129. Going up northward from Phoenicia we enter Syria, whose capital is Antioch. The persecution here was just as severe, but it was singular in that it preferred to attack Christian chastity and modesty, raging with wild fury against the women.

Pagan Antioch was already a center of corruption and it had remained much the same in Christian times. The Caesar of the East was Maximin, whom historians depict as a type of debauchery. Of the many unpleasant details mentioned by Lactantius (cf. *De mortibus persecut.*, 38) it is sufficient to record here that he had a well-organized body of his own servants who spied out among the houses of the town for women, married or single, noble or common, who could satisfy the desires of the Caesar. This happened in every town where he passed (*Hist. Eccl.*, viii, 14, 12). Since this was done by the head, it is only natural that his inferiors should follow his example. They, of course, lacked the power of a Caesar, but in recompense they showed themselves energetic persecutors of the Christians, or rather of Christian women, against whom any action was allowed as outlaws in the Empire.

Speaking in general, Eusebius records people who flung themselves from lofty buildings to escape their seducers, avoiding by their death the wickedness of the evil ones (cf. *ibid.*, viii, 12, 2). In particular, though without mentioning their names, he speaks of two young sisters, of noble birth, beautiful and rich, who, by the command of the servants of the devil, were flung into the sea. This can only mean that they had refused to be seduced (cf. *ibid.*, viii, 12, 5). He then speaks at greater length (cf. *ibid.*, viii, 3-4) of another episode which is mentioned also by Ambrose (*De Virginibus*, viii, 7) and by John Chrysostom (*Homilia*, 51; Migne, *Patr. Graec.*, 50, 629-640), who was of Antioch himself. Although the various relations disagree in minor details the substance of the story seems to have been the following.
130. Domnina, Berenice, and Prosdoche. Domnina had two daughters, Berenice and Prosdoche — these names are not mentioned by Eusebius. All three women were well known in Antioch. The mother was a zealous Christian and she had brought up her two daughters in the same religion. They led a life of prayer apart from the world. The outbreak and intensification of the persecution put them in the same dangers as the other Christians with the additional hazard that they were women, rich and beautiful, and therefore fair game for the pagans of Antioch.

They took the radical decision to leave not only faithless Antioch, but also Syria and to go as far away as possible. They crossed the Euphrates and made their home at Edessa, a town which had provided a home and refuge for Christians for very many years. For some time they remained untroubled. Their departure from Antioch had been noticed, however, and the anger of the pagans began to increase against them. The husband of Domnina, who was perhaps a pagan, had remained at Antioch and they began to work on him. Probably during the intensification of the persecution under Maximin, search was instituted for individual Christians, and relatives were forced to reveal their hiding places. The husband was persuaded to talk and he betrayed his wife and daughters. Edessa was a long way away, but the importance of the prize would compensate for the labor of the long journey. According to Chrysostom the husband himself accompanied the soldiers in their expedition. During their return to Antioch with their booty the tragedy occurred. The three women flung themselves into a river to attempt an escape not only from the tortures which awaited them, but also the certain loss of their chastity. The way in which this extreme resolve was carried out is described differently in the three accounts we have. Eusebius and Chrysostom make the women already captured by the soldiers from whom they were able to detach themselves for some reason or by means of a trick. Ambrose, on the other hand, supposes them not to be caught, but that when they found themselves trapped between the soldiers and a river, they chose the latter.

131. Pelagia. Eusebius does not record the similar case of Pelagia of Antioch, although he may have included her in his brief reference to those who suffered martyrdom by flinging themselves from heights (par. 129). Both Ambrose, however (cf. De Virginibus, iii, 7; Epist., xxxvii, 38), and John Chrysostom in two homilies in her honor (cf. Migne, Patr. Graec., 50, 579–586) refer to the historical Pelagia. (Other legendary Pelagias are derived from her sufferings.)

She was a fifteen-year-old girl who from the outbreak of the persecution had lived hidden in her house more for fear of her chastity than her life. One day some soldiers were charged to bring her to the tribunal and arrived at the house "when neither father, nor mother, nor sisters, nor nurse, nor slave girl, nor neighbor, nor friend" was at home. She realized what would happen to her in the solitude of her house and immediately made her plans. She opened the door to the soldiers with a welcoming countenance and asked to be allowed to retire to her room to put her best garments on so that she could present herself before the magistrates as worthily as possible. Taken in by such aplomb the soldiers suspected nothing and allowed her to do this. Pelagia went to her room, clothed herself in her finest clothes, made fervent prayer to God, went up to the top of the house, and flung herself down. The soldiers found only a corpse.

132. Lucian of Antioch. A martyr of Antioch worthy of particular mention is Lucian, celebrated from ancient times for his learned work on the Greek text of the Bible. According to Jerome his recension of the Bible was the most used in the lands from Constantinople to Antioch. What we know for certain about his death is found in Eusebius (cf. *Hist. Eccl.*, viii, 13, 2; ix, 6, 3). The sermon in his honor by Chrysostom (cf. Migne, *Patr. Graec.*, 50, 519–526) suffers from oratory and is rather vague in details. Later legends have developed his story considerably and added items derived from pagan mythology.

Eusebius tells us that Lucian was arrested and taken to Nicomedia where the Emperor, at that time Maximin, was residing. After he had defended his faith he was put in chains and finally executed on January 7, 312. His body was taken to Drepanum, a city on the coast of Bithynia which Constantine later called Helenopolis in honor of his mother Helena. She was very devoted to Lucian. Over his tomb a basilica was constructed.

ASIA MINOR

133. Our proposed journey (par. 99) now takes us northward from Syria into Asia Minor where Christianity had penetrated in the time of the Apostle Paul and, at the period with which we are dealing, was very widespread. Our principal guide, Eusebius, unfortunately now leaves us and there is no one who is able to take his place.

There is no lack of *Passions* of martyrs in these regions, but in general they lack authenticity. For the most part they are later relations which probably have authentic history in them but are mixed with much that cannot be trusted (par. 76, no. 3). Such is the *Passion* of the innkeeper Theodotus and the seven virgins which comes from Ancyra in Galatia and purports to be written by an eyewitness, Nilus, who was in prison with Theodotus. The story is full of incident and pleasant to read. Nevertheless among other things toward the end (*Passio*, cap. 33 ff.) there is an account of some asses burdened with bags of wine which is also told by Herodotus (ii, 121). The *Passion* of Taracus, Probus, and Andronicus may be rather more authentic. The author says that he bought the verbal transcript of their interrogation for two hundred pence (par. 69). This may well have been true, but the author has stuffed the whole account with fantasies and sited the various incidents in a number of different cities (Pompeiopolis, Mopsuestia, Anazarbus). Apart from all this the matters he relates are so peculiar that it is impossible not to doubt the whole affair historically.

134. Julitta the Widow. The story of the widow Julitta is not very long, but quite worthy of acceptance. She came from Caesarea in Cappadocia, and although we have no *Passion* for her, we have, in recompense, a discourse in her honor given by the great Basil who was himself a native of the same city (*Homil.*, v, 1–2).

Julitta was very rich, and owned lands, cattle, slaves, and a very well-furnished house. All this excited the jealousy of one of the principal citizens who by fraud and dishonesty began to extort her property from her. This was fairly easy in the case of a widow whose rights, as those of an orphan, were not properly safeguarded in antiquity, especially in the East. When he had got her lands and cattle, her persecutor turned his attention to her household furniture and other possessions which he began to remove a little at a time into his own house. The injured woman took him to court, but her powerful enemy not only bought up the witnesses and bribed the judges, but also arranged a more decisive attack which had great success. When Julitta had begun her explanation of her rights and the fraud and violence of her enemy, he came to the front of the hall and made a complaint about the procedure of the trial. The plaintiff, he maintained, could not be heard until she had made the customary act of worship of the gods of the emperors and had renounced the Christian faith. The thief had found the perfect defense, for the law allowed no rights to Julitta if she was a Christian (par. 56). The judge ordered that incense and fire should be brought immediately and that the plaintiff make the offering. Julitta refused point blank saying: "You may take my life as well as my possessions; I will lose my body before my mouth will utter any impiety against God my Creator." The judge became angry and insisted that Julitta should carry out the ceremony under pain of incurring legal infamy. She answered: "I am the handmaid of Christ." When she was finally given the alternative of sacrificing or dying by fire, she chose the latter and was executed shortly afterward.

135. The Martyrs of Pontus. The northeast of Asia Minor is taken up by the region of Pontus, which is bordered by the Pontus Euxinus (Black Sea) and had as its capital Neocaesarea. We have already mentioned the Christian forebears of Basil who avoided the persecution by taking refuge in the forests there (par. 85). Before leaving Eusebius, we must hear his short account of the cruelties perpetrated in Pontus during the persecution.

He says: "Terrible to hear were the agonies suffered by those

(Christians) of Pontus. Some had sharpened reeds thrust under their fingernails; others had boiling lead poured over their backs and their most vital parts burned in this way; still others suffered in their private parts tortures which were shameful, callous, and impossible to describe; these torments were inflicted by noble judges who respected the law; they made show of cruelty as if it were a wise virtue and in a wretched competition for new tortures attempted to beat their rival judges as if they were striving for a prize" (*Hist. Eccl.*, viii, 12, 6–7).

Apart from this short summary we have no particulars on the persecution in the Pontus. And even Gregory of Nazianzus, a friend and contemporary of Basil keeps to generalities in his references to the persecution.

MACEDONIA, THRACE, ILLYRICUM, RHAETIA

136.   Leaving Asia Minor we follow the example of the Apostle Paul and make our way into Europe by Macedonia. We make our first stop at Thessalonica which he evangelized.

Agape, Irene, and Chione.   When the edict was first published which ordered the handing over and destruction of the Sacred Scriptures (par. 47), there were at Thessalonica three sisters, who, instead of obeying the edict, carefully hid many copies of the Scriptures in their house and then fled to the mountains. They had beautiful and symbolic names according to the customs of the ancient Christians, Agape (charity), Irene (peace), and Chione (snow). After spending some time wandering in the hills they returned home, only to be arrested and taken before Dulcitius, the governor of Macedonia. With them was charged a man Agatho and three other women, Cassia, Philippa, and Eutichia, all Christians.

The Acts of the three sisters, in which the other martyrs figure in a secondary place, seemed to be based on their respective interrogations which a later author put together and embellished with an introduction and an appendix. The Acts contain, however, many obscurities. Their Greek text has been recently published. The Latin text published by Surius and by Baronius is not ancient, but is a rather poor translation made by Sirleto in the sixteenth century.

Toward the end of March, 304, the group of accused, one man and six women, was interrogated by Dulcitius. He began by having the account of their arrest read in court from which it emerged that the accused had refused to eat the flesh of animals sacrificed to idols. When the charge had been read he passed to the interrogation.

Dulcitius began by making a general complaint:

"What madness is this of yours that you will not obey the most religious commands of our emperors and Caesars?"

He then turned to the only man, Agatho:

"How is it that you did not follow the custom of those who are consecrated to the gods and take part in the sacred rites?"

From this it would seem that Agatho in the past had been one of "those who are consecrated to the gods"; possibly he had been a pagan priest or something of that kind. Agatho replied: "Because I am a Christian."

Dulcitius continued:

"You still persist in your purpose today?"

The reply was: "Yes, without any change."

Dulcitius then turned to the women:

"And you, Agape, what have you to say?"

"I believe in the living God and do not wish to have anything but good deeds on my conscience."

The replies of the other women, Chione, Irene, Cassia, Philippa, and Eutichia were the same. Eutichia was heavy with child, and so the judge demanded.

"Have you a husband?"

"He is dead."

"When did he die?"

"About six months ago."

"By whom are you bearing this child then?"

"By the man whom God gave me."

"How then do you find yourself with child if as you tell me your husband is dead?"

"No one may know the counsels of the omnipotent God. This is the will of God."

The last question of Dulcitius and the reply of Eutichia have been left out in the editions of the Latin translation (but not in Sirleto's original manuscript). Apart from their delicate nature they seem difficult to understand. The problem has been explained recently (Franchi de'Cavalieri) by the theory that Dulcitius had not believed that her pregnancy was so far advanced and that Eutichia had remarried after the death of her first husband and did not wish to expose her new husband, certainly a Christian, to the interrogations of the judge. Dulcitius continued:

"I beg you, Eutichia, to put away this madness and to think once more like a rational being. What do you say? Will you obey the royal edict?"

"I most certainly will not obey it for I am a Christian, a servant of the omnipotent God."

The judge then replied:

"Since Eutichia is with child let her be kept for a time in prison."

It is known that the Roman law protected expectant mothers when they were brought up for trial. In the past Felicity, the slave and companion in martyrdom of Perpetua, could not be fed to the wild beasts because she was pregnant. While the Christians with her were waiting for their martyrdom they had all prayed for her and she had given birth to her child although she was only in her eighth month. Thus she was able to join her prison companions in their death.

The judge continued the interrogations and admonitions with Agape and Chione. Of the latter he demanded:

"Have you in your possession any treatises or parchments or books of the impious Christians?"

"We have nothing; the present emperors have taken away all that we had."

When he saw that his efforts were in vain, Dulcitius wrote out and pronounced sentence. Since Agape and Chione had rebelled against the edict of the Augusti and the Caesars by practicing the execrable Christian religion they were condemned to be burned alive. The judge then added that Agatho, Cassia, Philippa, and Irene were to remain in prison at his pleasure.

137. The two condemned women were burned at the stake. Meanwhile, the judge continued his inquiries in the hope of finding some secret cache of the Sacred Scriptures and in an attempt to break down Irene, the only one left of the three sisters. A little later in fact, his police managed to discover hidden away in Irene's house, boxes and other containers which were found to contain considerable quantities of the Scriptures they were looking for. They found "parchments, books, tablets, small codices and pages of writing" (Acts, Chap. 5). All this had certainly been collected before their flight from individual Christians. We do not know exactly what had happened. Perhaps

Irene believed that the earlier searches, to which Chione had already referred in her answers to the judge, had disposed of all their Scriptures and therefore had told Dulcitius that she had none. It may be that one of the other two sisters had prepared the hiding place without informing Irene. Whatever the case, Irene had every right to answer in the way she did. Dulcitius was encouraged by this discovery and again interrogated Irene. The fact that the Scriptures had finally been found in her house was a clear demonstration of her obstinacy, as was indeed the tranquillity she seemed to possess even when faced with the execution of her two sisters. The judge referred to all this and said that in a rather foolish urge of generosity he would forget everything and set her free if she would eat some meat which had been sacrificed to the gods.

Irene answered:

"My answer is no, by the omnipotent God who created heaven and earth, the sea and all things that exist. The dreadful punishment of eternal fire is especially reserved for those who have denied Jesus, the Word of God."

The judge asked her who had persuaded her to keep the Scriptures in her house and Irene replied that it had been God, who required us to love him even unto death and to allow ourselves to be burned to death rather than hand them over. Then the judge asked:

"Who besides yourself knew that these writings were hidden in your house?"

Irene answered: "No one else, as God sees me, except the omnipotent God who knows all things; other than he, nobody. We consider our own people indeed worse than our enemies for we fear that they may betray us. Therefore I showed them to nobody."

The expression "our own people" refers to members of the household in general and not to their husbands as is the interpretation of the faulty Latin translation. It does not appear that any of the three sisters were married.

Dulcitius thought that the interrogation might produce new information and so continued:

"Where did you hide yourselves last year when the edict was published?"

This sort of question laid the way open to the giving of information which might bring into the net Christians still in hiding. Because of this danger Irene replied in a prudently vague manner:

"Where God wished. We remained under the open sky, as God is our witness, on the mountains."

"With whom did you live?"

"In the open air. Here and there on the mountains."

"Who provided you with food?"

"God, who provides for all."

"Did your father know of this?"

"No, by the omnipotent God! Indeed he was not privy to our plans and knew nothing about them."

"Who then of your neighbors knew what you were doing?"

"Ask the people on the spot if any of them knew where we were."

"After you had come down from the mountains, as you maintain you did, did you read these writings in the presence of anyone?"

"They remained in our house and we did not even dare to bring them out. This was a great distress to us for we could not occupy ourselves over them as we had been in the habit of doing from the beginning until last year, when we had to hide even those."

It was clearly useless to prolong the interrogation and Dulcitius decided to impose the sentence. The other two sisters had been burned, but some other penalty more severe was required for this one. The judge thought for a while and then turning to Irene announced solemnly:

"I will not see that you end your life quickly as your sisters did. I command that the guards and Zosimus the public executioner expose you naked in the brothel. Every day you will be given a loaf of bread from the palace and the guards will see that you do not escape."

He then turned to Zosimus and the guards and warned them that if he came to hear that the girl had left the brothel for a single moment, they would all be put to death.

But the experiment of Dulcitius failed. "Not one person," says the *Acts* (Chap. 6), "dared to approach her or to do or say anything wicked to her." The Governor was not beaten, however, and he had Irene brought back into the tribunal. He asked:

"Do you still persist in your temerity?"

"It is not temerity, but divine piety. In that I still persist." The sentence was then immediately written and proclaimed: she was condemned to be burned like her two sisters.

Irene was martyred, it would seem, on April 1, 304, and her sisters a few days before this.

We know nothing about the end of the other accused, Agatho, Cassia, Philippa, and Eutichia. Perhaps the compiler of the *Acts* gave the place of honor to the three sisters and did not bother to look for the transcript of the trial of the other martyrs.

138. Philip of Heracleia, Severus, and Hermes. Toward the east along the seacoast from Thessalonica we come to Thrace which forms the northern bank of the Propontis (Sea of Marmara). About halfway along this coast to Byzantium (Constantinople) is situated the city of Heracleia (today, Eregli; anciently, Perinthus). A group of three martyrs suffered here at the beginning of the persecution — Philip, the bishop of Heracleia, of advanced age, the priest Severus, and the deacon Hermes.

The *Passion* which we have was composed sometime between the fourth and fifth centuries on the basis of official legal accounts and other dependable information. The author indulged a certain literary ambition and amplified the severe replies of the martyrs, sometimes transforming them into sermons in which there are useful records for profane history. The general substance of the *Passion*, however, is worthy of historical acceptance.

Bassus, the prefect of Thrace, carried out the imperial edicts but failed to put his heart into the matter since, as the *Passion* says (Chap. 8), "his wife had served God already for sometime." It would seem that she was a Christian. In any case he had to obey his orders for he was very near the end of his period of office and there was the danger that his successor would denounce any failing on his part to the highest Augustus in nearby Nicomedia. One day, therefore, Bassus sent a police officer to close and seal up the doors of the church in Heracleia. When he got there he found Philip preaching to the people.

From a reference in the sermon where Philip says that "the holy day of the Epiphany" is near (*epiphaniae dies sanctus incumbit*, Chap. 2), it seems that the day was January 6, 304. If this is the correct interpretation, then this would be the most ancient mention of the Christian feast of the Epiphany which is of relatively recent origin. Against such an interpretation it has been observed (Franchi de'Cavalieri) that the Latin word *epiphania* is a simple transliteration of the Greek επιφάνεια. This word need not refer to the Christian feast, but rather to the second coming or "*parusia*" of the glorified Christ. St. Paul alludes to this coming frequently and especially in his two letters to the Thessalonians, linking it up with contemporary events and acts of supreme courage and with the end of the world. In fact, Philip, speaking of the *nutantis saeculi extrema* which were then unfolding themselves, emphasizes that Christians must overcome these tests of their courage and show themselves brave and strong. It seems unlikely, in any case, that the first edict of the persecution, published in Nicomedia in February, 303, should not yet have been executed in Heracleia by 304, when it was so short a distance from Nicomedia.

The officer therefore closed the church and sealed the doors. The following day he returned and, having made an inventory of the furniture, vestments, and sacred vessels, sealed the boxes in which they were kept. Even under such conditions the old Bishop did not abandon his people. Since he could not get into the church he sat in front of its sealed doors and preached to the faithful from there, preparing them for the coming trials and encouraging the timid.

At one of these discourses, Bassus appeared and demanded to know who was the head of the Christians. Philip replied: "I am the one you seek."

Bassus then followed the imperial edict and demanded the handing over of all the sacred vessels whether precious or not and all the copies of the Sacred Scriptures. After he had backed his request by the threat of tortures, Philip replied:

"If as you say you enjoy our torments then my soul is ready to endure them. Tear then with any torture you wish this weak body of mine. Over that you have power but over my soul you have none. If you want the sacred vessels you may take any you like for we can easily do without such things; we honor God not with precious metals but with fear. The beauty of our churches is less pleasing to Christ than the beauty of our souls."

We have already heard of the refusal of the Christians in other places to hand over the sacred vessels and the Scriptures. This reply of Philip seems, therefore, surprising at first sight. He was no coward like Paul, the bishop of Cirta (par. 80 ff.), and others for he was to lead the opposition to the persecution with great spirit and finally become a martyr. It appears that at Heracleia the matter of the *traditio* was considered differently. The sacred vessels were material objects which could easily be replaced (par. 84), and perhaps by his answer Philip wished to show himself to be free from any avarice or cupidity. As far as the Sacred Scriptures were concerned, later events will show that it was too late in any case to hide them and nothing could be done except to lay a formal protest.

139.   The prefect Bassus then called in the executioners, among whom was one called Mucapore well known for his pitiless cruelty. The deacon Hermes was already present and the Prefect commanded that Severus the priest should be brought for they were both the helpers and especially loved disciples of the Bishop. Severus, however, could not be found. Bassus was annoyed by this and put Philip to the torture. While this was going on the deacon Hermes exclaimed to the magistrate that even if the persecutors should destroy all the Sacred Scriptures there were on the earth, the future Christians would draw on the memory of their elders and their own spirits and would compose even more voluminous writings to teach the veneration owed to Christ.

The Deacon was flogged for his rashness. He was then ordered to accompany a certain Publius who was the assessor of the Prefect to the place in the church where the sacred vessels and the Scriptures were kept. Publius was a thief and he found in the collection a fine opportunity to provide for his own interests and began to put aside the things he fancied for himself. He was reproved for this by Hermes and became so annoyed that he struck Hermes on the face with such force that he drew blood. Bassus got to know of the affair and when he saw the Deacon with a bleeding face rebuked Publius and ordered that Hermes should have the care of a doctor. He then ordered that the Bishop with the rest of the Christians should be taken to the forum so that everybody could see them. When he had returned to his palace, he commanded that the roof of the church which was covered with very beautiful tiles should be demolished. At the same time, the soldiers carried the Scriptures to the square to throw them on to a bonfire.

Meanwhile Philip was seen in the nearby market and was told that the Sacred Scriptures were being burned. The compiler of the *Passions* now found a golden opportunity to allow the old Bishop to make a learned sermon which was presented to "Jews, pagans and all others of whatever religion or sect" (*Passion*, Chap. 5). Apart from a quotation from St. Paul at the beginning and a reference to the fall of Sodom, the whole sermon is a pleasant collection of not particularly religious incidents in history and legend.

To show that God makes special use of fire to combat idolatry,

Philip gives first the example of Sodom and then refers to an ancient myth about Mount Etna in Sicily (cf. *Photius Biblioth.*, 186, 43; in Migne, *Patr. Graec.*, 103, 580–582). He continues with Hercules and Aesculapius, and after this gives a list of famous fires — the temple of Diana (Artemis) at Ephesus, the temple of the capitol in Rome, another built by Heliogabalus on the Palatine in honor of the sacred stone of the Sun, the temple of Serapis at Alexandria, the temple of Bacchus at Athens, that of Minerva in the same town, and finally the temple of Apollo at Delphi. All this rather exuberant erudition is given by the compiler of the *Passion* to Philip who is made very eloquent, although he was a feeble old man who had just been tortured.

After various incidents, and another sermon by Philip against idolatry, Bassus turned his full attention to the deacon Hermes who in civil life had the post of decurion. Since he also refused to sacrifice, Bassus ordered him to be put in prison with his Bishop. On the way there, one of the crowd knocked the old man down, but he got up quite happily with the praises of God on his lips. After a few days in prison they were transferred to a house nearby, but so great were the crowds of Christians who came to visit them and listen to their words that they were put into prison again. Even here the Christians got to them through a secret tunnel which joined the prison to a neighboring theater and the crowds were as great as before.

140.　After some time Bassus was succeeded in office by Justinus, who was very anti-Christian. Despite all threats Philip refused to sacrifice at his new interrogation. Justinus had him dragged through the city with his legs bound hoping that he would die in the process. He did not oblige, and during the last stages of his journey he was held up by Christians until he reached the doors of the prison. It was at this juncture that the priest Severus, who had managed to remain hidden until then, gave himself up to the tribunal. He was treated to the usual exhortations and threats and was reminded by the judge that he had children dependent on him. He still refused to sacrifice. Justinus tried mercy to see what would happen and once more had the three prisoners transferred to a private house. This was clearly unsuccessful, for they were back in prison within two days and remained there for another seven months. After this Justinus sent them to Adrianople, the capital of Thrace, where he was going very soon.

At Adrianople, the first hearing was in the baths. Philip was brought in and the Governor asked him:

"Have you considered? All this time has been given you that you may change your mind. Sacrifice, therefore, and leave this court a free man."

The old man replied: "If our stay in prison had been voluntary and not forced, then we would have been grateful for the time you had given us. If, on the other hand, it was a punishment, why do you pretend that it was a kind favor? As far as I am concerned I have already told you that I am a Christian and this will be my reply at any future interrogations."

He was then flogged with such violence that his bowels were exposed and in this condition the old man was taken back to prison.

Three days later Philip and Hermes were taken back to trial not now at the baths, but in the usual tribunal. The Governor reproved Philip for his temerity in disobeying the Emperor, but the Bishop answered that this was not temerity but obedience to God.

"All my life I have obeyed the emperors and when they made just commands I hastened to do their will; the Scripture indeed tells us to render to God the things that are God's and to Caesar the things that are Caesar's . . . take notice of what I have said so often, that I am a Christian and refuse to offer sacrifice to your gods."

The Governor then turned to Hermes and begged him not to follow the example of Philip, a failing old man, but to offer sacrifice. In this way he would be able to enjoy life once more. The compiler once more produces a long discourse for the Deacon this time with quotations from the Bible to justify his refusal. The Governor became very angry and said to Hermes:

"You speak as if you would make me a Christian."

Hermes replied: "Not only you but all those who are present."

This little interchange is obviously inspired by the Acts of the Apostles (16:28–29). When he saw that his efforts were completely unrewarded the Governor consulted with his assessors (for such a consultation, cf. also the Acts of the Apostles, 25:12) and then gave sentence.

"Philip and Hermes, who by disobeying the command of the Roman emperor have lost the right to be called Romans, are condemned to be burned alive so that they may the more clearly know how great a crime it is to disobey the imperial commands."

141. The two condemned men were immediately taken to their execution. Philip because of his age and the tortures he had suffered had to be carried. Hermes followed on foot but even he walked very slowly for he was weakened by his protracted torments and sufferings. At the place of execution two small holes had been dug and at the edge of each a stake had been driven into the ground. The aged Philip was put down by his bearers with his feet in the hole. Then his hands, which were tied behind his back, were fastened to the stake and the hole was filled with earth up to his knees. Hermes was ordered to climb down into his pit, but since he was using a stick to assist his weak legs he burst out laughing and exclaimed: "Not here, O Devil, can you sustain me [*Neque hic me, diabole, sustinere potes*]." The devil, the true contriver of the martyrdom, was not looking after his own interests if he now ceased to help the martyr along to his death, so Hermes reproved him.

Men now began to heap up the wood around the two men. Before a light was put to it, Hermes called out to one of the Christians present and begged him in the name of Jesus Christ that he should afterward go to his son and remind him to give back to everyone their own property. He had, first as a civil magistrate and then as a deacon, received various sums deposited with him by private individuals. These people trusted him completely and expected their money back when they wanted it. The son would do honor to his father by restoring this property promptly. The message was accompanied with a moral warning: "You are a young man. You will have to get your living by hard work as you know your father has always done. You must remember that he has always been just to all people."

These were his last words. The fires were lighted and both the martyrs were choked by the smoke and finally burned in the flames.

As for the third prisoner, the priest Severus who had been left in prison, we only know that he was executed the following day.

By order of the Governor the bodies of Philip and Hermes were flung into the River Hebrus which flowed near Adrianople and came out into the Aegean. The Christians, however, were all prepared. They had provided themselves with nets, and after three days they found the bodies and buried them in a place twelve miles from Adrianople.

142. Going to the northwest from Thrace across the modern Balkan countries one comes into the imperial "diocese" of Illyricum which contained various provinces, First and Second Pannonia, Savia, Noricum (Mediterranean and Ripense), and others. These regions had given a number of emperors to Rome (par. 1), and in them also Christianity was widespread. It is not, therefore, extraordinary that there were many martyrs here in the Great Persecution. We will mention only those about whom we have secure information, and begin with those who suffered near Sirmium.

Irenaeus, Sinerus, the Five Sculptors. The city of Sirmium which corresponds to modern Mitrovica (Jugoslavia) was in Second or Lower Pannonia near the River Savus, tributary of the Danube. There, probably in 304, Irenaeus, the bishop of the city, was arrested and taken to Frobus, the governor of the province. Irenaeus was a young married man with children. It would appear that he came of a wealthy and influential family.

His quite authentic *Passion* is based on the actual transcription of the trial with only very small additions here and there from the hand of the compiler. It was put together toward the end of the fourth century.

He was asked several times to sacrifice and refused each time. The Governor became severe and said:

"Sacrifice, or I will put you to the torture."

"I shall be happy if you do, for then I shall be able to share the sufferings of my Master."

He was then tormented grievously. After a while Probus spoke again: "What do you say now Irenaeus?"

"With my endurance I am even now offering sacrifice to my God to whom I have always sacrificed."

Worse even than the torments were the urgings of his friends and kinfolk who were present at the torture. They wailed and lamented and begged him to submit. His parents tried to persuade him, his young children clasped his knees, his wife implored his "countenance and his age" as the author of the *Passion* has it. We must let his wife continue for a while for she talked well:

"On him was lavished the grief and lamentation of all his relations, the sobs of his servants, the wailing of neighbors and the cries of friends; everyone wept and said to him: 'Have pity on your own youth.'"

The martyr did not reply. Probus broke in again:

"What do you say? By the tears of these people turn away from your madness, look to your youth and sacrifice!"

The only reply to this was:

"I am looking to my eternal future if I do not sacrifice." Probus then had him taken back to prison where he underwent varied tortures.

After some days of this softening-up process, Probus tried him again, this time at night. The prisoner was brought in and the judge said:

"Now will you sacrifice, Irenaeus, and save yourself further torture?"

"You are doing what you are told. Do not expect me to do the same."

He was referring to the imperial commands, which the judge accepted. Therefore, he had to punish those who refused to obey them. Irenaeus did not accept such commands. Probus became angry and ordered him to be beaten. Irenaeus replied:

"I have God whom I learned to adore from my childhood; I adore him who comforts me in all things and to him I sacrifice. I cannot adore manufactured gods."

Probus insisted: "Why not escape death? Surely the torments you have already suffered are enough?"

"I am escaping death all the time by means of the punishments which you think are hurting me but which I do not feel. Through them I receive from God eternal life."

"Have you a wife?"

"No."

"Have you children?"

"No."

"Have you parents?"

"No."

"Who were all those people wailing at the last session?"

"There is a commandment of my Lord Jesus which says: 'He who loves his father or mother or wife or children, or brothers or relations more than me, is not worthy of me.' "

"Sacrifice at least for their good."

"My children have the same God as I have and he will save them. Do therefore as you have been commanded."

"Look to yourself, young man. Sacrifice or I will torture you again."

"Do as you wish. You will see now what patience the Lord Jesus Christ will give me before your wiles."

"I shall pronounce sentence against you."

"I shall be happy if you will."

Sentence was finally given:

"Irenaeus who has been disobedient to the imperial command is ordered to be flung into the river."

Irenaeus replied:

"I expected you to (carry out) your varied threats of much torment and to condemn me to the sword. You have done nothing. I beg of you to do something, so that you may learn how by their faith in God the Christians are accustomed to despise death."

Probus became very angry indeed and added death by the sword to his original sentence.

The condemned man was taken to a bridge chosen for the execution. It was probably a bridge over the little river, Bacantius, which flows past the city and finally goes into the Savus. There the martyr removed his own clothing and prayed to Jesus Christ for himself and his church at Sirmium. He was beheaded and his body thrown into the river.

The martyrdom, according to ancient testimonies, occurred on August 21 or 23, March 25, or April 6. This last date is the most probable.

143. In the lands around Sirmium the curious affair of Sinerus took place, which ended with his martyrdom. He was a Greek by birth and his name has been shown in various ways in documents — Sinerius, Sirenus, Serenus. Originally it must have been Sinerus. He did not suffer at the beginning of the persecution, but when it had been going for some time, perhaps in 307 or a little earlier.

His *Passion* is based not this time on transcriptions of his trial, but on the lively memory of eyewitnesses. These people could not forget the extraordinary events in which Sinerus figured, for the business was a seven-day wonder for the town gossips. The *Passion* can probably be assigned to the last years of the fourth century.

He was already quite old when he left Greece and came to Illyria where he earned his living as a gardener at Sirmium. He was a Christian, but when the persecution made normal life impossible for the Christians, he concealed himself. After a while he regained confidence and went back to his work, which did not cause him to mix very much with other people. He was not exactly a monk — he is called this in some versions of his *Passion* — but rather a solitary with pious inclinations. This tranquil existence, however, was completely upset by an unexpected event. One day a woman with two maids began to walk up and down in the garden where he was working. Since they gave no explanation of this uninvited visit, Sinerus asked the lady what she was looking for. She replied evasively and said it pleased her to walk in that particular garden. Sinerus was not very satisfied with such an answer and, speaking with the frankness of a simple man, said, "What kind of lady is this who comes for a walk here at such a late hour? It is already the sixth hour (that is about our midday) and it is obvious that you have not come here for a walk but to display yourself for some lascivious purpose. Therefore kindly get out and preserve your virtue as an honest matron should."

The storm then broke. The matron was furious not so much at her humiliation at the hands of this common gardener, but because her plans were no longer secret. She could not allow herself to be treated in this way for she was the wife of a high official and friend of Galerius. At the time her husband was away in service with Galerius. She went home and still blazing with fury wrote and told her husband about the insult, leaving out quite a deal and inventing a similar amount. Her husband was furious too and took his protest to Galerius.

"How can this be? While we stand at your side in the imperial service, are our wives to be subjected in their loneliness to such insults?"

Galerius immediately took the side of the husband and gave him a short leave of absence to allow him to vindicate the injury to his wife. Armed with a letter from Galerius he presented himself at the Governor's palace demanding justice. The Governor wanted to know who had committed this insult. He was told that it had been Sinerus, a common gardener. Sinerus was quickly brought to the Governor's presence who began to question him:

"What is your name?"

"Sinerus."

"What is your job?"

"I am a gardener."

"Why did you dare to injure the name of the wife of so important a man?"

"I have not injured any woman."

The Governor then ordered one of his officers to force Sinerus to confess who the woman was who had wished to walk in his garden. The defendant replied with all simplicity.

"I know that some days ago a woman was walking in my garden

at an inconvenient hour. I rebuked her and told her that it was not right for a woman to leave the house of her husband at that hour of the day."

To the husband, who was present in court, this was news indeed. The matter of the time had been omitted in the letter written him by his wife. He remained speechless especially since the open sincerity and humble manner of the old man were a clear proof of the truth of what he said. He was very ashamed of the affair and so kept quiet, refusing to ask any more of the Governor. The public undoubtedly had a fine time laughing behind their hands and making whispered interpretations of the affair. The Governor also became very thoughtful, for something very much like a scandal seemed to be looming over a very high personage. What would Galerius say after taking so much trouble in the matter? To free Sinerus, with the truth of his story confirmed, would be a humiliation not only for the husband but also for the Emperor. No. Sinerus must not leave the court a free man. This would lose the Governor his office. Some legal reason, some juridical pretext for condemning Sinerus had to be found.

After considerable thought the Governor finally hit on a good idea. Why — he reflected — was this old man so keen to break up the obvious tryst? Everybody had such appointments and took little care more often than not to conceal them; in any case no one would talk about them afterward. If this fellow protested then he must have some unusual principles which were not those of the ordinary people but which were derived from some particular prejudice. Therefore — concluded the Governor in his mind — he must be a Christian (Hic homo christianus est). This conclusion spelled safety: he could preserve his own career, the husband his social respect, the Emperor his prestige. And all this could be done without breaking the law but by following it. The Governor felt a new man and turned to Sinerus and asked:

"Of what kind are you? [Quod genus tibi est?]"

"I am a Christian [Christianus sum]."

With this confession everything was safe once more and the court was back on a legal footing.

"Where have you been hidden up to now and how have you managed to escape having to sacrifice to the gods?"

"It must have pleased God to have preserved me until this time. I was like a stone rejected by the builders but now the Lord wants me for use in his house. Since he wishes me to be discovered I am ready to suffer for his name so that with his saints I may have a part in his kingdom."

He was quickly condemned to decapitation and the sentence was carried out immediately.

The rolling of this head at Sirmium reminds us of another which was lost at Machaerus almost three centuries before. We know that there the head was carried on a tray to a princess who was very keen to have it. We do not know whether the head at Sirmium was carried to the lady, but she certainly did not desire it any the less. It may be that it was taken to the husband; if this did happen then the husband certainly told the right story to the end in defense of the injury to his wife's reputation. Sinerus was probably martyred on February 22 or 23.

The Christians of Sirmium buried the body in a cemetery, where a church later arose in honor of the martyr. Ancient memorials there mention him by name and express the desire to be buried close to his remains.

144. We have already mentioned that at Sirmium there were marble quarries belonging to the imperial treasury, in which Christians worked (*confessores metallici*) who had been condemned to forced labor (pars. 88–89). Since we are at Sirmium we will make a short visit to these Christians who have told us about some of their brethren there who ended as martyrs. They were sculptors, five in number, who worked in these quarries.

The *Passion* of these five martyrs of Pannonia has had a curious history. It has reached us after having had attached at the end, in a rough and ready manner, the story of four Roman officials (*cornicularii*) who really have nothing in common with the five martyrs of Pannonia. The united *Passions*, however, went around under the title of the *Passion of the Four Crowned Saints*. The first twenty-one chapters deal with the five sculptors and the twenty-second with the four Romans. The names of the first group were Claudius, Nicostratos, Simpronianus, Castorius, and then a certain Simplicius who is not always named with the other four.

The fusion of the two *Passions* has raised various difficulties which have so far not been solved. The greater part of the book which concerns the martyrs of Pannonia seems to have been written about the end of the fourth century or in the first half of the fifth. It is not based on official records of the trial, but on very precise and fresh eyewitness reports. The author is given as one Porphyry, a Christian, who had the office of *censualis a gleba actuarius*, that is, he worked in the office which controlled the land taxes. A summary of the facts is as follows.

The five Christian sculptors were very able in their work. For this reason, Diocletian himself approached them in regard to some work he had in mind. The Emperor here is shown for what he was, a great builder. We find him, therefore, in the time just after his abdication when he was carrying on with the decorations and embellishments of his grandiose villa at Salona (par. 59). Diocletian came to the quarry and ordered various decorative works from the five Christians, among which were statues of winged victory and some cupids (*victorias, cupidines*). The sculptors carried out this assignment to the satisfaction of the highest Augustus. They were ornamental objects without any idolatrous significance and the Christian consciences of the artists were at ease in working on them. There was more, however. Earlier they had carved a group showing the Sun on his chariot drawn by four horses (*simulacrum Solis cum quadriga*); this condescension of the Christians need not astonish us for without any reference to idolatry the group could quite easily portray the celestial phenomenon spoken of so often by the poets. Other Christians put such scenes on sarcophagi and obviously gave them an allegorical significance (par. 89).

Now, however, Diocletian ordered them to fashion a statue of Aesculapius which was clearly intended for idolatrous use since he was the god of good health. Their Christian consciences were troubled by this and they refused to carry out the work. "*Asclepium simulacrum non fecerunt*": "Asclepius" stands for Aesculapius. Their refusal brought them to martyrdom. They had a rapid trial from Diocletian, were closed like corpses in boxes of lead and flung into the river. This probably took place on November 8, 305.

They had been brought to Christianity by Cyril, the bishop of Antioch who was their companion in hard labor (par. 89). When he heard of their death he himself died of grief.

145. Other Martyrs of Illyria. The governor Probus, who had been responsible for the death of Irenaeus of Sirmium (par. 142), had two other victims who are known to us. Probably a little while prior to his condemnation of Irenaeus he ordered the execution of Montanus who was a priest of the church of Singidunum (Belgrade), although he seems to have suffered at Sirmium.

His other victim was Pollio, a lector of the church of Cibali, a place which has not been positively identified. Of Pollio we also have a *Passion*. He was reported to Probus who asked him what kind of work a lector among the Christians did. Pollio replied:

"He reads the divine eloquence to the people."

"Oh!" said Probus. "Then you are one of those who lead stupid girls by the nose telling them they must not marry and persuading them to a barren chastity."

Pollio replied:

"You can try out our stupidity and vanity today."

After a fairly long discourse by Pollio on Christian faith and morals and on the happiness of the future life, Probus delivered himself of a reflection which was typically pagan: "How does it help a man if when he dies, he no longer sees the light and loses all the powers of his body?"

Pollio was invited, with threats, to sacrifice. He refused and was condemned to be burned alive. Sentence was carried out a mile outside the city. He died in 304 but after Irenaeus, probably on April 27.

An important city of the province of Savia, also in Illyricum, was Siscia. The bishop here, called Quirinus, died a martyr. We have a *Passion* of Quirinus, and he is mentioned in a hymn of Prudentius (*Peristephanon*, vii). The *Chronicon* of Jerome assigns his death to the 271st or 308th Olympiad (ed. *Helm*, p. 229; or to the 273rd Olympiad, ed. *Schoene*, p. 189). He was arrested at Siscia and sent by the court to Amantius, the governor of Pannonia Prima, who held his trial in the public theater of the city of Sabatia. He refused to sacrifice and was thrown with a millstone around his neck from a bridge into the river. The martyrdom probably occurred on June 5.

Another illustrious victim in Illyria was Victorinus, the bishop of Poetovio in Noricum, which was famous in antiquity for its culture. Jerome had a weak spot for him and considered him a compatriot, but Victorinus must have been Greek in origin, for he spoke that language much better than Latin. Jerome speaks of his numerous writings (*De viris illustr.*, 74), but, unfortunately, almost nothing has come down to us. From a fragment of his commentary on the Apocalypse it appears he had Millenarist ideas. Of his life, apart from the fact that he was a bishop, we know nothing. Jerome says that he died a martyr and one martyrology assigns him to the persecution of Diocletian.

Going to the north from Poetovio, but remaining in Illyria, we come to the city of Lauriacum in the Noricum Ripense (Lorch in Upper Austria). Here we find the martyr Florianus. His *Passion* was written in the fifth century, perhaps with the use of official records. There is a recension which is somewhat longer, but of later date and of doubtful authenticity.

The facts of the story seem to fit with the year 304. In the full cry of the persecution the governor Aquilinus came to Lauriacum to search out the Christians who were hiding in the mountains and the surrounding caves. He captured forty of them whom he kept in prison for a long time, and whom he placed under torture. Florianus was also a Christian in secret; he had in the past held the office of the *princeps officii* of the Governor, but at this time was living privately in the little city of Cetium. He learned of the troubles and the danger of the forty imprisoned Christians and of his own accord went to Lauriacum to share their fate. As he was entering the city he met some old companions in arms who were looking for Christians. He saved them some trouble by giving himself up to them and was taken to Aquilinus. He was beaten and finally condemned to be thrown into the River Anesius (Enns) with a stone tied to his neck. His body was then buried by a Christian woman named Valeria. Later a basilica was built over his tomb. The martyrdom occurred on May 4.

146. Leaving northern Illyricum, and going toward the west, we come to the "diocese" (smaller than a prefecture) of Italy which contained various provinces of which the most northerly were the Prima and Secunda Rhaetia. Rhaetia Secunda was above the Prima, and its capital city was Augusta Vindelicorum, the modern Augsburg. Here we find the martyr Afra who is an exceptional figure, for before she became a Christian she had been a prostitute.

It was inevitable that such an unusual case should lead to all kinds of stories about her conversion. These have been collected in her *Passion* which is a general congeries of legends and history. In general one can distinguish two sections; the first treats of her conversion and the second her trial and death. We must dismiss the first part, for it is obviously a series of fables tacked together with huge errors of historical fact. The second is worth more than the earlier story, although even here there are inexact or suspect elements. This second part of the *Passion* was probably put together in the first half of the fifth century and was based on secure facts. Besides the ancient martyrologies, Venantius Fortunatus (cf. *Vita S. Martini*, iv, vv. 640–643) in the sixth century makes mention of the martyr and of the honor she received at Augsburg.

Probably when Afra was arrested she was a practicing Christian, but was only a catechumen and not baptized. We do not know when she discontinued her disgraceful trade; certainly the memory of its continued sins remained firmly fixed in her mind and she was fervently desirous of making up for them. She conceived a hate for the money she had gathered by prostitution and wanted to give it away to the poor. The Christians, however, poor though they were, refused to accept it. Already in the Old Testament we find that the money obtained by such practices was considered unclean (Deut. 23:18; Mich. 1:7).

She was arrested, probably in 304, and the judge Cajus invited her to offer sacrifice. She was reminded that it was more pleasant to be alive and happy than to die in torment. Afra replied that she had committed enough sin when she still did not know God and refused to add another one to her already long list. Cajus insisted:

"Get along to the capitol and sacrifice."

Many colonies and boroughs of the empire had their own "capitol" in imitation of the Roman one.

Afra replied:

"My capitol is Christ whom I keep before my eyes; to him every day I confess my crimes and my sins."

"From what I understand you are a prostitute. Sacrifice therefore, for you cannot be of the God of the Christians."

"My Lord Jesus Christ said that he had come down from heaven for sinners. The Gospels indeed show that a prostitute bathed his feet with tears and had her sins forgiven her."

"Sacrifice, for then you will be as acceptable to your clients as before and they will give you much money." But Afra said that she had already unburdened herself of her money which had been so tainted that the Christian poor would not accept it, although she had offered it on the condition that they prayed for the forgiveness of her sins. Cajus insisted however:

"You have lost any chance of Christ thinking you worthy of him.

You have no proof for saying that he is your God for he does not recognize you."

These words show clearly the high opinion the pagans had of the Christians although in practice they had no intention of following their moral teachings.

"I do not deserve to be called a Christian as you so rightly point out; but the mercy of God which judges not according to merit, but in conformity with his own mercy, has allowed me the honor of this name."

"How do you know that he has shown you such mercy?"

"I know that I have not been cast off by God since I am being allowed to confess his glorious name through which I believe that I shall receive pardon for all my sins."

"This is all nonsense. Better to sacrifice to the gods through whom you will receive your safety."

"My safety is Christ who hanging from the cross promised the happiness of paradise to the thief who confessed to him."

"Sacrifice or else in the presence of your lovers who have dealt in filth with you I will order you to be beaten with 'cathomis'" (uncertain meaning).

"I am not ashamed of anything except of my sins."

"Sacrifice to the gods; already I have demeaned myself by continuing to argue with you. If you will not sacrifice, you will be executed."

"This is what I desire if I am worthy so that I may come to eternal rest."

"Sacrifice, or else I will have you tortured and then burned alive."

"The body with which I have sinned will accept the torments but I will not stain my soul with the sacrifices of the devil."

The judge then pronounced the sentence:

"Afra, public prostitute, who has professed herself a Christian and that she does not wish to offer sacrifice, is to be burned alive."

The condemned woman was immediately led to a little island on the river which flowed by the city. There the executioners stripped her and tied her to a stake. Meanwhile she prayed and cried with her eyes lifted to heaven. The wood was piled about her and set afire. When the flames reached their height, her voice was heard thanking Jesus Christ and offering herself as a sacrifice to him.

The martyrdom probably occurred on August 7.

ITALY AND THE REST OF WESTERN EUROPE

147. Now we come to Western Europe. Here the prefecture of Gaul comprised the various imperial "dioceses" of Spain, Gaul, Viennensis, and Britain. We then come to the prefecture of Italy, which was divided into the diocese of the City (peninsular Italy and the islands) and the diocese of Italy (north of the River Po). In this large area, the persecution differed in manner and intensity from what we have seen so far.

In general, the persecution caused less suffering here than in Eastern Europe or North Africa. Within Western Europe itself there was not the same severity in all the regions. The explanation is simple. We know already that Constantius, who governed the greater part of Western Europe, did not approve of the persecution and as far as possible softened the harsh edicts of his superiors (pars. 51, 162). Then Severus, who was first his Caesar and then an Augustus (pars. 59–62), did not last very long, and in any case was not particularly zealous against the Christians. Maxentius, who was not exactly the "tyrant" that he is called by the writers of the Constantinian court, showed himself neither the friend nor the enemy of Christianity (pars. 63, 156). In the territories which were under his care, the true persecution cannot have lasted more than a couple of years — that is, from the beginning of the persecution in the East until the first proclamation of Maxentius in 306 (par. 61). Nevertheless, many suffered in Italy before the time of Maxentius, and in other parts of Western Europe the enthusiasm of fanatical magistrates kept the persecution alive.

Unfortunately we have little information about these Western martyrs. Although they are very celebrated we know in many cases only their names and a few vague generalities. Those fine documents, simple and informative, which tell us of the martyrs of Eastern Europe and Northern Africa do not exist for these Western martyrs. All we have are records which are sometimes poetical, often vague, with plenty of imagination and little historical worth. As we have already pointed out (par. 77), this does not prove that a martyr did not exist. His *Passion* may well be legendary while his historic reality is shown by authoritative documents and inscriptions.

148. Roman Martyrs. Let us first consider Agnes, one of the most celebrated martyrs of Rome, who probably suffered under Diocletian.

Her *Passion* has been erroneously attributed to Ambrose, but is really later than the fifth century and has little historical value. Nevertheless there are references to Agnes, vague and sometimes contradictory, in the *Depositio Martyrum* of 336, the *Martyrology of Carthage*, in the *De virginibus*, i, 2, and *De officiis*, i, 41, of Ambrose. She is named in the hymn of Pope Damasus which is still preserved on the original stone in the wall of the Roman basilica of the martyr. Prudentius mentions her in *Peristephanon*, xiv, as do others. The information given by these writers can be checked by the archaeological data provided by the basilica mentioned above and the little estate surrounding it. From all this, we gather that Agnes was killed at the age of about twelve years, perhaps by beheading (Ambrose, *Prudentius*), perhaps by fire (Damasus). Her martyrdom is connected with her vow of virginity; the *Passion* and *Prudentius* give the episode of her exposition in a brothel (cf. the case of Irene in par. 137).

The body of Agnes was buried in a Christian cemetery on the left of the Via Nomentana. Over her tomb, Constantina, the daughter of Constantine, built a basilica shortly before 350. This basilica was repaired and enlarged at various times and the nearby cemetery was discovered and explored methodically by M. Armellini and G. B. de'Rossi from 1865 on.

Another very well-known martyr of Rome is the soldier Sebastian. The events of his martyrdom were bound up with those of the martyrs Marcus and Marcellianus, Castulus and the four *cornicularii* (par. 144) for no particular reason. This *Passion*, which is of the fifth century, presents a life already well equipped with legend. Sebastian is said to have come from Narbo, and to have been educated at Milan. He was beloved by Diocletian who gave him command of the "first cohort." By means of this high office he was able to assist Christian prisoners in Rome during the persecution; he converted pagans and worked miracles. Finally he was discovered and denounced to Diocletian who in his rage forgot his usual benevolence and treated the martyr with great cruelty, condemning him to be killed by arrows. After the sentence had been carried out, Sebastian was left for dead on the ground. He was brought in and was looked after by Irene, the mother of Castulus. He recovered his strength and then presented himself to Diocletian to reprove him vigorously for his cruelty. He was immediately flogged to death. His body was thrown into the Cloaca Maxima, but was recovered by the matron Lucina and buried *ad catacumbas* along the Via Appia. The *Passion* is written in a lively manner and shows an intimate knowledge of the topography of Rome, so it would seem to have been written there.

The crypt where the martyr had been buried was put in order at the beginning of the fifth century. The basilica which stands over it (Basilica Apostolorum) was first dedicated to the Apostles Peter and Paul perhaps because their bodies were taken there for a time in the third century (this matter has not been absolutely proved as yet). At any rate, from the ninth century the church was commonly given the title of St. Sebastian (par. 207).

It is possible, but not certain, that Sebastian was a victim of the purge in the army which came before the general persecution (par. 37 ff.), but his direct relations with Diocletian in Rome itself are certainly legendary.

149. Sicilian Martyrs.   From ancient times, Sicily could boast of two martyrs with just as great a popular following as Agnes and Sebastian. These were Agatha and Lucy. Though little that is certain about them has reached our times, there is no doubt that they existed. Their names appear in the Canon of the Mass where they were probably put by Gregory the Great. They are also mentioned in the *Gelasian Sacramentary* and in other ancient documents.

Agatha is given to the city of Catania by all the documents which have any value (par. 78). Her dates are most uncertain, for the *Passion* puts her in the persecution of Decius and other records make her suffer under Diocletian. The *Passion*, which is no older than the sixth century, incorporates popular stories, pagan reminiscences, and local traditions. The cult of Agatha, found from ancient times in Catania, soon spread to parts of Italy.

Lucy was martyred at Syracuse under Diocletian, perhaps in 304. Her *Passion*, which is earlier than the fifth century, is mainly legendary though there may be some historical facts embedded in it. She was honored as a martyr from the beginning of the fifth century and a little later in the churches of Milan and Ravenna. In this last city the saint is shown in a group of virgins in St. Apollinaris Nuovo.

Also a Sicilian was the martyr Euplius, who suffered at Catania under Diocletian, probably in 304. His *Acts*, which exist in various Greek and Latin versions, are of good quality, depending, apparently, on the verbal transcript of the trial. They date back to the end of the fourth century or the beginning of the fifth, but have been touched up somewhat and variously interpolated. Euplius underwent two interrogations by Calvisianus, the "corrector" of Sicily, one on April 29 and the other on August 12 (the dates, however, differ in the manuscripts). At the first hearing he presented himself with a book of the Gospels in his hand. This roused a protest from a friend of Calvisianus who was present as an assessor. He was asked to read something from his book and first read: "Blessed are those who suffer persecution for justice' sake for theirs is the kingdom of heaven" and then went on to "Who wishes to come after me, let him take up his cross and follow me" (Mt. 16:24).

Calvisianus asked:

"And what does this mean?"

"It is the law of my Lord which I have been given."

"By whom?"

"By Jesus Christ, the Son of the living God."

This seems to have ended the first hearing and Euplius was put back in prison. The actual sequence of events is not very clear, however; neither is the connection between the first and second hearings; this may be owing to a retouching of the documents.

When the interrogation was renewed, Euplius made the sign of the cross and confirmed that he was a Christian and that he read Sacred Scripture despite the emperors. He was then tortured and thanked Christ for this favor, begging him to give him the strength to suffer in patience. Calvisianus suspended the torments and exhorted him to adore the gods, and to venerate Mars, Apollo, and Aesculapius.

The three names brought to mind the Divine Trinity of Christianity. Euplius therefore replied:

"I adore the Father and the Son and the Holy Ghost. I adore the Holy Trinity and outside these Three Persons there is no God. I am a Christian."

The tortures were renewed more fiercely than before. The martyr once more thanked Christ for them and asked for strength. When he no longer had the power of speaking aloud, he weakly formed his lips to the prayer. Calvisianus then sentenced him to decapitation. To his neck was hung the book of the Gospels which had caused all the trouble; while he was being taken to the place of execution a herald went before him proclaiming: "Euplius the Christian, the enemy of the gods and of the emperors." Each time this was announced Euplius replied joyfully: "Thanks be to Christ my God."

After the execution the Christians managed to obtain his body and to bury it.

150.   In the other parts of Italy we have an abundance of names, but very little certain and accurate information even in the case of well-known martyrs.

Vitalis and Agricola (the former was the slave of the latter) are mentioned by Ambrose and Paulinus. They were martyred at Bologna, perhaps under Diocletian. Their bodies were buried in a Jewish cemetery and were discovered by Ambrose in 393.

Cassianus of Imola has been very handsomely treated by legend writers. It is certain that already in the fifth century there was a church dedicated to him in Imola. Prudentius (*Peristeph.*, ix) says that in this city he saw a picture showing a naked man being attacked by boys who were stabbing him with the *stilus* they used in school. Prudentius was told that this represented Cassianus, a schoolmaster who had been condemned to be executed in this way for refusing to sacrifice to idols. There can be no doubt that Prudentius saw this picture, but it can be questioned whether the actual picture was not perhaps a representation of a similar incident recorded by Titus Livius (v. 27), and Sozomenus (*Hist. Eccl.*, v, 10). The date of his death is uncertain.

151.   This poverty of information increases when we go out of Italy to the rest of Western Europe. There is nothing certain to be found in Britain, almost nothing in Gaul; there is a great deal in Spain but only of bare names unaccompanied by any certain information. Again, it should be noted that this lack of information does not mean that there were few or no martyrs for we have proof that there were many. What was lacking was someone to report accurately and faithfully the story of their trials and sufferings. To give but one example, Prudentius in one of his hymns (*Peristephanon*, iv) gives the names of some thirty martyrs. Since he was a Spaniard living in the second half of the fourth century, it is natural that he should speak of martyrs who suffered rather close to his own time and who were of the same nationality as himself. For us today, however, the names in this hymn are just a bare list, a litany, from which little further than the actual names can be gathered.

Most celebrated, both in Spain and in other countries, was Vincent, a deacon of Saragossa (*Caesaraugusta*); Prudentius dedicates a long hymn (*Peristephanon*, vi) to him; and he is mentioned by Augustine as having a *Passion*. A *Passion* has come down to us, but much of it must be accepted with considerable reserve.

Another well-known martyr was Eulalia of Mérida, who is also honored by a hymn of Prudentius (*Peristeph.*, iii); she is spoken of by Augustine, Hydatius, Gregory of Tours, and Venantius Fortunatus. The *Passion* which we have is very late and lacks historical authenticity. As early as the fifth century there was a church at Mérida in her honor and the martyr is shown in the group of virgins in St. Apollinaris Nuovo at Ravenna.

III. FINAL STAGES OF THE PERSECUTION

1. *End of the Tetrarchy and the Edict of Toleration*

152. The death of Maximian (par. 67), with which we ended our relation of the political situation, did not change the general condition of the Empire. Maximian was no longer recognized as a member of the tetrarchy and had been marked by Constantine with the *damnatio memoriae*; he presented the figure of an inconvenient ruler who was now out of the way. One should note that while the dead man had been given the Constantinian *damnatio*, his son, Maxentius proclaimed him *divus*, not so much to make up for the lack of gratitude shown by him to his father as to do something different from Constantine. Already Constantine and Maxentius had little love for each other — they were now the only rulers in the West and any lessening of the power of the one meant an increase to the other.

The real changes in the Empire came in the following year (311) and were most unexpected. As early as March of 310 the senior Augustus Galerius complained of bad health, certainly caused by evil living. A sore which first appeared on the sex organs, began to spread despite all the efforts of the doctors; weakening hemorrhages alternated with fitful improvement and the sick man sank frequently into delirium. The more the doctors cut, the larger and deeper grew the ulcer. When medical action failed and the surgeons had done their best, the gods were called in. Aesculapian Apollo seemed even less effective than surgery, for his state became much worse, his bowels began to putrefy, and all the lower part of his body started to decay and filled with worms.

There is no point in repeating the description given by Lactantius (cf. *De mortibus persecut.*, 33) of every horrifying detail. Sufficient to say that the stink of the decaying imperial flesh filled the palace and spread to the neighborhood. Galerius became a wizened pack of bones in the upper part of his body while from the belly down he was enormously swollen.

153. Galerius was desperately in need of help and he began to think that if the gods of his own empire could not help, perhaps something might be got from the God of Christianity. It would seem that this was suggested to him by one of his doctors, perhaps a Christian, who told him plainly that man could do nothing in the face of this disease for it had been sent by God; if the Emperor would atone for the terrible suffering inflicted by him on the Christians he would certainly find a cure.

Whether this story is true or not, the sick man did try this last remedy. The proud ruler, who had first started the persecution and had slaughtered vast numbers of Christians, now whimpered like a child and to propitiate the God of the Christians, promised to rebuild His ruined temples and do penance for his crimes. The God of the Christians, however, quite reasonably distrusted promises extracted by the agonies of a frightful disease; some positive proof of sorrow was needed. Galerius saw this and desperately hastened to show his good will toward the Christian God.

In any case, even before his illness Galerius must have taken stock of his own position and the result of the persecution. By the latter he had gained nothing. The tetrarchy existed only in name, for every dynast thought first of himself and then of keeping a wary eye on his colleagues. Galerius himself, who in theory governed all people and all things as senior Augustus, had no power either in Rome or in Italy, in Africa, Gaul, or Britain. Far from destroying Christianity, the persecution had strengthened it and purged it of many ills. The Empire, however, had been sorely damaged as was evident by a comparison between those regions where the persecution had raged and those which had remained virtually untouched.

These facts were clear and undeniable. Courage was needed to confess them openly and this Galerius did not have; it seemed to him that he would deny his very self and commit moral suicide. To avoid his imminent physical death he compromised; the result was a masterpiece of contradictions and incongruities which was called — the "Edict of Toleration."

154. The edict published at Nicomedia on April 30, 311, was copied and sent to all governors from Serdica where Galerius was staying with Licinius. The text has been preserved by both Lactantius (cf. *De mortibus persecut.*, 34) and Eusebius (cf. *Hist. Eccl.*, viii, 17, 3–10). The most important difference between these two versions is that that

of Lactantius lacks the prologue containing the names of the dynasts who issued the decree. Eusebius gives a translation from the Latin beginning with the names of Galerius, Constantine, and Licinius. Maximinus' name is wanting, for he had been awarded the *damnatio memoriae*. In some codices the name of Licinius is left out because of his quarrel with Constantine; in the first edition, however, Licinius' name appears, for this was before the quarrel.

The first impression made on the reader of the edict is that the author respects Christianity but insults it, that while he is retreating he is threatening. At the end he recommends himself to those he has insulted and threatened. This was one way of covering up capitulation; the threats and hard words refer to the past while the surrender regards the present. Here is the substance of the famous edict.

The emperors wished in the past for the good of the State to reorganize laws and customs according to the ancient Roman tradition; they therefore reminded the Christians of their duty when they had abandoned the religious institutions of their ancestors (*veterum instituta*). Through some spirit of pride, of their own accord, they (the Christians) made new laws and began to hold assemblies in various places. The emperors published edicts in an attempt to lead them back to their former religion; some submitted in fear, some were condemned to punishment of various kinds; many however, persisted in their stupidity. The emperors now realize that these did not offer the veneration due to the gods and do not venerate even the God of the Christians (this last refers to the prohibition of holding meetings which was made at the beginning of the persecution). According to their normal indulgence, they therefore pardon all and permit that there may be Christians once more (*denuo sint christiani*) and that they may hold their meetings provided that they do not cause any disturbance. In return for this clemency, the Christians must pray to their God for the health of the emperors, for the State, and for themselves so that public affairs may be prosperous and that they may lead a tranquil life in their own homes.

After the rebukes at the beginning of the edict and the reference to former edicts of persecution, the reader of this document expects a storm of thunderbolts and fiery darts against the Christian rebels. Instead, he finds a rather embarrassed indulgence and the greatest shock of all — *admiramini et obstupescite!* — a request for prayers. In practice, this edict meant that Christians could announce themselves as such once more (liberty of conscience), and could hold their meetings (liberty of worship). The condition that they should not disturb the peace was no handicap, for this meant that they must obey all other laws which were not directed against the Christians.

155. Galerius lived only a few days after the publication of this edict. Licinius hastened to his bed both to help his dying benefactor and to safeguard his own interests in the matter of succession. Galerius recommended to him his wife, Valeria, the daughter of Diocletian, and his son Candidianus; then he died. His death was made known at Nicomedia on May 15.

The Edict of Toleration was published in all territories under the jurisdiction of Galerius, Licinius, and Constantine. For his part, Maxentius, who was officially outside the Empire, had little to do to put himself in line with the prescriptions of the edict. Though officially he ignored it, the Christians in his territories already had practically the same freedom. Much the same could be said of the lands of Constantine. By Maximin the matter was handled differently. He received the edict as usual but did not publish it. He told Sabinus, the prefect of his praetorian guard, to notify the governors of the provinces that the emperors no longer intended to persecute the Christians for religious reasons. We have a copy of the letter sent by Sabinus to the governors (cf. *Hist. Eccl.*, ix, 1, 3–6), but this comes from preceding editions of Eusebius, for codices depending on the last edition do not have it. The letter of Sabinus, which reflected the attitude of Maximin, is much less condescending than the edict and leaves some points vague; Maximin profited by this when he started the persecution again.

In all the territories of the Empire, however, the edict had a wonderful effect. It was, as Eusebius says (cf. *Hist. Eccl.*, ix, 1, 8 ff.), as if a great light had burst out in the middle of the darkest night. In the towns, the Christians began once more to hold public meetings and celebrate their services. The prison doors were opened; Christians came out from their dungeons and passed through the streets singing the praise of God; the survivors from the forced labor camps returned to their houses in triumph. And it was not just the Christians who rejoiced; the pagans themselves who witnessed with surprise so sudden and unexpected a change joined in the common happiness and, as it was said, "proclaimed the God of the Christians great and true." The Christians pitied those who had surrendered during the persecution, and those who repented their fall were reconciled.

156. The death of Galerius was felt immediately in the political field. Both Licinius and Maximin, without troubling themselves about the rules which governed succession in the tetrarchy, hurriedly took over the territories which Galerius had ruled. Maximin occupied all of Asia Minor as far as the Bosphorus, while Licinius seized the lands to the north of the Propontis (Sea of Marmara); their forces with their ready arms gazed fiercely at each other from opposite banks of the Bosphorus. After some violent arguing, however, the matter was settled; Maximin kept the territories of Galerius in Asia and his opponent those in Europe (cf. Lactantius, *De mortibus persecut.*, 36).

While all this was going on Maxentius in Rome roused himself from his indolence. He had taken quietly the rebellion of the Phrygian general, Alexander, who had robbed him of his dominions in Northern Africa (par. 64); in the long run, however, this usurpation proved very harmful, for the City did not receive the supplies of grain which came mainly from that part of the world. Maxentius had made preparations for an expedition against Alexander some time before and now he put his plans into execution (in 311) giving the command of his army to the brave general Rufius Volusianus. The campaign turned out to be an easy one, for Alexander had made no preparations to meet it. In a few battles his armies were put to flight; Alexander himself was shut up in Cirta and, when he finally surrendered, was put to death.

Revenge against the rebels was bloody. Cirta was destroyed, and also Carthage. Very many were condemned to death, especially people of good families, for the treasury at Rome was empty and African money was as good as any other. Quite a few Christians were involved in these sanguinary measures either by mistake or because they had quite reasonably joined in with the rebels. Among those compromised was Felix, a deacon at Carthage, who had written a pamphlet against Maxentius; for this he was sought out and arrested by the magistrates. He was sent to Maxentius but managed to escape and took refuge with his bishop Mensurius (pars. 82–83) who refused to hand him over. The magistrate informed Maxentius of the situation and the latter, with much condescension, invited Mensurius to Rome to explain his position. Mensurius got on well with Maxentius; his explanation was accepted and he was sent back to Carthage in freedom. On his return journey, however, the Bishop died. It should be noted that this favorable attitude of Maxentius toward the Christians was nothing new; at this very time in accordance with the edict of Toleration, which had so far been officially ignored, he had restored to the religious authorities the Christian churches in Rome which had remained in the hands of the treasury. The word "tyrant," applied to Maxentius among others by the court panegyrists of Constantine, was quite unmerited so far as his treatment of Christians is concerned. The civil government of his subjects, however, especially in the last two years of his rule, might give him more merit to the title.

157.   While Maxentius was strengthening his position in his own lands, Constantine was doing the same. At this time, the latter certainly included Spain in his territories (things may have been different earlier, par. 13). The West, therefore, was divided into two great bands of territory; Britain, Gaul, Spain, and a small part of Africa south of Gibraltar depended on Constantine; Italy, the land beyond the Alps to Rhaetia, the islands and the African coast to the Cyrtis Maior belonged to Maxentius. The rest of the Empire was divided between Licinius and Maximin on the basis of the agreement made between them after the death of Galerius (par. 156). Licinius ruled Greece (including Crete) and the lands to the west, the Balkans as far as Noricum and the Danube, while Maximin had Asia Minor and the lands to the south to Egypt, Libya, and the Thebaid.

The four dynasts were personally in very different positions. The weakest of all was Maxentius, not only because he was officially a rebel and an intruder in the tetrarchy, but also because neither Constantine nor Licinius liked him. Maxentius and Constantine were brothers-in-law, for Fausta, the wife of the latter, was the sister of Maxentius, but family relationships counted for little in face of political expediency, and this inevitably put the brothers-in-law in opposition. Toward Licinius, Maxentius could feel nothing but anger and jealousy, for it was by the former's election at the meeting of Carnuntum (par. 64) that Maxentius had remained outside the official tetrarchy. The territory of Maxentius to the north of the Alps penetrated like a wedge between the lands of Constantine to the west and into those of Licinius to the east. There was therefore the ever present danger that his two neighbors could move in and destroy what they surrounded. Where could the anxious Maxentius find help and allies? There was only Maximin. Maximin was not on good terms with Licinius, who had given him most unwillingly the territories of Asia Minor in the agreement made on the shores of the Bosphorus (par. 156).

158. Negotiations for an agreement between Maxentius and Maximin had to begin in secret, especially since it seemed at that time that Constantine and Licinius would end by uniting against the other two dynasts. In this way the tetrarchy would be split in two; the Western Constantine was allied with the Eastern Licinius and Western Maxentius with Eastern Maximin.

The twofold agreement was indeed reached and the first results of it were clear. Maxentius prepared to avenge his father Maximian who had been put to death by Constantine, and at the same time reinforced his military bases in northern Italy both in the West against Constantine and in the East against Licinius. To raise money he increased the Italian taxes and those in Rome, and thus he lost the regard of the Senate which had been especially hit by the forced contributions and decimated by killings, and the affection of the people who lacked food as a result of the war in Africa. Only the soldiers — and especially the praetorians — gave orders in the city now for they were the only power that Maxentius had. To them everything was allowed and their continuous thieving among the citizens led to numerous bloody conflicts with the people.

It should be added that Maxentius was not inferior to his ally Maximin in licentiousness (par. 129). Without going through the unpleasant details given by ancient historians, it will be sufficient to mention the affair of the Christian matron Sophronia, the wife of the prefect of Rome. Her husband was terrified by the threats of Maxentius and handed her over. When the praetorians appeared at the door to take her to Maxentius, she asked for a moment or two to dress herself more suitably and in the privacy of her room plunged a sword through her heart (*Hist. Eccl.*, viii, 14, 17; the name Sophronia is given by Rufinus). If this was the kind of conduct favored by the supreme commander, we can easily imagine what his underlings did and the sufferings of the people as a consequence. All this was known to Constantine who kept a quiet watch on Rome from a distance; he got to know, also, that monuments were being erected in Rome showing Maxentius and Maximin together. The alliance between these two was obviously signed and finished.

Constantine now realized it was better not to await the attack of Maxentius, but to strike first. This would give him the advantage of surprise and Maximin would be too far off to give speedy assistance. He could trust Licinius; this alliance was cemented by a marriage between Licinius and Constantine's sister, Constantia. Constantine could show himself as the liberator of the oppressed Roman people; in the eyes of the Christians he would seem a friend for in his territories, even in the time of his father, there had been no persecution and, in any case, behind Maxentius was Maximin, who at that very moment, was relighting the fire of persecution in his own lands. Looked at from a military point of view, things were not so hopeful; but against the many and grave difficulties presented by a campaign in Italy Constantine hoped to place his characteristic speed and audacity of operations.

159. This was to be no hasty expedition. At the beginning of 312 he was still on the frontiers of the Rhine as a guard against the barbarians; and when the news from Rome became more and more threatening, he called a council of war to decide what should be done. When the aims of such a campaign were explained, the generals of his army showed themselves reluctant or even openly in opposition. Recent expeditions in Italy attempted both by Severus and by Galerius (par. 62) had met a disastrous end. The lesson seemed clear: an invasion of the peninsula meant a rapid lengthening of supply lines and every mile forward meant a deeper penetration into a blind alley where retreat and communications could easily be cut. If there was an enormous superiority in numbers the danger would not be so great; but there would not be even this advantage, for Constantine could not take all his armies with him for the invasion, since this would lay bare the frontiers to the depredations of the barbarians.

Maxentius, on the other hand, had been enlarging his forces for some time; Mauri and Carthaginians from Africa; new levies in Sicily and Italy; the veterans of his father's army and his own faithful praetorians had been in continual training. He had special trust in his troops on armored horses (cataphracti or cataphractarii and clibanarii) to which the infantry had no answer. With all these forces, possibly 100,000 men, Maxentius intended to march up to Rhaetia and then, swinging westward, to strike deep into Constantine's territories. For the present, this plan could not be realized for his armies were not prepared nor fully trained.

160. In spite of the opposition of his generals, Constantine decided on the expedition so as not to lose the great advantage of being first and of launching a surprise attack. Once the decision had been taken he acted like lightning. As a guard against the barbarians he left the

majority of his men, who actually were not fully trained, and took with him about 40,000 chosen soldiers. He crossed the Alps at Mont Cenis and was before Susa (Segusio) while Maxentius thought he was still on the Rhine. Maxentius now had to abandon his project of an offensive, and think of defending his own land. Susa was encircled by strong walls and here were stationed part of the troops which Maxentius had placed to guard the passage of the Alps; the greater part of his men retreated toward Turin. Constantine's men burned down the gates of Susa and slaughtered the enemy troops.

Before Turin, Maxentius' army was ranged in perfect battle order; the armored horses were in the middle, and two bodies of flanking infantry reached up to hilly ground. Constantine directed the battle in person and ordered an attack on the center of the opposing army; this was its strongest point, for it was made up of a compact mass of horses and men in armor. Such an attack could not hope to break through.

After this feigned attack, Constantine ordered his men to retreat in apparent disorder; the cataphracti followed them up, thereby opening their own ranks and sacrificing the original compactness of their force. Constantine then threw in his reserves armed with heavy maces, since lances and swords were useless against armor. The horses were struck down with mighty blows on the head, and in a short while the charge was weakened and the armored cavalry were in flight. With the center missing, the two enemy wings were soon dislodged from their positions and the whole surviving army of Maxentius was in full flight for Turin.

Turin was hostile to Maxentius and closed its gates to the fugitives. Under the walls there was a slaughter of the fleeing army caught between the mighty walls of the town and Constantine's army. The same evening the city opened its gates to Constantine. The disciplined behavior of his soldiers who entered into the city without committing the usual violence against the inhabitants confirmed the benevolence of the town to the conqueror. The example of Turin was followed by other cities; even Milan, at one time the seat of Maximian, opened its gates with joy, and Constantine took up residence in Maximian's palace and let his men rest in the city.

161. This rest was very short. Northern Italy had been conquered only to the west, while in the east large forces of Maxentians under the command of Ruricius Pompeianus barred the Alpine routes. Constantine did not fall into the mistake of Severus and Galerius, and

before going forward to Rome wished to secure his rear by disposing of these forces. He pushed toward the east, met a body of cavalry near Brescia and drove them back toward Verona. This city constituted a grave obstacle, for it was defended by a large body of troops, had the natural defense of the River Adige which surrounded the town, and to the west was protected by marshy ground which provided a further line of defense. A siege was necessary to take the town, even though Constantine was in a hurry and was worried by enemy troops scattered in the Veneto. He did begin a siege and attempted to cut the line of supplies which came by water from the Veneto. Ruricius Pompeianus who meanwhile had collected a strong army from his scattered men advanced to take Constantine at the rear.

Constantine, imitating the strategy of the ancient consul Claudius Nero against Hannibal, replied with daring and bravery. He left a mere covering force before Verona, and with the major part of his army turned to meet Ruricius Pompeianus. The encounter was savage. Constantine encouraged his men by fighting in the front line; more than once his loyal legionaries had to rush to protect him; the battle went on until dark and by then the destruction of the enemy was complete. Ruricius Pompeianus, as was to happen later to Maxentius, was found dead in the marsh. After this victory, Verona surrendered and the occupation of Aquileia and Modena soon followed. All northern Italy was now free, and Constantine had arrived at the territories of his ally Licinius. The territory to the rear was now safe and he was able to direct his forces to the enemy capital.

Along the Via Flaminia Constantine moved by forced marches toward Rome. He had no occasion to exclaim at this decisive moment — like Julius Caesar at the Rubicon — "*Alea iacta est.*" This was no gamble for Constantine, for he was absolutely certain of victory.

Why was he so certain?

2. "*Instinctu Divinitatis*"

162. Before he began his expedition into Italy, Constantine had worked out not only his strategy, but also his religious policy. He had asked the opinions of his generals and they had attempted to dissuade him (par. 159). After human advice he sought divine; he consulted the gods and through their haruspices the inhabitants of Olympus had condemned the venture and urged him to abandon it. Constantine,

however, went on with his plans *contra consilia hominum, contra haruspicum monita*, as the anonymous panegyrist says, who in 313 recited the praises of the victorious emperor (*Panegyr.*, ix, 2). Two points stand out clearly. On the eve of the campaign Constantine had recourse to pagan auspices; and he was quite ready to forget such advice if it displeased him.

At this time Constantine was officially a pagan. To learn what he really was we can only go to ancient authorities. He was not a thinker searching out philosophical truth; he preferred tangibles; he was a man of action and in the political field he turned out to be a fine organizer. Nevertheless such qualities require that subtle intuition which guides the man of action and keeps him in touch with reality. Even in religious matters Constantine had his intuitions; little by little they were modified and influenced in various ways.

The first influence was that of his father, Constantius, and his mother Helena (par. 11). His father was a tolerant pagan who never showed any dislike for Christianity. His mother was certainly a pagan while she was living with her son, though she possibly showed even then some predilection for Christianity. Nothing certain about this can be gathered from ancient historians. A possible indication is that one of his daughters was given the name of Anastasia; this could easily have been due to Christian influence (*Anastasis* — "resurrection"), but could also be the result of the idle fancy or love of novelty which is so frequent in the choice of names.

From his father's house, Constantine passed to the imperial court of Nicomedia where Christians held high positions, and at the outbreak of the persecution gave their lives for their faith (par. 49). He already knew — and found out more later — that in other parts of the Empire most of the Christians resisted the persecution. All these facts could not but have had some influence on his keen mind, and at least make him see the Christians as a force of the first order in religion and politics.

163. Officially he continued with the ceremonies of paganism, sacrificing to Apollo (the Sun) before the campaign on the Rhine (par. 66), and consulting the haruspices before his expedition into Italy. Pagan panegyrists speak also of secret communications made him by Apollo in Gaul. We need not wonder at all this, for paganism was the official religion and he had no decisive motive for abandoning its external ceremonies. We do not know what he was thinking. It is very probable

that the cult of the god Sol pleased him since, like so many others, he believed that such a poly-monotheistic system would not only fit in very well with the State religion but would respect the convictions of the Christians (pars. 27–29). If Constantine at this time was no longer a convinced polytheist he was only following the footsteps of his father who, as we are told, "had broken away from the religions of the Greeks" (cf. Socrates in *Hist. Eccl.*, i, 2). It is almost certain that Constantius, after deserting polytheism, welcomed the apparent monotheism of the god Sol while he was treating the Christians with kindness.

If we are to understand Constantine, we must take into account his personal character, all dash and ambition, longing to do something and to advance himself even though this might mean personal suffering and the gravest risks. When in such a person first efforts meet with success, a conviction is gradually formed that he is protected by some superior force; that he rejoices in the safekeeping of some mysterious *Arcanum* which transcends human affairs. This *Arcanum* was called by the pagans "Fortune" (*audaces Fortuna iuvat*), and was given different lodgings on Olympus. For those who had rejected the gods of that mountain, it could be identified with the greatest god, *Sol invictus* and *Deus sol*, whose supremacy and oneness could be proved by reasoning and whose nature seemed to correspond very well with that of the God venerated by the Christians. Later when Constantine, although himself still a pagan, was openly friendly to the Christians, more than once he put forth the idea that he had been chosen for mysterious purposes. He then talks about "Divine Providence" (*Hist. Eccl.*, x, 5, 18; Constantine is reported in some writings to have used similar expressions on other occasions).

That Constantine had walked this hidden *itinerarium mentis* is no conjecture, for we know he did. There are also various supporting indications. As long as Constantine was subordinate in the tetrarchy to the other dynasts, he uses the tutelary deities of the tetrarchy, the Jupiter of Diocletian and the Hercules of Maximian (par. 5). When these two Augusti left the stage, Constantine put Jupiter and Hercules aside and brought out the divinity Apollo-Sol, connecting him with Claudius II, the Goth from whom his servile courtiers made his father Constantius descend (par. 11). From 310 — the death of Maximian — in court panegyrics and on his coins Constantine is depicted as surrounded by the light of "Sol." In the panegyrics the Sun is the companion (*comes*) of the majesty of the emperor. Inscriptions on coins echo this idea (*soli invicto comiti*), and show the Sun pouring out his rays or even Constantine shining forth in the guise of the Sun-God.

164. It was in such a condition of mind that Constantine set out for Italy. Such feelings were bound to assume a special importance for him because of the political conditions. His adversary Maxentius was not hostile to the Christians, but he was hated by his subjects for his wretched government (par. 158). Anyone who rose against such a "tyrant" would wish to take a position different from his on the question of Christianity, not showing himself as a simple neutral in the battle of religions, but as the friend and protector of the followers of the Cross. In such a case, political and religious considerations would combine to suggest a policy.

The God of the Christians, who had by now become the *signum contradictionis* of the Roman Empire, had clearly shown his terrible power when he forced the Empire to surrender before the unarmed crowds of the followers of the Cross. Who had removed from public view the first of all the tetrarchs, Diocletian? Who had reduced to a heap of worms the principal persecutor, Galerius? Who had forced this Galerius to recommend himself to the very God whom he had persecuted? To ask these questions one did not need to have a great philosophical mind; practical sense and experience would suffice, and these Constantine had in abundance.

When all this was clear, Constantine made another step forward. Was this Christ perhaps the last and most powerful manifestation of the Supreme Divinity who had conquered and finally embraced the various gods of the Empire? Could he not easily be the latest appearance of the *Deus Sol dominus imperii Romani* in whom the mind of Constantine had found a reasonable solution of religious problems? This was very possible. All that was needed to transform this possibility into certainty was some sign, some proof. Just as his father Constantius had spared Christian blood, and therefore avoided the miserable end of the persecutors; so also in this daring expedition against Rome, Christ must show that he was protecting Constantine. He must assist one who had now decided to protect the followers of the Cross. After Constantine had come to these decisions, "he prayed to the God of his father" (Eusebius, *De vita Constant.*, i, 27–28). What happened after this is told by both Lactantius and Eusebius, but with some difference in their stories.

165. Lactantius (cf. *De mortibus persecut.*, 44) says briefly that on the vigil of the decisive battle near Rome, "Constantine was warned in his sleep to mark on the shields of his men the heavenly sign of the God and thus to go to battle; he did as he was commanded and putting the letter X on its side turned back the top arm (*transversa X littera, summo capite circumflexo*) thus making the name Christ." After this the battle began.

About twenty years later, Eusebius (cf. *De vita Constant.*, i, 27–30) tells the story in another way. The divine message came not near Rome on the vigil of the final battle, but many months earlier while Constantine was preparing for the campaign. In this account, it was during a march he was making with his army "toward a certain place" somewhere in Gaul (*ibid.*, 28). In the midst of a consideration of military affairs, Constantine realized that he had great need of divine assistance and began to work out "in which God he ought to put his trust" (*ibid.*, 27). He reflected on the wretched end of the persecuting dynasts, and prayed to the God of his father Constantius. Then there came a miraculous portent. If this sign had been simply written about by authors (continues Eusebius) readers would have difficulty in accepting it; but the event was narrated to Eusebius by the emperor Constantine himself a considerable time after he had received him into his confidence; the story was confirmed by an oath. In the later part of the day when the sun was going down, Constantine saw in the sky "a trophy in the shape of a dazzling cross in front of the sun and with it a motto saying 'With this sign thou shalt conquer'" (τούτῳ νίκα). He and all the army with him on the march saw the miracle and were seized with wonder. Constantine did not understand the meaning of the vision and when night came he was still thinking about it. But "while he slept there appeared to him Christ of God with the sign he had seen in the sky, who told him to make standards of that shape to serve as a protection in his conflicts with the enemy."

166. It is not to be wondered at that later Christian writers mention some divine communication or vision to Constantine with similar variations in their stories. More interesting, however, are the references to be found in pagan authors although such references are only vague and couched in generalities. The panegyrist of 313 asked Constantine rhetorically what God it was who made him decide on the expedition "*contra consilia hominum, contra haruspicum monita*" (par. 162). The panegyrist supposes that Constantine must have had some secret relation with a divine mind which, while leaving the care of ordinary mortals with minor gods, took special interest in the Emperor. After summarizing the campaign in a few words, he concludes that under the care of this superior divinity, Constantine marched toward "*non dubiam*" but "*promissam divinitus victoriam*" (*Panegyr.*, ix, 2–3).

Passing over references even more vague and uncertain, we must mention the inscription which still survives in Rome on the triumphal arch of Constantine which was decreed him by the Senate and dedicated in 315:

> "To Constantine, the Great, general, Caesar and priest, Pious and Happy Augustus, because with the guidance of divinity and the loftiness of his own mind he freed with his army the Republic from a tyrant and all his machinations at one blow by just force, the Senate and the Roman people dedicates this worthy arch to his triumphs."

> (Imp. Caes. Fl. Constantino Maximo
> P.F. Augusto S.P.Q.R.
> Quod instinctu divinitatis mentis
> Magnitudine cum exercitu suo
> Tam de tyranno quam de omni eius
> Factione uno tempore iustis
> ultus est armis
> Arcum triumphis insignem dicavit.)

Some scholars of the past century thought that the words "*instinctu divinitatis*" were not in the original inscription since they were too openly Christian; they considered that they had been substituted for some idolatrous expression which spoke perhaps of Jupiter or some other god. In 1863, however, when Napoleon III was having some sketches made of the carvings of the arch, G. B. de'Rossi with other experts was able to go up on the scaffolding and examine the joints of the slabs and the veins of the marble. From this examination it was quite evident that no slabs had been changed and no writing had been altered. The two words in question must be considered part of the original inscription.

These two words, however, mean considerably less than they might seem to at first. A Christian would approve them but so also would a pagan. They say that Constantine was guided by some divinity or even by one divinity. They have the general meaning that, in the opinion of the Senate who put up the arch and certainly also in the estimation of the pagans, the victory of Constantine was obtained not only by military strategy, but also by means of superhuman and divine assistance. But this is for us far too little a confirmation of the two stories of Lactantius and Eusebius.

167.   What is the relation of the stories to each other? In common they have the divine warning given or at least confirmed during sleep; they differ completely in time, for Eusebius makes the affair happen many months before Lactantius. For the rest, the "heavenly sign of God" mentioned only by Lactantius must correspond with the "sign seen in the sky" described at length by Eusebius. The sign placed on the shield according to Lactantius must correspond to the standard fashioned by Constantine according to Eusebius. It is not reasonable to doubt the good faith either of Lactantius or Eusebius for we know so much about them as writers in other matters. It would be most difficult to maintain that there were two different divine warnings, one in Gaul and the other near Rome. Keeping to what is related by both writers, the warning during sleep, it would seem more secure to accept the story of Eusebius who bases himself on the confidences made him by Constantine and confirmed by oath. If we do this, we must understand that when Lactantius assigns the divine warning to the vigil of the battle he is really referring to the vision in Gaul the effects of which were seen so clearly in the battle near Rome. The ancient historians are known to have preferred the linking of the argument in their grouping of incidents to chronological precision. (Many modern exegetes consider that the casting out of the buyers and sellers from the temple which is told by John at the beginning of the public life is the same incident as that narrated by the other three Evangelists at the end of the public life, that is, more than two years later.)

The standard made by Constantine is the *labarum* of which Eusebius gives a description (cf. *De vita Constant.*, i, 31). The word is unknown in classical Latin and a certain etymology has yet to be discovered. The *labarum* consisted of a gilt pole which had a small bar at the top thereby forming a cross; from the transverse bar hung a square piece of purple cloth ornamented with gold and precious stones. At the very top of the upright was fixed a circle of gold and precious stones and in the center of this circle was the monogram of Christ, composed of the two first letters of the Greek Word (XPIΣTOΣ); the X was combined with the P in such a way that the P came in the middle of the X. In later times the medallions of Constantine and his sons were attached to the cloth. Comparing this monogram with the sign put on the shields according to Lactantius, we find a difference for Lactantius speaks of a combination as follows:

This shows the letters joined into one; the monogram of Eusebius, however, does not fuse the letters, but puts one on top of the other:

168.   Some modern scholars have opined that the monogram of the *labarum* and the sign on the shields was derived from some symbol for the god Sol already commonly used in Gaul. There is no adequate proof of this. The enormous popularity of the monogram and the *labarum*, which was achieved almost immediately, is astonishing. Reproductions of it are found everywhere and especially on the coins of Constantine and his successors. The mint at Siscia in Pannonia in 317 struck coins with the figure of Constantine bearing the monogram on his helmet. It appears frequently in Christian art particularly in the catacombs (graffiti, stones, and sarcophagi); one of the best specimens is that found in the catacombs of St. Agnes at Rome.

Eusebius also says (cf. *Hist. eccl.*, ix, 9, 10–11) that after Constantine's victory a statue was erected to him in Rome. He desired that this statue should hold in one hand "the trophy of the saving passion (of Christ)," that is, the Cross; he had inscribed on the pedestal: "With this saving sign [σωτηριώδει] true proof of bravery, you liberated your city saving it from the yoke of the tyrant, etc." Some scholars, however, have considered that Eusebius misinterpreted both the trophy and the inscription; the cross of the statue could have been an ordinary *vexillum* (a military standard) and the inscription, given by Eusebius in Greek, may have said, not "saving sign" (*signo salutari*), but "excellent sign" (*singulari signo*). This is the reading of Rufinus who refers to the text in Latin. In this way it could have a military meaning.

3. Saxa Rubra

169. Constantine continued his march down the Via Flaminia and was now approaching Rome (par. 161).

Maxentius had not taken the threat very seriously at first, for he did not expect Constantine to deal so successfully with his troops on guard at the foot of the Alps. When his armies were put to flight one after the other, and the route down Italy stood open and unprotected, he was terrified and lost all sense of strategy. He had never been a military genius; now his terror was such that it did not even allow him to see that though his position was very dangerous, it was not really desperate. He controlled the sea; Rome had solid walls; the earlier shortage of food had been remedied by the provisions which he had been collecting from all parts in preparation for his campaign against Constantine. In his frenzy, however, he did not consider all this, and did not realize that Constantine with a small force in enemy land would have every reason to avoid laying siege to so well provided a city as Rome. In fact, Maxentius would quite probably have been able to outlast any siege Constantine could mount.

Maxentius was laboring under the disadvantage of being cordially hated by the nobility and even the ordinary people of Rome; on the other hand, the soldiers and especially the praetorians were very loyal and any popular rising would have been quickly crushed.

Filled with terror, Maxentius remained shut up in his palace. He dared not even go down to the nearby Sallustian gardens, for he said that he had been informed through a haruspex that if he left the gates of the city he would die. During the night he would start from his bed and wander wildly through the rooms and corridors of his palace; once he decided to move into a neighboring house with his wife and children at night. To gain some courage, he called up all the forces of pagan religion; every day haruspices and fortunetellers were called to the royal apartments so that the future could be examined. The most filthy rites of magic were employed; pregnant women are said to have been disemboweled and young babies killed so that their entrails could be examined; even lions had their throats cut and spirits were con-

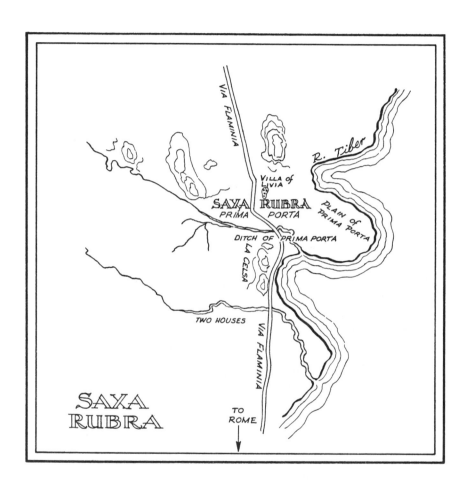

VIA FLAMINIA

R. Tiber

VILLA OF
LIVIA

SAXA RUBRA
PRIMA PORTA

PLAIN of
PRIMA PORTA

DITCH OF PRIMA PORTA

LA CELSA

TWO HOUSES

VIA FLAMINIA

SAXA
RUBRA

TO
ROME

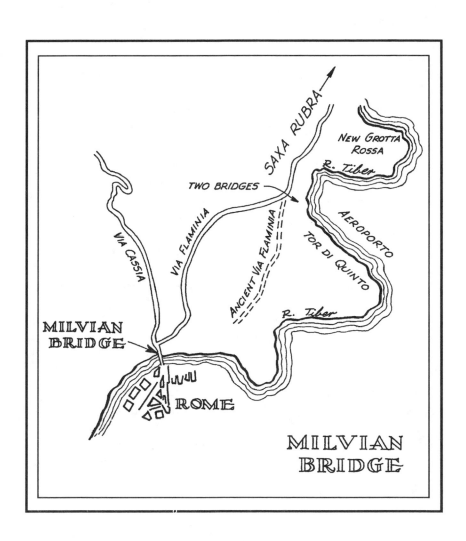

MILVIAN
BRIDGE

sulted in the dark of night. This mobilization of magical force did not slow the pace of Constantine's march on the city.

Maxentius' one comfort was the praetorian guard. He concealed the defeats in the North and called them to him singly or in groups demanding: "Am I not the only emperor?" They replied: "Yes, the only one, the unconquerable one." Handfuls of money were showered on them; "Enjoy yourselves, spend freely." Meanwhile in the distance were seen the advance guard of Constantine's force.

170. If a brief reference by Lactantius (cf. *De mortibus persecut.*, 44, 3) is correct, the first meeting between the two armies was unfavorable to Constantine (*Dimicatum, et Maxentiani milites praevalebant*). This must have been a mere clash between scouting parties somewhere well away from the city. October 27 was near and Maxentius would then have completed five years as elected emperor; the occasion would have to be celebrated with great festival, with shows and the circus. The whole city was in an uproar partly because of the festivities and partly on account of the news which was arriving from outside the city; it may be that Constantine had got agents into Rome and that they were busily engaged in seeking support for their master. In the streets the people were talking excitedly and, during a performance in the circus, the spectators suddenly began to shout that Constantine was invincible.

Maxentius was horrified and sought counsel from the *Sibylline Books*; the reply was that the enemy of the Romans would die that very day. The words were typically sybilline, for the answer did not include the name of the enemy. Maxentius naturally presumed the prophecy meant Constantine; he was much encouraged and suddenly grew active; disregarding the warning by the haruspices against leaving the walls of Rome, he went out and took his place in front of the army which was already drawn up for battle.

171. After the preliminary unsuccessful skirmish, if it took place, Constantine continued along the Via Flaminia to a place called Saxa Rubra (Red Rocks) about nine miles from the city. The place is known exactly. It is a district along the right bank of the Tiber where the river makes a great semicircular bend. Directly to the north of this bend on a little hill was a villa called anciently *ad gallinas albas* at one time belonging to Livia, the wife of Octavianus Augustus. This part is called the *Prima Porta* and the half circle of land closed in by the river is the Plain of the Prima Porta. The word "red" is derived

from the color of the surrounding land which is formed from a pinkish
tufo of the Roman *pozzolana* type. In various places and especially
around the villa of Livia ancient disused quarries of *pozzolana* are to
be found and reference to this is seen in the names of two places a
little to the south called the "old Grotta Rossa" and the "new
Grotta Rossa."

Flowing through this enclosed piece of land is a small water course
called the Ditch of the Prima Porta. It comes from two little streams
which join a little to the west; it passes by a hill — *La Celsa* — which
presents a steep rocky face to the Tiber and after crossing the semicircle enters the main river.

The army of Maxentius was spread out at the Saxa Rubra with
the main intention of barring the approach to Rome along the Via
Flaminia. The road leaves some small hills to the north and runs
between La Celsa and the right bank of the Tiber; the gap is very
narrow with an average width of a hundred yards. Besides this, the
narrow passage goes on for some hundreds of yards forming a corridor
between the river and the hills which come after La Celsa. If this
passage could be blocked, then any invader would be forced to move
across to the Via Cassia much farther to the west, thereby losing
much time and spreading out his forces.

172. Maxentius' army was disposed in the following order. On the
right wing in the semicircle formed by the Tiber were the mercenary
infantry, Italians and Africans; they were placed there protected almost
completely by the river, since their courage and determination in the
face of the enemy were doubtful. The center, which was placed in
position across the Via Flaminia, was much more important, and
therefore the hard core of the army was allotted to this place, the
cataphracti which Constantine had already met at the foot of the Alps
(pars. 159, 160). Their rear was protected in part by the hill La Celsa
while in the front they were perhaps protected for part of the way
by the Ditch of the Prima Porta. The left wing, which was also very
important, was protected to some extent by the small hills and the
streams of the Ditch; to make this section firm, the praetorians were
stationed here for they were most loyal and quite brave.

At the rear of his forces was the Milvian Bridge providing communication with Rome and a possible line of retreat. A pontoon bridge
had been thrown across in a great hurry, but it was not very strong.
Ancient historians do not tell us exactly where this bridge was con-

structed, but it was probably at the point where the Via Flaminia —
which in ancient times ran much farther to the south than nowadays —
turned sharply from the river directly toward the Milvian Bridge.

173. Aurelius Victor (cf. *De Caesar*, 40, 43) says that the meeting
of the two armies was at Saxa Rubra. Aurelius Victor was prefect of
Rome and therefore knew the ground; his statement is confirmed indirectly by Zosimus and by the panegyrists. Lactantius, on the other
hand, names the Milvian Bridge as the site of the battle. This discrepancy is only apparent. A battle usually has an initial or principal
location and then smaller areas of fighting. In our case, the first and
most important part of the battle was at the Saxa Rubra, for it was
here the defeat of the army of Maxentius began. Then followed two
important episodes, one at the wooden bridge and another at the
Milvian Bridge, where the fighting was fierce but only because the
Maxentians were trying to escape.

If Maxentius made a grave strategic error in not allowing himself
to be besieged, his general committed no less a one in choosing Saxa
Rubra for the battle. The land has been examined in recent times
by military experts, including the famous Moltke, and they have all
agreed that much more suitable positions for Maxentius' army can
be found in the vicinity. There was little possibility of maneuver for,
on the right, the way was closed by the curve of the Tiber; the center
had many advantages, but La Celsa and other hills at the rear stopped
any change of position in an orderly and compact way; the left wing
had little protection and no tactical junction with the right. For a
defensive battle, the narrow stretch of the Saxa Rubra would have
been ideal for soldiers who were willing to die rather than retreat a
step. Maxentius' soldiers, however, were not the warriors of Leonides.
They had been softened up in the Roman brothels, and only the praetorians would fight to the death.

The fact is that the choice of Saxa Rubra was made hastily in a
frantic desire to bar the Via Flaminia to the invader. Since every
effort of the magicians had proved useless in the face of Constantine's
steady advance, it was thought that the narrow passage between the
Tiber and La Celsa would be a suitable spot to halt his armies by
human means. A wider vision would have seen that quite another
strategy was demanded. The Via Flaminia and all the other roads
leading to Rome should have been left open so that Constantine could

arrive easily as far as the city walls. The height and thickness of these walls was Maxentius' real power.

174. The most difficult sector for Constantine was the center where he was opposed by the *cataphracti*; if they could be broken, then the two enemy wings would offer little trouble. It was against the center, therefore, that Constantine first attacked, leading his troops in person. The conflict was hard and long, and it is probable that Constantine used the same tactics which he had used to defeat the *cataphracti* before Turin. The frieze of the Arch of Constantine has preserved for us a scene which according to many archaeologists shows these armored troops being thrown into the Tiber. This interpretation of the sculpture is doubtful, however. It probably shows the later crossing of the Milvian Bridge, rather than the fight at Saxa Rubra, since it was there that the *cataphracti* were flung into disorder and dispersed with the blows of maces; perhaps, however, some units later made a stand at the Milvian Bridge and it was these who were thrown into the Tiber.

The defeat of his cavalry was a great tactical loss for Maxentius, and a very heavy blow to the morale of the troops. The infantry were left open on their flank nearest the center; when they saw the rout of the powerful cavalry on which their highest hopes were fixed they were filled with panic. The mercenary infantry collected from here and there, and insufficiently trained soon gave way under the charges of the Gallic and German cavalry of Constantine. The praetorians, on the other hand, showed great courage. These survivors of imperial Rome, who had for centuries made and unmade the governors of the world, fought to the death. A few days later in Rome the conqueror Constantine abolished the praetorians, dismissing the survivors of the battle.

175. Of the troops of Maxentius who had been put to flight, some jumped into the Tiber, and if they managed to get across, fled over the open country. Others retreated toward Rome in the hope of reaching the wooden bridge, or the Milvian Bridge. Soon the crowd of fugitives on the former, which was nearer, became very large, and as is usual in hurried retreats, very disordered. Under the weight of such numbers the badly constructed bridge collapsed, and those on it fell into the river which was swollen with the autumn rains. Many tried to continue their crossing by means of the boats, which had supported the bridge or by hanging on to the supports which were left. One of the crowd of fugitives was Maxentius. It is not known

whether he fell with the rest when the bridge collapsed, or whether he was attempting to cross on horseback; it seems that he managed to get within reach of the opposite bank, but was dragged down in the mud by his heavy armor. There he died and his body was found the next day by Constantine's soldiers; they removed his head and sticking it on a pike, carried it in triumph to Rome.

As soon as victory was obvious at Saxa Rubra, Constantine decided to take advantage of it by intercepting the retreat toward Rome. For this he had to occupy the Milvian Bridge as quickly as possible — the wooden bridge was no longer usable. From the story given on the Arch of Constantine, it seems that he managed to do this. He probably sent a strong force over the Via Cassia more to the west down which they came a little later on to the Via Flaminia once more. The Milvian Bridge stood at the junction of these two roads, and though when these fresh troops arrived at the bridge many fugitives had already managed to cross, the greater part of the rout arrived at the bridge to find it blocked by Constantine's men. The fugitives among whom were perhaps the surviving cataphracti, tried to force a passage but were destroyed or thrown into the river. By now the gates of Rome were being opened.

It was October 28, 312.

4. Constantine in Rome

176. The following day, October 29, Constantine entered Rome.

As was to be expected, it was a triumphal entry. Aurelius Victor says that the conqueror of the day before was received laetitia et gaudio of the people and the Senate; Lactantius and Eusebius say the same. The citizens in general were pleased with the victory for they could now breathe again; the Christians rejoiced even more for they saw in the hero a possible protector of their religion. Constantine was received by enormous crowds and among the masses one could distinguish senators and knights. They all shouted the more cheerfully since they no longer felt that their heads were under the danger of Maxentius' sword or that their wives and their wealth were threatened by his agents. They accompanied Constantine to the royal palace occupied by Maxentius two days before and stayed in front a long time, cheering and asking him to show himself. All admired his magnificent physique and also

a quality which had not been seen for some time in their masters —
a modest bearing. Constantine had this trump card in reserve and
knew the opportune moment to play it.

177. He gave proof of this moderation with his first official orders.
As usual on such occasions, the people demanded not only reparations
for the abuses of the past, but revenge on those who had perpetrated
them. Had Constantine listened to the furious demands of the people,
half the population of Rome and certainly all the members of Maxentius' household would have been headless. This did not happen; the
son of Maxentius and some of his more crime-stained collaborators
were executed; what was left of the praetorian guard was disbanded
(par. 174); the military of the city were reduced in numbers and spies
were punished. Those of Maxentius' agents who had shown themselves moderate were maintained in high office; so far as possible
Constantine compensated the victims of the fallen regime, freeing
prisoners, recalling exiles, and restoring confiscated property. Those
who were in great need were helped with money and food. The most
important political event was the order to destroy the statues of
Maxentius and Maximinus which were a testimony of their secret
treaty (par. 158).

Constantine wished to show deference to the Senate, and so revived
the ancient usage by which generals reported on their victorious campaigns to the Conscript Fathers. In a solemn session he described how
much he had done for the glory of the Empire and further revealed his
plans for the future. He would bring back to the Senate its old importance and restore the glorious dignity of which only the memory
remained. The old men of the Senate took these announcements
seriously and rejoiced to see the old times of the republic with them
again when a Roman senator was worth more than an Oriental monarch. Such joy could not remain sterile, and so the Senate outdid itself
in acts of homage to the generous conqueror.

178. The Senate first of all accepted without discussion the payments
demanded for the costs of the war. Then, carried away by Constantine's
trust in them, they decided the status of the remaining dynasts of
the tetrarchy; Constantine was given the title "First of the Augusti,"
and given precedence over Licinius and Maximin. All this was very
pleasant, but had no practical results. Two buildings were assigned
to the honor of Constantine which had already been built by their
preceding master. One was the *heroon* raised by Maxentius in honor

of his son Romulus to whom he had been devoted and who had died in 310. Until a few years ago it was believed that this *heroon* was a small round temple on the Via Sacra which had been joined later to the Church of SS. Cosmas and Damian. Recent studies have shown that this temple was the *Templum Sacrae Urbis* (also put up by Maxentius), while the *heroon* was beside the Via Appia near the stadium of Maxentius. The second of the buildings given over to the honor of Constantine was the basilica of Maxentius mentioned earlier (par. 63). Some changes in it were ordered by its new patron.

The construction most widely known was the famous Arch of Constantine which bears the inscription with which we have already dealt (par. 166). There has been much — perhaps too much — discussion about this monument. There are some who maintain that it was first put up by Domitian, and that it had served for various emperors until it was finally transformed and dedicated to Constantine by the Senate. It is certain that to prepare the arch in as short a time as possible, material was collected haphazardly from earlier monuments of Trajan, Hadrian, and Marcus Aurelius; the material thus brought together was built into the arch without a great deal of care. It is evident after even a summary examination that persons and scenes are represented on the arch which are not particularly suitable to Constantine and actually clash with each other. This fact can be attributed partly to the artistic decadence of the times and partly to the speed with which the monument was erected; there are no real arguments to show that the actual arch had been built earlier than Constantine.

179. The general and well-founded opinion is that the arch was dedicated in 315, a little more than two years after the victory at Saxa Rubra; this was the celebration of the decennials of Constantine at Rome. Some students have suggested a later date, but with little proof.

Constantine stayed in Rome no more than a couple of months after his triumphal entry. In this time — as Nazarius the panegyrist says — he solved many problems. The first was that of the Christians. It is possible that during the two months Constantine met and discussed affairs with Miltiades, the bishop of Rome. It is a fact, however, that less than a year later, in the October of 313, the synod which was held to discuss the Donatists (par. 238) was held in the *domus Faustae* at the Lateran, once the property of Fausta, the sister of Maxentius and the wife of Constantine. The only explanation of this is that the Lateran Palace had become the property of the Roman Church, for since there were at least twenty-five ecclesiastical properties in the city, it would have been unreasonable to hold the council in some private secular building. This gift of the *domus Faustae* must have occurred about a year before the council — that is, during the meetings between Constantine and Miltiades where restitution and indemnities in the Roman Church were discussed. The first Lateran basilica incorporating the *domus* was built later (par. 206).

The Roman Church came to possess many other buildings in the city during the government of Constantine. Before we can deal with this, however, we must look at the later political developments.

5. *Persecution of Maximin — His Death*

180. After the two months in Rome — that is, in the first days of 313 — Constantine went to Milan to celebrate the marriage of his sister Constantia to Licinius (par. 158). This was no love match, for the bride was a mere girl and her bridegroom rather old and quite different in character. Politics, however, required the union for it would strengthen the political alliance and proclaim it to the Empire. For this reason the marriage was to be celebrated with every pomp and even the aged Diocletian was invited; though he was almost forgotten now his presence would increase the solemnity. The solitary of Salona refused the invitation and kept to his gloomy hermitage. This seems to have annoyed Constantine.

It is not very difficult to imagine that the two Augusti who met at Milan occupied themselves less with the coming nuptials than with affairs of State. The most urgent problem was of course the attitude they were going to adopt toward the third Augustus, Maximin, of whom they were very suspicious. After this, they had to decide on the legal standing of Christianity in the Empire. The two problems were to some extent connected.

Maximin had been quite happy to execute the edicts of persecution, but during 307 he began to moderate his zeal perhaps for financial reasons for he now preferred to send Christians to the mines of the State for forced labor rather than kill them off immediately. After July, 308, however, he took up the persecution to the death even more fiercely and with more effective methods. When Galerius' Edict of Toleration was published Maximin was forced to accept it, but from the beginning avoided obeying it, as we have already seen (par. 155). He did not publish the edict, but notified the governors of provinces that the emperors were now abandoning their attempt to recall the Christians to the worship of the gods and that they did not intend to persecute them any longer. This was a very vague order and it allowed Maximin and his governors to harass the Christians under other pretexts. After a short while Galerius died and Maximin took his place in Nicomedia. Officially he did not withdraw the Edict of Toleration, but in practice he conducted a clever offensive against Christianity.

181. In this way Maximin anticipated by fifty years Julian the Apostate who fought Christianity by removing its friends and blackening its character. He forbade the Christians to restore their ruined churches and even to hold their meetings in cemeteries; the reasons given were, however, connected with public order and morals. The pagan temples, however, which had fallen into decay were hurriedly restored and with an entirely new arrangement the priests serving these temples were placed in a regular hierarchy corresponding very much to that of the Christians. In the cities and provinces there now appeared not only priests, but archpriests, bishops, and archbishops, all pagan. They were given a distinctive dress, furnished with administrative and punitive powers and ordered to favor idolatrous cults and put every obstacle in the way of Christianity.

To take away the good name of the Christians, the so-called "Acts of Pilate" were widely circulated; these are a very coarse collection of attacks on the person of Christ. The book had probably been compiled some time before this, perhaps at the beginning of the persecution (pars. 32–35) but had remained unknown. Maximin saw to its diffusion both by giving away a large number of copies free and by having it publicly read and explained; it was also made an obligatory subject in the schools (cf. *Hist. Eccl.*, ix, 5, 1). The methods were not new and they are still in use.

Another ancient method of attack (and still not out of date) was to expose the debauchery practiced at Christian meetings. In earlier centuries Tertullian and other apologists had recorded such calumnies but by the time of the Great Persecution the same charge was made again. The private life of Christians, however, was well known for they were to be found in all classes of society and their conduct was a clear contradiction of such disgusting stories. In view of the absence of new charges the old ones were used again and an attempt was made to give them some legal backing. In Damascus, therefore, some streetwalkers were arrested and were induced without great difficulty to declare themselves Christians and to confess that they had taken part in secret meetings and in the filthy deeds which were practiced at them. Their statements were written down and a copy was sent to Maximin; he had numerous copies made of it and ordered it to be distributed in the cities and villages and put up in public places where the people could read it (*Hist. Eccl.*, ix, 5, 2). Such actions seem to have made little impression on the population for they knew how little right Maximin had to put himself up as a protector of public morals (par. 129).

182. Petitions then began to come in from the pagans begging Maximin to protect them, and their gods, from Christian impiety. They asked that Christians should be expelled from all inhabited places. As always happens under tyrants, these requests were presented as spontaneous, provoked purely by the hatefulness of the Christians; It never appeared that they had been inspired by the servile agents of the monarch or by magistrates wishing to gain his favorable attention (cf. Lactantius, *De mortibus persecut.*, 36; Eusebius, *Hist. Eccl.*, ix, 2 ff.). An inscription found in Arycanda of Lycia (cf. *Corpus inscr. Lat.*, iii, 12132) gives the petition of its citizens who implore the clemency of Maximin (and of the other two Augusti for the sake of form) to save them from the Christians. The reply which is partially recorded in the inscription tells them that their request was very near the Augustus' heart. Similar petitions were sent by Tyre, Antioch, and Nicomedia (cf. *Hist. Eccl.*, ix, 7, 3–15; ix, 2–3; ix, 9, 17–19).

The usual favorable answer to the petition from Tyre has an unusual characteristic. Maximin not only produces theological arguments against the Christians, but furnishes a kind of pagan catechism embellished with poetic favors and pompous phrases. He points to the prosperous and fertile lands (it was the summer of 311) and concludes that the gods are looking after their cultivators rather than after those who cultivate Christianity.

The petition of Antioch had special authority, for the statue of Zeus Philios (Friendly Jupiter) venerated there had spoken with its own mouth the oracle demanding the expulsion of Christians from the city and the whole territory. How the statue was given the power of speech would have been explained by Theotecnus the "curator" of Antioch who had studied magic and in his other capacity of a clever mechanic had directed the construction of the statue (cf. *ibid.*, ix, 11, 5–6) (par. 193).

183. Despite these moral and mechanical successes, things were not going as well as Maximin had expected. While the crops had promised well at first, the end of the summer and the autumn were disastrous, drought ruined the harvests, especially in Syria. It was unfortunate that prophet Maximin was thus proved false; the famine and want that followed were even more serious. Such famines still occur in Eastern countries where everyone is sustained by the annual harvest, and no thought is given to keeping a stock or importing food from other countries.

Barns filled with corn were only a memory and it now was a fortune to be able to find some grass. Every kind of property was sold to obtain food; for a meal, parents even sent their children into slavery. Many collapsed in the streets too weak to ask for help; once rich matrons carried what few valuable garments they had left to sell them for food.

Epidemics soon broke out and especially an unknown disease, some kind of carbuncle, attacked the face and the eyes. The dead were numberless; those who survived the famine were disposed of by the plague. Whole families, and indeed the population of whole villages disappeared altogether; when the imperial tax collectors came they found nobody from whom to demand payment. Bodies lay along all the streets; they did not putrefy for countless dogs disposed of them. Orders were actually given to kill all dogs in an attempt to stop the spread of the plague (cf. *Hist. Eccl.*, ix, 8).

In all this distress and upheaval only the Christians, persecuted in the past and now once more, did what they could to help their enemies. They buried the abandoned bodies, for they had been the temples of God; they collected and distributed the few victuals they could find, for those dying of hunger were the children of God. The pagans who saw this could not believe their eyes, and moved by their good works — far more deeply than by any philosophical arguments — lauded their mercy and gave praise to their God.

184. Maximin was not moved and his fury against the Christians continued. Precise dates are lacking, but it must have been now that he made the expedition against the Armenians which is mentioned only by Eusebius (cf. *Hist. Eccl.*, ix, 8, 2–4). These Armenians seem to have been the inhabitants, not of the true kingdom of Armenia, but of those five territories on the other side of the Tigris which had passed to the Roman Empire after the defeat of Persia (pars. 19, 85). They were for the most part fervent Christians and therefore could not have been pleased with the persecution in the lands of Maximin. The precise reason for the expedition is not known — there were probably several reasons. It was well known that the Armenians received the fugitives from persecution (par. 85); perhaps they had also sent help to those who remained in the Empire. None of this can have been to Maximin's liking. One can conjecture that along the borders the Christians had been holding meetings with the idea of intervening with force on behalf of their fellow Christians. Nor is it beyond belief that Maximin attempted in his pagan fury to convert the Armenians *manu militari*; this would also have solved a political problem.

The expedition was led by Maximin himself. It was begun under bad auspices, for the army set off from Syria while those regions were suffering under the famine and the plague; the campaign ended when the news came from the West that Constantine and Licinius were preparing some unpleasant surprises for Maximin. We have no precise details of the expedition — it was probably not a glorious one.

185. Pagan zeal did not allow Maximin to look after his political and dynastic interests properly. On his deathbed Galerius had entrusted his wife Valeria to his friend Licinius and she had stayed for a while in her protector's territories; she presently decided to move with her mother, Prisca, over to the lands of Maximin. It would seem that she did this to avoid any suspicion of her conduct, for Licinius was still single while Maximin, the grandson of Galerius, was married. It may have been that such prudence was due to some remaining favorable feelings toward Christianity; Valeria and Prisca were the daughter and wife respectively of Diocletian and had been forced by threats to sacrifice to idols (pars. 31, 49). Unfortunately, when Maximin discovered their presence in his territory he decided to marry Valeria. His intentions were only political. If he could become related to Diocletian, the founder of the tetrarchy, his rather insecure position would be strengthened. His present wife was a problem, however, the more so since her conduct was nothing but honorable. Maximin declared that he was ready to repudiate her the moment that Valeria agreed to marry him. Valeria refused flatly. She said that she was still

wearing her widow's weeds and that the ashes of her husband were still warm; she added that his present wife had done nothing to deserve repudiation (Lactantius, De mortibus persecut., 39–41). In any case she declared that Diocletian's daughter would die univira following the example of the ancient Roman matrons.

This refusal and his deluded ambition drove Maximin to fury. From that time he persecuted the two noble ladies and their household. He killed their servants, harassed their friends, and confiscated their goods. They were forced to move from one place to another at the orders of Maximin given under the pretext of security. The two women ended up by being exiled in the Syrian desert. From there, Valeria managed to send a message to Diocletian telling him of their sufferings and begging his help. Her father sent representatives asking for the restitution of his daughter, but Maximin refused. Diocletian even sent one of his relatives, a person of great authority and of high position in the army; this time the reply was the same but couched in overbearing and insolent language. The old man, the onetime Father of the Empire, who had created at his will Caesars and Augusti and had himself given the purple to Maximin, was now not even able to save his daughter from insults or to have her with him in his retreat at Salona. The two women continued their wanderings while their persecutor sank deeper in his vile debaucheries (par. 129). A shadow of despairing sorrow now came down on the sumptuous palace of Salona which would only be dispelled by Death the Liberator.

186. The bad government of Maximin soon brought disaster. He had failed in his plan to hitch his wagon to Diocletian's star by marrying Valeria; he had not succeeded in getting any help from Maxentius (par. 158). The Empire appeared quite determined to be divided into two parts — the East and the West. The two Augusti, Constantine and Licinius, were firmly in alliance, but even for geographical reasons such a union was not possible for Maximin and Maxentius. The commercial connections between East and West were breaking up and soon would disappear completely; ships and merchants did not trade between the two regions and travelers avoided passing from one to the other for they ran the danger of being taken for spies, harassed, and tortured. This was the beginning of the process which would later cause the total separation between the East and the West which still exists in our own times.

In this confusion came a sudden shock — no less surprising for the fact that it had been half expected. Constantine made his sudden march down the length of Italy and Maxentius was defeated at Saxa Rubra. Why did not Maximin go to help Maxentius at least by threatening the territories of Licinius, Constantine's ally? The first difficulty was certainly geographical and Maximin was not prepared for such an expedition. At any rate, quite possibly at this time he was engaged in his war against the Armenians. The disaster which Maxentius suffered opened his eyes, however, and he could see the real danger of his position. Information came to him that Constantine had found in Rome the statues of Maxentius and Maximin as allies and had destroyed them (par. 177). He also knew that letters had been found there which proved the secret alliance between them and that if there had been any doubt before, Constantine must know now that he had been plotting against him. Maximin knew, therefore, that even the official friendship of Constantine was lost beyond all hope; he had therefore no support in the West and was mortally exposed to the power of the two allies, Licinius and Constantine.

187. Constantine showed his diplomacy again. He did not publish the compromising documents found in Rome; he made use of the title "First Augustus" given him by the Senate and acting as such sent an official notification to Maximin telling him of the defeat and death of Maxentius. Constantine took occasion to invite Maximin to stop persecuting the Christians (cf. *Hist. Eccl.*, ix, 9, 12; Lactantius, *De mortibus persecut.*, 37).

Maximin, though he did not see eye to eye with Constantine, considered that this was not the moment to announce his opinions. To continue, therefore, in the official favor of the powerful Western dynast, he made the best of a bad job and sent to Sabinus, the prefect of the praetorians, other instructions on the treatment of the Christians. But even this rescript which was given right at the end of 312 had no real effect and was intended only to gain time (cf. *Hist. Eccl.*, ix, 9, 14–22). Maximin presents himself as a firm supporter of religious toleration even in regard to the Christians. It is true, he says, that he has been attempting to recall his subjects to the traditional worship of ancient gods of the Empire, but he has always used kindness and persuasion. If some subordinate magistrate has been using physical inducements, then the people should know that this was never the intention of the Augustus and that he now formally forbids it. From now on, he concludes, there must be liberty and respect for all — even for those who refuse to return to the worship of the old gods.

Very pretty words these, but devoid of meaning for those who knew the real state of affairs. Maximin might be wearing sheep's clothing for the moment, but the Christians knew quite well what animal was hidden by this new and innocent front. The new law was, as usual, very vague and did not decide whether the Christians were allowed to hold meetings or to rebuild their places of worship. For reasons of safety they did neither and so things remained as they were before. Constantine had excellent sources of information in the East, and he was no more fooled than the Christians by the innocent bleatings of Maximin.

188. This unstable politico-religious situation lasted only a few months and it was Maximin who made the first move.

At the beginning of the spring of 313 Maximin considered the time was ripe. The other two Augusti were far away in Milan deep in their discussions on the forthcoming marriage celebrations and conferring on their future attitude toward the Christians and other problems of the Empire; the eastern frontier of the territories of Licinius were only thinly held by skeleton forces; Constantine's regiments on the Rhine were threatened by one of the periodic invasions of the Franks. Maximin had already recalled his troops from their expedition against the Armenians; he now strengthened them with forces from Asia Minor. With a powerful army he conducted a fatiguing winter march — which did nothing to boost the morale of his men — along the northern coasts of Bithynia. He crossed over the Bosphorus, penetrated into Thrace, and took Byzantium and Heraclea after short sieges.

The happy bridegroom, Licinius, broke off his honeymoon and rushed to his frontiers gathering what troops he could on the way; Constantine went off to the Rhine to do what was necessary against the barbarians. The short resistance put up by the garrisons of Byzantium and Heracleia was of great value to Licinius, for it gave him time to confront his enemy with a reasonably powerful array. Though he was inferior to Maximin in numbers, the morale of his troops was very high for they felt they were companions in arms of the conquerors of Saxa Rubra.

189. It was a war of religions from the beginning. Word went around that Maximin had made a vow to Jupiter that if he was granted victory he would destroy Christianity once and for all. This rumor only confirmed in the minds of Licinius' men that they were fighting for the

same cause as those who had battled at Saxa Rubra; they were certain
of victory. Licinius could not but encourage such sentiments among
his soldiers, for their morale had never been higher. He was not a
Christian and had no real sympathy with Christianity as we shall
see later. For the moment, however, it was convenient that he should
appear to share the sentiments of his ally Constantine and should be
held by his soldiers as a defender of the God who had triumphed
at Saxa Rubra. Lactantius tells us that a short while before the battle
an angel appeared to Licinius in his sleep and taught him a prayer
to the highest God which he was to use with his soldiers; as soon as
he awoke, Licinius called a secretary, dictated the prayer, and ordered
copies to be distributed to his troops before the battle.

This supernatural communication is evidently intended to correspond
with what happened to Constantine before Saxa Rubra. The heavenly
privilege had little effect on Licinius, for a few years later he was a
wholehearted persecutor of Christianity. It is worthy of note that only
Lactantius reports this vision and then merely as a peg on which to
hang the words of the prayer (cf. *De mortibus persecut.*, 46). It
should be noted that he was writing before the persecution of Licinius.
Eusebius, on the other hand, who wrote after the persecution and the
death of Licinius, reports neither the prayer nor the dream.

190. Without bothering about the dream part of the story there are
no serious reasons for calling into doubt the authenticity of the prayer.
Its character of vague monotheism fits in quite well with the inscription placed by the Senate on the Arch of Constantine (par. 166). It
could have been accepted easily by Licinius. His skepticism was sub-
merged by the needs of the moment, for the prayer would not fail
to arouse the ardor of his military already in high spirits at the success
of Saxa Rubra. The prayer says:

> Highest God, we pray Thee.
> Holy God, we pray Thee!
> We recommend all justice to Thee;
> We recommend our safety to Thee;
> We recommend our empire to Thee!
> We live through Thee;
> We are conquerors and happy through Thee!
> Highest, Holy God,
> Hear our prayers.

We stretch out our arms to Thee;
Hear us, Holy, Highest God!

The prayer is in the form of a litany which rendered it very suitable to be recited by a large crowd, such as an army. Litanies found in the Hebrew psalms were much used by Christianity and perhaps in pagan liturgies also, especially in the rites of the mysteries. Whoever made up the prayer did nothing but follow forms and sentiments already well known.

191. Right to the end Maximin hoped to bribe the soldiers of Licinius to desert. The two armies finally came face to face on a desert plain of Thrace, called Campus Serenus, a little to the south of Adrianople. Under the eyes of their armies, Maximin and Licinius held a parley but no agreement was reached. The meeting had been fixed by Licinius for May 1, on which Maximin completed the eighth year of his reign (even here there is similarity with the time sequence of Saxa Rubra, cf. par. 170). Maximin, however, anticipated it by a day and it occurred on April 30. The soldiers of Licinius, before the parley, had momentarily laid down their shields and helmets, and raising their arms had recited the official prayer three times. The battle line of their enemy had heard the murmuring roar of the prayer and were impressed. The trumpets sounded and the fight began.

From the start, things went badly for Maximin. His infantry in which he had great hopes fought wretchedly and were soon put to flight; a little later his personal guard deserted and joined the enemy. Seeing his imminent peril Maximin saved himself by disguise; he flung away the eye-catching purple and dressed up as a slave. He fled over the country and hid himself in the surrounding villages. The army was left to itself. Those who still fought on discovered what Maximin had done and they either followed the imperial example or surrendered. Before long Licinius' army had no enemy to fight.

192. The flight of Maximin developed into a miracle of speed. In a day and a night he covered 160 miles and crossing the straits at Byzantium came to Nicomedia; he did not stop even there, but taking his wife, children, and members of his court continued his flight across Asia Minor, never stopping until he reached Cappadocia. Here in the middle of his territories he could pause for breath and, feeling once more master of himself, began to think how he could repair the disaster.

His strategy now was to defend himself in Cilicia, shutting himself up in the mountains of Taurus, whence he had easy communications with Syria and Antioch. He acquired another purple cloak and began to gather an army. Licinius, however, had not stopped long in Nicomedia. He pursued him and attacked on his right flank, in the lands which join Syria with Cilicia. The defense was badly organized and morale was low; Maximin could not hold Licinius who, after a succession of small engagements, closed Maximin in the narrow strip between the Taurus Mountains and the sea. He was now cut off from all his territories; in despair he took refuge at Tarsus, where three centuries earlier St. Paul had been born. Lactantius and Eusebius say that there he poisoned himself and died after long and terrible torments — which they both describe with complacent detail. Aurelius Victor, however, merely says that he died without mentioning either poison or torments. 193. Before he died, Maximin made two provisions which may be attributed partly to his character and partly to the circumstances in which he found himself. He published an edict, reported by Eusebius (cf. *Hist. Eccl.*, ix, 10, 7-11), in which he gave full and absolute liberty to Christianity. This edict competed with those of Licinius a little earlier at Nicomedia of which we shall speak later. But since with this edict Maximin had acknowledged, willingly or no, the victory of Christianity, his brutal temperament wanted revenge. This he showered on the pagan priests and on all those who had urged him to war, declaring that he had been tricked. He made a wholesale massacre of the new scapegoats a little before his declaration in favor of Christianity (cf. *ibid.*, ix, 10, 6). By now the summer of 313 was well advanced.

With the death of Maximin there disappeared another dynast of the old tetrarchy and his territories passed into the hands of Licinius, who thus became the only Augustus of the East. To obtain a feeling of security in his new possessions, Licinius, instead of following the mild example of Constantine after his entry into Rome, began to chop off heads; anybody who had any connection with the deceased dynast was executed. Although he owed everything to Galerius, he condemned to death his widow Valeria and her mother Prisca. At least the lives of these two noble ladies had been spared by Maximin (par. 185). It is hardly necessary to add that Maximin's wife, children, relatives, and numerous assistants and governors were executed. The statues of these people had a similar fate; they were thrown down, mutilated, and defaced in various ways. Not even the pagan priests and their supporters were spared. This was due to no antipagan zeal, but to a general reaction against the fallen regime. It was now that Theotecnus lost his life — the engineer who had designed the mechanism of the statue of Zeus Philios at Antioch (par. 182).

194. What was left now of the tetrarchy, the great creation of Diocletian? There was really nothing; the two Augusti left in power were where they were through their own strength, with no reference to the general rules of succession which had been laid down. Now it was that the creator of the system disappeared.

There have been from ancient times various versions of the death of Diocletian. He counted for nothing in politics any more; he had outlived his own work. No one now bothered about what he thought. In the solitude of Salona he was not even able to have his wife and daughter; it is even probable that they were executed in his own lifetime. The Christians he had persecuted had their triumph; those who had accepted the purple and honors from him paid him no attention and caused him sorrow. Not until all this had happened, did long-desired Death (par. 67) come to liberate the unhappy old man.

According to Lactantius (cf. *De mortibus persecut.*, 42–43), it would seem that Diocletian died before Maximin; this is judging from the order of events as related, but not too much store can be put on this. Eusebius says that he died after a long and painful illness (cf. *Hist. Eccl.*, viii, appendix 3), but does not record the date. There is a suggestion, echoed by Aurelius Victor, that he died of self-starvation; the *Fasti Hydatiani* make him die in December, 316; other documents provide other dates.

With Diocletian went one of the greatest emperors of Rome. His authority, although finally it was completely lost, was always firmly fixed in the conscience of his old subjects. The Roman Senate decreed him the title *Divus*, although he was no longer emperor; this was the sole occasion when a private person was raised to divinity. His body, wrapped in purple, was closed in the sarcophagus which he had prepared for it at Salona; the bas-reliefs on it represent Meleager killing a boar in the hunt, thus alluding to the manner in which he had begun his political career (par. 2).

IV. THE TWILIGHT OF THE GODS

1. "We, Having Met Under Favorable Auspices at Milan"

195. The year 313 saw a shower of imperial decrees, all of them favorable to the Christians. The weather had changed; after the storm came the calm and pleasant plants and flowers grew in the wilderness. The flowers were planted by the same person who a year or two before had unleashed the storm — Maximin. Another cultivator in the Christian garden was Licinius, who a little later was to destroy his work with another tempest of persecution. The past was forgotten and the future unknown. For the moment the order of the day could have been the words of Virgil (and of Dante) "*Manibus date lilia plenis!*"

We have already seen that Maximin published an edict of liberty for the Christians (par. 193). This edict was not without precedent and Maximin published it only that he might not be the odd man among the dynasts. Then came the war between him and Licinius and after the latter's victorious entry into Nicomedia the conqueror issued on June 13 a rescript giving full liberty to Christianity. This rescript aroused the emulation of the fugitive Maximin and induced him to publish *in extremis* his own new edict of liberty. A few weeks later he was dead and all his legislation was abrogated by Licinius. Thus only the rescript of the latter remained.

What was the origin of this rescript? It is presented as the result of an agreement between Constantine and Licinius when they met at Milan for the nuptial ceremonies mentioned in paragraph 180. The text of the rescript is given by Lactantius (cf. *De mortibus persecut.,* 48), and also by Eusebius (cf. *Hist. Eccl.,* xi, 2–14). The latter gives a Greek translation of the original Latin, but gives a brief introduction (cf. *ibid.,* 2–3), which is absent in Lactantius' text.

196. The text of the rescript beginning with the preamble given by Eusebius follows:

"We have thought for a long time that religious liberty cannot be denied and that everyone should be given permission to regulate himself in matters of religion according to his own opinion and preference. We therefore ordain that anybody — including the Christians — may observe the faith of their sect and cult. Since in the earlier rescript granting this later additions and conditions were made, many may have been hindered in the observance of their religion."

It cannot be doubted that this preamble is from an official document. Since it comes immediately before the text of the rescript, which is also found in Lactantius, we must conclude that the introduction was added by Licinius when he published the rescript on June 13. In other districts the rescript was without the introduction and it was from one of these that Lactantius took his version.

The reference to a preceding law giving everyone liberty of conscience and worship has caused some scholars to suppose that Constantine had himself made such a law directly after his entry into Rome before going to Milan. There was one well-known archaeologist who considered it "very probable that this was done in a solemn meeting before the people in the Roman Forum." He gives as confirmation one of the scenes depicted on the Arch of Constantine. Leaving aside gratuitous hypotheses, it must be recognized that we have no record of any law made by Constantine in the period before he went to Milan for the meeting. The words of the preamble undoubtedly refer to the Edict of Toleration of Galerius in 311 (par. 154). What is meant by "later additions and conditions" is uncertain — possibly later legislation by Maximin or restrictive clauses added by Galerius which have not come down to us.

197. After the introduction comes the body of the rescript in the report of which Lactantius and Eusebius are in substantial agreement:

"Having met under favorable auspices at Milan, we, Constantine Augustus and Licinius Augustus, have discussed all things pertaining to the public safety and utility. Among those things which appear to please the majority of our peoples we wish to put first the honor given to the Divinity. We therefore give to Christians and to all others, the freedom to follow their own religion. In this way all that is divine in Heaven may be placated and will assist us and all those who are under our government. With salutary and evident proof we see fit to decide that no one should be denied the practice or observance of Christianity or of whatever religion to which anyone may have dedicated himself according to his opinion. The highest Divinity among whose worshippers we number ourselves will therefore show his usual favor and benevolence. Your Excellency [the magistrate to whom the document is directed] may know in consequence that we are pleased to remove all conditions which were contained in earlier letters from this office in regard to the Christians; such conditions seem utterly hateful and alien to our clemency. Anyone now who is pleased to hold with the Christians may do so with all liberty and freedom and without hurt or hindrance. We see fit to communicate all this to your Solicitude so that you may know that we ourselves have given free and absolute permission to the Christians to practice their religion. Since this has been given to them your devotion will understand that similar open and free observance of their own religion has been allowed to others so that in matters of the divinity all may have free choice. This has been done so that it may not seem that we wish to detract anything from the honor or the religion of anyone.

"Furthermore we judge it opportune to decide in the matter of those places where the Christians were in the past accustomed to have their meetings. If they have been taken over in obedience to earlier letters from this office and have been confiscated by our Treasury or any other body they are to be restored to the Christians freely without any charge, objection or fear; those who may have received them as gifts must restore them to the Christians immediately. If those who have been given Christian buildings or bought them wish compensation, they may apply to our Vicar who will see to this out of our clemency. Everything must be given back to the Christians immediately and without delay. It is known that besides the places where the Christians were accustomed to meet they also had other buildings belonging by right to their society — not however to individual persons. These are to be included in the order. You are to order that they be restored without any delay or hesitation to the Christians or to their society or church, being mindful however, of the principle that those who make restitution in this way without indemnity may hope for something from our benevolence. In all these matters you must hasten with your powerful mediation so that our Command may be fulfilled in regard to the Christians with the greatest speed and in this way ensure the public peace through our clemency. As we have said earlier the divine favor which has already been seen in our regard will thus continue for all time toward all our efforts for the public good.

"So that the words of this ordinance of our benevolence may come to the notice of all, it will be convenient for you to show this rescript everywhere on your notice boards; in this way all may know about it and the evidence of our graciousness may not remain hidden."

198. This document is a "rescript" (*rescriptum*), that is, an official copy of a legal disposition sent by the lawgiver to magistrates for their information and guidance. In our case the lawgivers named in the document were Constantine and Licinius who were at the time the only Augusti in the Empire. Since Lactantius in reporting the rescript expressly names Nicomedia as the place where Licinius promulgated it, it is probable that that is where he copied it. Eusebius does not say, on the other hand, where he copied it, but when we remember that the rescript occurs in the later part of his *History* (Books VIII–X), which he wrote at various times from 312 to 324 (par. 72), it is probable that he took it from a copy in the archives of Caesarea.

These documents of Nicomedia (Lactantius) and of Caesarea (Eusebius) presuppose an earlier official text from which they were copied. This is clear from the reference at the beginning to an agreement between Constantine and Licinius when they "met happily at Milan." In the East under Licinius, this treaty was made public by the documents of Nicomedia and Caesarea; there must have been rescripts in the West under Constantine. There, therefore, must have been an official publication of the edict at Milan itself immediately after the agreement between the two Augusti; this was the original text which was copied by the different rescripts.

It was the famous "Edict of Milan."

This is theory. Unfortunately there is no rescript deriving directly from the edict published in Milan. This is not a matter for wonder. Those most interested in copying and spreading the text were without doubt the Christians; the rescripts we have come to us from the Christians Lactantius and Eusebius. Pagan authors do not mention the new law. This pagan silence really confirms its authenticity, for if the whole affair had been false and invented by the Christians, then there would certainly have been cries of protest and easy confutation.

It must be noted that Lactantius and Eusebius lived and wrote in the East where documents regarding the great persecution — and naturally of its cessation — were collected industriously (par. 70 ff.). In the West such documents were not collected or were soon lost (par. 147). It is not extraordinary, therefore, that such carelessness extended even to the document which ended the persecution. This is one of the many historical cases where the absence of information constitutes an *argumentum a silentio* which after all proves nothing. 199. The constitution of Constantine and Licinius of 313 was a great advance on the Edict of Toleration of Galerius in 311 (par. 154). Galerius did not condemn the preceding persecution, and in fact rather defended it. Now, as a matter of political expediency, he unwillingly ordered that the persecuted peoples should be tolerated. The true religion of the Empire, however, remained that of the traditional gods. The law of 313 goes much further. It looks at the subjects of the Empire and is not worried about the traditional gods. Knowing that besides the worshipers of the gods there are numberless worshipers of the God Christ, it guarantees full liberty to all. It speaks no more of a traditional religion of the Empire — this had been an important part of *veterum instituta* of Galerius in his edict — but is concerned simply with the people of the Empire who could now be pagans or Christians as they wished.

It was a true revolution in the Roman concept of the State. From the beginning the State had included the veneration of the gods of the fathers. Even if in recent centuries foreign religions had been tolerated, the fidelity to the ancient gods had never officially been denied. Now the Empire took up a neutral position.

200. Before such a startling development it was only natural that the pagan majority of Roman subjects should be worried. Very many foresaw that it would not be long before the supreme head of the Empire, sacred to the gods, would be a Christian. If this should happen, it would not be difficult to envisage a persecution of the pagans by the Christians. This is why the rescript attempts, from the beginning, to dispose of these fears. It is obvious (cf. G. Boissier, *La fin du paganisme*, ch. ii, 2) that there is great emphasis in the edict on the fact that religious liberty is given equally to Christians and pagans. Such emphasis is necessary because "*en effet il parlait un language qu'on n'avait pas encore entendu.*"

The fear of the pagans that the head of the State might be a Christian would not have disturbed Tertullian for he considered such a possibility absurd (cf. *Apologet.*, xxi, 24). Elsewhere, however, he had taught it "to be necessary that a Christian should love the emperor, that he should revere and honor him, that he should wish him security with the whole of the Roman Empire as long as it lasts; for it will last long" (Ad Scapulam, 2). What does this mean? The Roman Empire will always remain, but must it always be governed by a pagan? Did Christ die for all except the Roman Emperor? Many years had passed, however, and the times had changed, and no one knows if Tertullian who changed his mind on various things in his lifetime would not have also changed his opinion here had he lived at the time of Constantine.

In regard to the other forecast of the pagans — of a new religious persecution — this unfortunately did happen. But, as usual, the human prophecy was not quite correct and instead of Christians persecuting the pagans, it was the other way around. This new persecution was ironically ordered by Licinius, one of the two Augusti to order tolerance for all in 313.

201. This edict was not the only one favorable to Christianity. Notwithstanding the paucity of our sources of information we have clear proof of other minor regulations. We have evidence also of practical provisions in favor of the lately persecuted religion. They were all the effect of the tolerant climate created by the meeting at Milan which gradually spread all over the Empire.

We have a copy of an imperial letter sent at the beginning of 313 to Anulinus the proconsul of Africa which orders the restitution "to the catholic church of the Christians in the different cities and other places" of their earlier possessions even if they were now the property of citizens or others and that this should be done with all speed and thoroughness (cf., Hist. Eccl., x, 5, 15–17). Although this is an order given to one magistrate, such commands must have been given to others — perhaps to all the magistrates in the West under the direct jurisdiction of Constantine. They would be merely a confirmation of the edict of Milan which ordered the restitution of confiscated goods.

Another document gives more information. Constantine understood that even when property had been restored there should be compensation for other losses in the persecution. In a letter directed to Caecilian, the bishop of Carthage, he therefore empowers him to collect from the procurator of Africa the sum of 3,000 folles (about 250 denarii), which is to be distributed according to the list already sent him by Hosius, the bishop-adviser of Constantine. If this sum is not enough, Caecilian may ask a further payment from another official who has been notified of this arrangement (cf. ibid., x, 6, 1–5).

202. In the spring of 313 there was a second letter to Anulinus on the matter of public offices and Catholic clergy. Because these public offices (munera civilia) lost much time and money for those who held them, they were generally avoided and a formal order was needed before anyone would accept them. Constantine shows his attitude toward the Church by recognizing that the clergy should be wholly dedicated to their spiritual ministry (here also one can see the influence of the bishop Hosius mentioned in the preceding paragraph). He orders Anulinus to exempt them from public office "so as not to take them away from the service of the Divinity" which "will bring great advantage to public affairs." This exemption, however, did not include all the clergy, but was given to "those in the catholic church of which the head is Caecilian who minister personally in the sacred rites and who are commonly called clerics" (ibid., x, 7, 1–2; cf. Cod. Theodosian., xvi, 2, 2, law of October 21, 319). This restriction was aimed at excluding the Donatist clergy who opposed and detested Caecilian, the legitimate bishop of Carthage. Such exemptions were already in common use among the Romans for certain classes of people, such as doctors, public teachers, and so on. When it was applied to the Catholic clergy, however, such exemptions soon fell into disuse (par. 212).

With the legal arrangements also came gifts of buildings, old and new. This leads us to examine more fully Constantine's government, even for many years after 313.

2. Constantine in the Guise of Christian Legislator

203. Dante Alighieri, following the usual opinion of his age, saw Constantine as the emperor who gave Rome as a "dowry" to Pope Sylvester, and then retired to Constantinople as a "Greek," taking with him the Roman laws and the imperial eagle. This picture tears from the Ghibelline poet the famous words:

> "Ah, Constantine, of what great evil was the mother
> Not your conversion but that dowry
> Which the first rich Father accepted from you."
>   (Inferno, 19, 115–117)

The imperial eagle is in paradise and therefore is very eloquent and speaks quite naturally in imperial tones. Although it gives glory to Constantine among the blessed, it complains of him because —

"with the laws and me
With good intentions but unhappy outcome
Made himself a Greek to give place to the Shepherd."
(*Paradiso*, 20, 55–57)

One cannot question too deeply the meaning of a poet, but Dante speaks of the same thing again in Latin prose and without hesitation pictures Constantine as the one who weakened (*infirmator*) the Roman Empire:

"Oh happy people, Oh Ausonia glorious through you! If only that weakener of your Empire had not been born or if his pious intentions had not been misguided!" (*De monarchia*, II, 13, reply 11.) We already know how Constantine had been a "weakener."

The legend of this gift by Constantine to Pope Sylvester rises to the fifth century in part, but had layers of invention up to the eighth century. As is customary with legends, there was some basis or historical "provocation" to which further details were added. The "provocation" was precisely this shower of moral and material benefices which the government of Constantine let fall on the Church. These are not in any way legendary.

If one compares the conditions of the Church under Diocletian and Galerius with those under Constantine, the difference is wonderful and paradoxical. The people of the time were even more amazed, for they could see at firsthand the material gifts, the privileges, the favors, and the buildings donated. All that glistens, however, is not gold. Under the pleasant splendor there were spiritual miseries which made many people lament the heroic martyrs of a few years before. The pagans and many of the Christians stopped at the appearances, and these certainly presented a complete change-over from the time of the persecution. If things continued in this way, how would they all finish? After such grave upheavals, when would some kind of equilibrium be reached?

In reality no one was able to answer such questions, perhaps not even the main cause of the changes, Constantine himself.

204. The external situation seemed to reflect the internal condition of Constantine. Like his political world, he found himself in gradual evolution; he was a being *in fieri*, repelled and attracted by opposing forces.

Although he was not officially a Christian, he was very friendly toward them. He became a true catechumen only in the last days of his life (par. 282), while earlier he had been a sympathizer with Christianity, waiting for death to approach his bed before deciding to receive baptism. Meanwhile in his court, the Christians became more and more numerous. The education of his son Crispus he entrusted to the Christian Lactantius (par. 74). Among his counselors the most powerful were bishops belonging to the various Christian beliefs among whom some were full Arians like Eusebius of Nicomedia who baptized the Emperor at the point of death; semi-Arian like Eusebius of Caesarea (par. 71); or even orthodox such as Hosius of Cordoba. Although the figure of Hosius never emerges too clearly, he was possibly the most influential of all the Christian advisers in the imperial court.

Hosius was born about 257, and died a centenarian about 358. We do not know when Constantine first had connection with him. Perhaps they met in Gaul, and the possibility cannot be excluded that the expedition for the conquest of Rome was made on the advice of Hosius against the opinions of the generals and the malediction of the pagan haruspices (par. 162). At the end of the third century, Hosius was bishop of Cordoba and took part in the Council of Elvira (par. 54). In 303, in the persecution of Maximin, he confessed the faith and underwent tortures, the marks of which he bore until his death. In 313 he was at the side of Constantine helping him in the distribution of subsidies to the Christians affected by the persecution (par. 201). After this he was sent by the Emperor to Alexandria where he fought against Sabellianism (cf. Socrates in *Hist. Eccl.*, iii, 7). He then arranged and presided at the Council of Nicaea, figuring as the head of the orthodox clergy; he also presided at the Council of Serdica in 343. Some years after the death of Constantine, he was exiled under Constantius to Sirmium for his opposition to Arianism. In the weakness of extreme old age he signed the "second formula of Sirmium," favorable to Arianism, but retracted this on his deathbed.

Without consulting facts it is easy to suppose that such a man would have great influence on the spiritual evolution of Constantine. In any case we have the law given by Constantine on April, 321, preserved in the *Codex Theodosianus* (iv, 7, 1), which assisted the manumission of slaves through the churches and which is addressed to Hosius. It was probably inspired by him.

205. Many other laws advised by Hosius or other Christians, or

arising purely from the will of Constantine were passed from the earliest years after the meeting at Milan. They were laws inspired by Christianity and were later collected in the *Codex Theodosianus* and in *Justinianus*. One law of June 23, 318, allowed a legal cause to be transferred from the ordinary courts to those of the bishop (cf. *Cod. Theodos.*, i, 27, 1); other laws gave the power to clerics to free their own slaves without any legal formality, and bit by bit the powers of the bishops were brought up to equal those of civil magistrates.

The influence of Christianity was even more obvious in social legislation. The Sunday (*dies solis*) was to be considered a festival day especially in law courts; nevertheless it was permissible to emancipate slaves on a Sunday (*Cod. Theodos.*, ii, 8, 1; law of July 3, 321). The ancient sanctions of Octavian Augustus against celibacy and barren unions were abolished (cf. *ibid.*, viii, 16, 1; law of January 31, 320). Conditions of slavery were mitigated; among other things the killing or torture of slaves was prohibited (cf. *ibid.*, ix, 12, 1; law of May 11, 319); it was also forbidden to separate father, mother, or children in the division of property (cf. *ibid.*, ii, 25, 1; law of April 29, 325); adultery of a mistress with her slave was punishable by law (cf. *ibid.*, ix, 9, 1; law of May 9, 329). The bloody spectacle of the gladiatorial fights were forbidden and those who had formerly been condemned to be gladiators were now sent to the mines (cf. *ibid.*, xv, 12, 1; law of October 1, 325). This last law issued by Constantine shows a deep change in his social ideas, for in the past he had been accustomed to celebrate his victories with bloodthirsty shows in the circus at Treviri (par. 63). Other social dispositions were due to Constantine; laws against rape and against prostitution in public taverns; in defense of imprisoned people; for the protection of orphans, widows, and unwanted children; against the custom of branding the faces of runaway slaves; against the use of the cross as a means of execution. These last provisions, and in fact all the rest, show evident Christian inspiration to one who remembers the pagan laws and true conditions of Roman society until these courageous innovations.

206. While Constantine was building up a Roman-Christian legislation he was also going ahead with the material construction of the Christian church. Places of worship were restored as had been determined by the convention of Milan, and at the same time new churches were built with the assistance of the imperial treasury. There was a great deal to be done, for the persecution had left ruins every-

where and had impeded the multiplication of churches to keep step with the increase in numbers of the Christian population.

Eusebius refers frequently and with evident complacency to this building activity (cf. *Hist. Eccl.*, ix, 11, 1; x, 2, 1; x, 3, 1). He records that when the building was finished, bishops and people from far-distant places came to celebrate the dedication. For example, the great church of Tyre was dedicated about 316, whose construction had lasted some years and which appears to have been the most sumptuous of Phoenicia. Many bishops came for the ceremony, and the sermon preached before them was by an orator "of little merit" as he calls himself with praiseworthy modesty. The preacher was Eusebius himself. His modesty, however, did not prevent him from reporting his interminable oration in full (cf. *ibid.*, x, 4, 1–71). The matter of the sermon has many harmless passages in the usual run, but there are also occasional expressions which have a bitter Arian taste (cf. *ibid.*, 10 and 65).

It was natural that Rome and the surrounding districts should receive the greater part of the Constantinian generosity. Special record of this has been kept in the *Liber Pontificalis* when it treats of Pope Sylvester. Although this document comes from two centuries after the events, and its authority is not completely beyond question, in this matter it is worthy in substance of credibility because of the well-known character both of the buildings and of the information in regard to their origin. With the *domus Faustae*, which had been the property of the church of Rome from October 1, 313 (par. 179), a basilica was soon joined, similar in architecture to profane basilicas. This church became the meeting place for the Roman Christians instead of the cemetery of Priscilla along the Via Salaria and the cemetery of Callistus on the Via Appia; enlarged and transformed at different times, it has remained through the centuries as the *ecclesia mater* of Rome.

A little less than a mile from the Lateran near the boundaries of the city was the *domus Sessoriana* where Helena, the mother of Constantine, lived. Here also arose a Christian basilica. When Helena returned from her pilgrimage to the Holy Places of Palestine (327–329) made at an advanced age, she placed in this basilica her various finds and the objects she had collected. Among these was the relic of the True Cross. For this reason the Sessorian basilica figures as a little Jerusalem, and in the passing of time was called the basilica of "The Holy Cross in Jerusalem" at the Sessorium.

207. As was natural, the basilicas received the most celebrated saints buried in Rome beginning with the Apostles Peter and Paul. Here we must listen to the *Liber Pontificalis* when it says that such basilicas were built *ex suggestione Silvestri episcopi*. The basilica erected over the tomb of Peter was of moderate size and on the triumphal arch was inscribed in mosaic the two lines:

> "Because with your leadership the world triumphantly
> reached to the stars, the conquering Constantine raised
> this building to you."
> ("Quod duce te mundus surrexit in astra triumphans
> Hanc Constantinus victor tibi condidit aulam.")

Of much smaller size were the basilica built over the tomb of the Apostle Paul and that over the martyr Laurence. The Basilica of St. Paul was orientated in a way opposite to modern custom, since it had the entrance on the old path of the Via Ostia, where the apse of the rebuilt basilica stands today. This ancient church lasted until 386 when Valentinian II demolished it and replaced it with a much larger basilica orientated in the usual way. The basilica of the martyr Laurence on the Via Tiburtina communicated with the crypt beneath with a double flight of stairs; near it other buildings arose later.

Besides the Sessorian Basilica, the Empress Helena built another on the Via Labicana in a Christian cemetery where the martyrs Marcellinus and Peter had been buried. These had been killed in the last persecution and without doubt there must have been many people still alive who had known them personally. Constantina, the daughter of the Emperor, lavished her care on the tomb of the martyr Agnes (par. 148) on the Via Nomentana, which was near the imperial villa in which Constantina lived. A basilica was built there with an acrostic inscription of the word Constantina, and also a mausoleum (the so-called Mausoleum of St. Constantina) in which later the Princess was buried in a magnificent porphyry sarcophagus still in existence (Vatican Museum).

The basilica called today St. Sebastian's (par. 148) dates from Constantine. It was first called *Basilica Apostolorum* and is on the Via Appia in the place called *ad catacumbas*. Many scholars have maintained that the name *apostolorum* is due to the fact that the bodies of the Apostles Peter and Paul were taken there in 258 and remained there for some time. Other scholars deny this. It is certain that the Constantinian basilica incorporated not only the crypt of the martyr Sebastian, but also a place of veneration of the two Apostles (cf. *Triclia apostolorum*). The spot was visited by many pilgrims, who as usual expressed their sentiments by "graffiti" on the walls. Very many of these graffiti invoking Peter and Paul are preserved today and are to be dated half a century before the erection of the basilica.

208.   All these Roman basilicas were given funds from the imperial munificence for maintenance and use. The *Liber Pontificalis* gives a detailed list of such resources; there are properties in the city itself (*domus et horrea*), a little outside the city (*suburbani*) or even at some distance from Rome (*suburbicarii*); there are sometimes gifts of property in distant regions or even across the sea (*transmarini*). The Basilica of St. Peter, for example, had properties in Antioch, Alexandria, and in the lands of the Euphrates; that of St. Paul in Egypt, Tyre, and Tarsus. This last place is clearly chosen purposely, for Paul was born at Tarsus. So also since he was martyred in Rome *ad Aquas Salvias*, the grounds of this place were destined by Gregory the Great for the maintenance of his basilica.

Chance discoveries have occasionally confirmed the existence of such properties. One of the more curious is the collar of a watchdog (illustrated by De Rossi in *Bullet. di archeol. crist.*, 1874, p. 63) bearing an inscription which names a *Felicissimus pecorarius* belonging to the *basilica apostoli Pauli et trium dominorum nostrorum*. De Rossi dates the inscription as before the year 394; and believes that Felicissimus was a shepherd engaged in the raising of flocks belonging to the Basilica of St. Paul, and that such possessions must have been in existence long before the year 394 — that is, practically from the time of Constantine.

It can be recorded briefly that other Constantinian buildings arose in Italy and abroad at Ostia, Albano, Capua, Naples, Cirta in Numidia, etc. without counting Constantinople and Palestine (par. 221 ff.).

209.   Despite all these favors toward Christianity, Constantine remained at the head of the paganism of the Empire for he kept the title and office of *pontifex maximus*. It is true that this was now merely a formal title and that Constantine was anything but zealous in exercising the corresponding office. Still the absolute irreconcilability of Constantine as *pontifex maximus* with the profession of Christianity

always remained, and this was one of the reasons which had made Tertullian announce the absurdity of a Roman emperor who was a follower of Christ (par. 200). In any case the unbaptized Constantine was not a formal Christian.

This was, therefore, a period of transition during which what could not be discarded was continued, but was inevitably to disappear. Constantine saw this clearly, but what was nearest to his heart was the strength and peace of the Empire; this would be greatly endangered if there occurred a rough change from paganism to Christianity, either in the Emperor personally or in the Empire in general. He chose to make the change gradually, and there was a period in fieri which corresponded fairly accurately with his personal feelings.

Although the sympathies of Constantine for Christianity became more obvious with time, this did not mean that his pagan subjects were going to imitate him. They could remain in their idolatry provided that the peace of the Empire was not disturbed; the future would show which of the two religions they would embrace if they were given full liberty. The Emperor personally saw the victory of Christianity, but as the sovereign of both pagans and Christians he was solicitous for both. We find, therefore, that while he continued to be the pontifex maximus of paganism he presents himself to the Christian bishop as the "bishop of those outside" (ἐπίσκοπος τῶν ἐκτός) (Eusebius, De vit. Const., iv, 24).

This expression has caused the labor of many scholars, but it is probably no more than an expression taken from the Bible and which is also found in rabbinical literature. In the Bible "those outside" or "outsiders" (Hebrew hīsōn) are the profane in opposition to the sacred Jews (cf. 1 Chronicles, 26, 29; Neh. 11:16); Eusebius himself designates the pagans as "those outside," as opposed to the "sacred" Christians (Hist. Eccl., viii, 7, 2 and 5); a similar expression appears in the title of the short work of Hermias which is presented as a "Derision of the philosophers outside."

The bishops of the Christians are their "overseers" according to the etymological meaning of the Greek word. Here Constantine, speaking to Christian bishops and wishing to show himself benevolent to their religion, says that he is the "overseer" of the pagans. He does not mean that in his office as high priest of idolatry, but insofar as he is a friend of Christianity and seeks to lead the pagans gently to the doctrine of Christ.

He gave himself, therefore, the office of a Christian apostle to the pagans, but exercised it prudently and with a certain dissimulation for political reasons. This appears to have been the feeling of the Byzantine Church, which, besides venerating Constantine as a saint, had given him the title of "pari-apostle."

210. There can be no doubt about the Christian sentiments of Constantine. It is true that his colleague and brother-in-law, Licinius, did for a little while follow a path favorable to Christianity, but he did this for political reasons, and feeling no real sympathy for the new religion he did not intend to join it. Though the Christian sentiments of Constantine were unformed, gross, and defective, they were absolutely sincere although subordinate as always to the supreme interests of the State.

It is instructive in this regard to consider his attitude to Arianism. When the Arian crisis became acute toward 323 Constantine found himself in a new world and became dismayed. Why should this have been? By now the Empire was completely dependent on him and the Christians saw themselves governed by a favorable sovereign. They should therefore have kept themselves in concord and tranquillity to contribute to the general peace of the Empire which afforded them protection. Instead, Arius arrived and proceeded to turn Egypt and the East upside down, and at the same time Alexander and others appeared to give him a flat contradiction. Why? Was there any danger of being forced to sacrifice to idols as under Diocletian? None whatsoever! All this upset was merely an attempt to decide whether the Word was the same substance as the Father or not. All this stupidity and shouting — thought Constantine — for so little. "Much ado about nothing!" Surely it would be sufficient to know that there was only one God and not numberless pagan divinities. In the face of such inexplicable stupidity Constantine was taken aback — much more than he had been by the *cataphracti* at Saxa Rubra. There at least he had been able to see his enemy in front of him, whereas now he could not see where his enemy was and could see no real danger before him. As a consequence, in the face of the Arian problem his behavior was uncertain and wavering (par. 249 ff.).

In the Donatist controversy he was very willing to compromise and please everybody; here, however, he was dealing with concrete facts regarding the organization and hierarchy of the Christian society. It was in hard facts that Constantine found himself in his element.

211. Constantine showed himself less and less in sympathy with Greco-Roman paganism, though he was never directly hostile or a persecutor. The agreement at Milan had guaranteed religious liberty, even to the followers of the ancient cults of the Empire, so clearly and insistently that it would have been too obvious a contradiction to deny such liberty in practice. Pagan temples remained open beside the Christian churches, notwithstanding requests in some cases that they should be closed. It seems that at one time Constantine was toying with the idea of closing them, but the all-important reason for him — the State — made him discard it (cf. *De Vita Constantini*, ii, 60).

In his role as emperor and *pontifex maximus*, he did make some provisions against paganism but for reasons of security. The temples of Aphaca in Lebanon, of Aegea and Heliopolis (Baalbek) in Phoenicia, which were notorious in antiquity for the immoralities practiced in their ceremonies, were shut (cf. *ibid.*, iii, 55–58; on Socrates in *Hist. Eccl.*, 1, 18). The use of magic and haruspices was forbidden in private houses — where it often led to licentiousness — but was allowed in public (*Cod. Theodos.*, ix, 16, 1–3; years, 318, 320); indeed, when lightning struck the imperial palace or other public buildings the haruspices were to be officially consulted according to ancient custom (cf. *ibid.*, xvi, 10, 1; year, 320). Later many temples were despoiled of their statues and other works of art for utilitarian reasons — for the decoration of Constantinople which the Emperor was building (par. 224). This would not have caused much of a stir, for frequently the objects were taken from unused temples, in places where the people had all become Christians.

Sometimes, as at Gaza in Palestine, the population remained obstinately pagan; at Heliopolis also after the closing of the temple, and possibly in protest, the people remained pagan despite the many advantages offered to attract them to Christianity.

A change took place in the coinage. As early as 314 the mint at Tarragona struck money with the sign of the cross on it, and in 317 coins were issued at Siscia with the effigy of Constantine carrying the monogram on his helmet (par. 168). From 320 there are no more pagan allusions in the inscriptions on coins, but only neutral expressions such as *Roma aeterna*, *Saeculi felicitas*, etc. Manifestations in honor of the conqueror of Saxa Rubra and his *gens Flavia* took place more or less everywhere, and as was natural had a somewhat religious coloring. In Africa, a college of priests was set up to celebrate the cult of the Flavian family and to preside at periodic games in its honor (Aurelius Victor, *De Caesar*, 40). Before these manifestations of official paganism, Constantine kept himself prudently reserved as appears from the inscription of Spello (Hispellum), a town near Foligno in Umbria (cf. H. Dessau, *Inscript. Latinae selectae*, i, 705). The inhabitants had asked, about 330, for permission to erect a temple to the Flavian family and obtained the rescript given in the inscription just referred to. Permission was granted but the condition was added that "the edifice dedicated to our name is not contaminated by the frauds of any dangerous superstition." Experts generally understand this to refer to idolatrous practices, at least those of any note. Nevertheless, it seems that the official cult of the *gens Flavia* at Spello did not remain purely civil, but had some elements of paganism for another local inscription speaks of a *pontifex gentis Flaviae* (cf. *ibid.*, ii, 1, 6623).

212.   These imperial favors did not always have a good effect on Christians; sometimes they brought evil with them. In the first place, there were the usual profiteers, the men of affairs, who had little time for spiritual goods, but were very much on the alert when material advantages were to be won. By now the open profession of Christianity was able to offer opportunities for a career, to make money, to possess social authority. Many people, therefore, adapted themselves to the new circumstances and, making a show of their new faith, began to frequent the places of government, the law courts, military praetoria, and even the imperial court where they plotted and intrigued to their advantage. In the very places where only a few years before the martyrs had shed their blood in the confession of Christ, the profiteers now came to collect pleasant but empty favors. If St. Paul could have come there and met such Christians, he would have repeated his complaint: "all seek their own advantage and not that of Jesus Christ" (Phil. 2:21). Even some of the laws which were made by the Emperor with perfectly good intentions brought abuses with them. We have seen, for example, the exemption from burdensome public offices granted to Catholic clergy (par. 220). This made many people become clerics purely for material profit — so many that it became necessary to forbid members of municipal courts and others to take on the clerical state (*Cod. Theodos.*, xvi, 2, 3; law of July 18, 320).

Also, another much worse industry began, brought about by sordid cupidity in the guise of Christianity. It had been customary even during pagan times to attempt to influence the wills of old people and the rich.

Now in the new Christian society ecclesiastics and ascetes of apparently austere habit began to frequent rich households, especially those of widows and orphans. There they looked around for possible victims, and having got them into their greedy hold persuaded them to bequeathe them handsome gifts or even their whole property — always, of course, under some religious pretext. This evil became very grave and widespread, and probably many families were ruined by it. Finally a law had to be made explicitly condemning such practices (Cod. Theodos., xvi, 2, 20). The law was directed against *ecclesiastici vel ex ecclesiasticis vel qui continentium se volunt nomine nuncupari* who *sub praetextu religionis* did what is described above. The law is of July 30, 370, and therefore is after Constantine, but the origin of such evils was old and went back before the death of Constantine. It is noteworthy that this law, issued in the names of the Christian Valentinian, Valens and Gratianus, is directed to Pope Damasus. This would seem to show that Rome was particularly infested with such confidence men.

Jerome refers to the same law with words which are as frank as they are impartial: "It is shameful to have to say this; pagan priests, actors, seers and prostitutes receive legacies; only for clerics and monks is this forbidden, a law not made by persecutors but by Christian princes. I do not complain of this but sorrow that we should have merited it" (Ad Nepotianum, epist., 52, 6; the year, 394). But about ten years before this the same Jerome wrote a letter in a rage (cf. Ad Eustochium, epist., 22; years, 383–384) against the decadence of Christian habits in Rome and especially against the morals of the clerics. We can believe him easily enough not only because he speaks from personal experience, but also because similar things were denounced by Eusebius in the East. During the period mentioned by Eusebius there was a truce between the Empire and Christianity, whereas the time of Jerome was the period when favors and privileges were showered on the Church.

213. Was Dante right when he said that the "dowry" given to the Church by Constantine was the "mother" of great evil? Dante Alighieri was a very sincere Catholic — one who moved by the "reverence of the highest keys" (Inferno, xix, 101), went on his knees before a pope who was still suffering for sin in Purgatory (Purg., xix, 127). We would, therefore, have expected that since the poet clearly distinguished conversion and dowry, he would have been able to make some distinction between the dowry and the use that was made of it.

Dante himself affirms that Constantine had "good intentions" (par. 203), although as a Ghibelline he could not pardon him for preferring Constantinople to Rome, and thus causing the split in the Sacred Roman Empire which according to Dante was founded by God. This last point, however, does not concern us — nor the supposed gift by Constantine to Pope Sylvester which is lamented by Dante. Without this gift what remains of the "dowry" of Constantine? There is still the legislation of Christian inspiration and the material gifts to Christianity. So far as legislation is concerned Dante could not have deplored the laws in favor of slaves, prisoners, and waifs, those against gladiatorial shows, nor many others which we have mentioned briefly (par. 205) or not at all. In regard to the material gifts we must keep in mind that these were an endeavor to compensate the Christians for their incalculable losses in the great persecution (par. 206). The whole affair was regarded from the typically Roman legal viewpoint which required, first, that property be restored *unicuique suum* and then eventually that evil be put right and losses repaired. Maxentius had already begun to make such restitution (par. 156). This was the first impetus and at the same time the legal basis for the conferring of material benefits. If such benefits tended to increase gradually, this was owing to the sympathies of the quasi-Christian Constantine and to other causes mentioned earlier.

Was the "dowry" understood in this way the "mother" of great evil? One cannot say that it produced only good; but if there were evil results, then these were beside the "good intentions" of Constantine. The truth is that this material dowry was immediately put to bad use, and the fault for this lay first at the door of Christians in general who had rapidly become unworthy of the earlier martyrs, and then at the door of those clerics who were denounced by St. Jerome.

The dowry was therefore very dangerous — so dangerous that not long before Dante, St. Francis of Assisi also considered that the tottering Lateran of Constantine would have stayed up more easily if it were not burdened with the weight of that dowry. The opinion was worthy of a saint — a very great saint. Practically speaking, however, as is usual in matters of this kind "*non omnes capiunt verbum istud, sed quibus datum est*" (Mt. 19:11).

3. Constantine and Licinius: The Forty Martyrs: Death of Licinius

214. The two Augusti were too different in temperament to get on well together for very long. One was an idealist and religious and the other was greedy and a sordid materialist. Their alliance against Maxentius and Maximin (par. 180) had been a mere political expedient without any spiritual ties, and when external dangers ceased the two brothers-in-law began to cast hostile glances at each other. The anxious Constantia, sister of one and wife of the other, tried to mediate — sometimes successfully. It could not be expected, however, that a woman would be able to change their policy. The alliance was doomed to collapse.

The reason for open conflict was not long coming. Constantine's sister, Anastasia, was married to Bassianus, a person eminent in court and favored by the benevolence of his august brother-in-law. The latter suggested his nomination as Caesar. Constantine would give him Italy and Licinius was supposed to hand over Illyricum. What happened at this point is shrouded in the gloom which seems to come on at various periods in the life of Constantine. It appears that Licinius was not disposed to cede Illyricum. What is more — and worse — it was discovered one day that Bassianus, together with his brother Senecio, were in secret communication with Licinius. This looked very much like intrigue and treason. So Constantine immediately took action, with disastrous results. He executed Bassianus, and demanded that Senecio, who had taken refuge with Licinius, should be handed over. This request was refused and war broke out between the Augusti. We know only the result of the contest. Licinius was beaten first at Cibali in Pannonia and then again in Thrace; he obtained peace by handing over Illyricum. This was at the end of 314. Not two years had passed since the meeting at Milan, when it seemed that eternal peace had been established between the Augusti.

It was precisely that meeting which was the first cause of the trouble. The edict in favor of Christianity had the approval of Licinius purely for political reasons, and without the backing of any internal convictions on his part. While it was advantageous to follow the path of the fortunate Constantine, Licinius did so but reserved his own opinions

on the worth and opportuneness of the edict. When Constantine
defeated him, and took Illyricum away from him, Licinius could think
only of getting his own back. His revenge would not be just on Constantine, but also on Christianity itself which was the favorite child
of the Conqueror and underlay much of his political action.

These plans, however, had to remain very secret — the disposal of
Bassianus made this clear — and things must be done slowly and with
patience. Constantine watched from a distance. At close quarters, poor
Constantia labored to soften the blow and smooth difficulties; she was
also able to act as an informer of the intrigue in the court of Licinius.
215. To all appearances relations could go on as before — peace was
agreed upon and everything was tranquil and innocent. In 317 the sons
of the two Augusti became Caesars; in 318 Licinius and Crispus, the
eldest son of Constantine, took up the consulate. About the same time
Eusebius of Caesarea in his sermon at Tyre (par. 206) praises both the
Augusti as dutiful protectors of Christendom, which would seem to
show that Licinius was keeping up appearances. The fire of discord
was hidden, but it would not be long before it broke through to the
surface.

The first provisions by Licinius against Christianity were indirect,
and were somewhat similar to the initial steps taken by Diocletian;
they began between 319 and 320 and rapidly became more frequent.
Details are given of them by Eusebius (cf. *Hist. Eccl.*, x, 8, 10 ff.; *De
vita Constant.*, i, 49 ff.). Christian clerks were dismissed from the court;
soldiers were obliged to sacrifice to idols under pain of degradation and
expulsion from the army; the visiting of prisoners, a common custom of
the Christians, was forbidden — in this way the food and other help
given by them to starving prisoners was now wanting. If visits were
made by some stratagem and the Christian was discovered, then he
would be liable to the same penalty as the person he was helping.

Difficulties were then placed in the way of Christian meetings. As
Licinius followed Maximin in his immoral habits (par. 129), so also
he wished to imitate him in his guardianship of public morals (par.
181). Although he acted as procurer for his officers, he found it unfit-
ting that men and women should come together in Christian services,
and further that women should receive instruction from men. He,
therefore, gave orders that separate gatherings should be held for the
two sexes; that such gatherings should not be held in private but in
the open and outside the city; that women should be instructed by

members of their own sex. Restrictions unknown to ancient Roman legislation were imposed on Christian marriages and burials. Bishops were hindered in various ways in the exercise of their duties, and were forbidden to leave their dioceses or to hold synods and meetings.

Licinius then got down to business and began to look for profits. As avaricious as he has been described by pagan historians, he now commenced to make money by extraordinary taxes, with a new and oppressive tribute. Although there is no absolute proof, it would seem that such exactions fell especially on the Christians. A war with Constantine was obviously very near and like all wars money was needed to conduct it; this money was exacted from the Christians.

216. This time, also, the persecution brought many evils besides apostasies. Many officials and soldiers were out of work for their persistence in Christianity; others, on various pretexts, were given burdensome civil offices or were sent to labor in the mines or even in the imperial stables; others became the property of the treasury and were sold into slavery. To avoid such troubles many Christians fled to a wandering life in the hills and the woods, just as they had done during the persecution of Diocletian. Churches were closed or destroyed especially in the region of Pontus where the persecution was particularly severe and there were many martyrs. In the city of Apameia, the capital of the province, then called Diospontus and later Helenopontus, Basil, the metropolitan of the province, fell a victim to the persecution. On this occasion a new kind of torture was employed: the bodies of the martyrs were cut into small pieces by strokes of a sword and then thrown into the sea as food for the fishes.

Many Christians, however, had not the courage to resist and were not even willing to disturb their normal life by flight. They fell into more or less complete apostasy. We have no means of reckoning the number of these new *lapsi*, but it was not small, as is shown by the fact that the Council of Nicaea itself (canons 10–14) dealt with them and made provisions in their regard (par. 267–268).

There are very few records worthy of faith regarding individual martyrs in this persecution. Particular mention, however, should be made of a group known in hagiographical tradition as The Forty Martyrs.

THE FORTY MARTYRS

217.   We have discourses on these martyrs by the Cappadocians, Basil and Gregory of Nyssa, and by the Syrian Ephraem. They are all of the same authority for they were near the region where the events took place. The *Passion* of the martyrs has little value, but the "testament" which they made just before their execution can be considered authentic.

They were enrolled in a legion which guarded the boundaries of the Empire. It seems certain that this was the XII Legion — Fulminata — which had taken part in the assault on Jerusalem in A.D. 70, and was later placed in the East with its center at Melitene in Armenia Minor. There was a kind of Christian tradition in the legion, for it had counted Christians in its ranks already in the third century, and perhaps earlier. Through friendships and intermarriage there must have been other connections with Christianity during the legion's stay in Armenia where the Christians were numerous (par. 184). The martyrdom took place a little to the north of Melitene, in the city called Sebastia (more exactly Sebaste) where the legion probably held a large garrison.

The forty legionaries were very young — about twenty years of age. In their "testament" where they sent their last wishes to their dear ones, only one speaks of his wife and small son; another one, his betrothed; while all the rest salute their parents. They must, therefore, have all been in early manhood. When the news arrived at the garrison that Licinius had ordered all soldiers to sacrifice to idols, they refused. They were immediately arrested, bound with one very long chain, and imprisoned. Their imprisonment continued for a long time, possibly because the legion authorities were waiting for orders from their superiors or — in view of the gravity of the case — from Licinius himself. During this wait the imprisoned soldiers foreseeing their certain fate, wrote a collective "testament" by the hand of one of their number called Meletius.

In this profoundly Christian document they exhort their relations and friends to leave the useless goods of the world for the joy of heaven. They salute the persons dearest to them. Finally, thinking that the possession of their bodies might lead to disputes between the Christians — as had happened so often in the past over the remains of other martyrs — they declared that they wished to be buried in the village of Sarein near the city of Zela. The document bears the names of all forty men and they have been copied in other documents with a few small differences of spelling.

The sentence finally arrived. They were to die by being exposed naked at night in the middle of winter on a frozen pool. The place chosen for the execution appears to have been a large space in front of the baths of Sebastia where the condemned men would be withdrawn from the curiosity and sympathy of the public and could be watched by the attendants in the baths. There was a large reservoir in the place, a kind of lake, which connected with the baths. Basil says that the place was in the middle of the city and that the lake was near the city. Perhaps the reservoir for the baths was drawn from a lake outside the city.

218. The tortures of the naked bodies on the frozen water at a very low temperature must have been frightful. To increase the agony of the victims, the entrance door of the baths was left open from which came light and steam from the *calidarium*. For the martyrs this was a dreadful sight; a few steps would have taken them out of their sufferings and allowed them to grasp the life which was leaving their bodies moment by moment. There was, however, an insurmountable barrier — the invisible Christ whom they had to deny. The hours passed in dreadful monotony; none of the condemned men left the ice; the attendants of the baths assisted at the affair as if it were a nightmare.

All of a sudden one of the men, overcome by the agonies of cold, dragged himself toward the lighted door. As was only natural, as soon as he was surrounded by the hot steam he died. At this, one of the guards enthusiastically decided to take his place, making the number up to forty; he tore off his clothes, proclaimed himself a Christian, and took his place on the ice with the others.

The dawn showed pitiful heaps of corpses. One only was still alive — he was the youngest, called Meliton by some documents. This tenacity for life terrified his mother, a Christian of wonderful faith who was present when the bodies were heaped on the cart to be taken to be burned. When she saw that her son was left behind because he was not quite dead, she took him in her arms and carried him to the cart so that he might not be defrauded of the common crown. The arms which had clasped him to her breast only a few years before now were strong enough to bear the young hero in his triumph. The young man died in his mother's arms.

The guard who was converted is called in certain documents by the name Aglaios. Various investigations of the different records and testimonies lead us to suspect that the one who abandoned the struggle and died on the steps of the baths was Meletius the writer of the "testament." This is, however, little more than a conjecture.

The story has some doubtful particulars; in general substance it can be securely accepted.

The veneration of the Forty Martyrs was very widespread in the East. In the West, at the end of the century, Gaudentius of Brescia speaks of them. The scene of their martyrdom is preserved in Rome in a seventh- to eighth-century fresco in an oratory joined to the Church of St. Maria Antiqua in the Roman Forum.

219. For both political and religious reasons, the persecution in the East was naturally followed with great attention in the West. Constantine had copious information from his sister Constantia and asked his colleague several times to change his attitude toward the Christians. Licinius made excellent promises, but did not keep them. He preferred to continue a "cold war" until he had made all his preparations for the ultimate struggle. For his own part, Constantine maintained careful watch. His most important aim was not to allow his rival the initiative of time or place; these must be the choice of Constantine.

The chance came in 323 — some say it was 324. As the Augustus of the East, it was Licinius' duty to defend the frontiers of the Empire which were marked by the lower course of the Danube. Though the barbarians in these parts were very dangerous, Licinius had placed his troops more with a view to the coming struggle with Constantine than with the intention of countering any barbarian threat. As a result, in this year a wave of Goths managed to open a wide gap in the Danube border, and having crossed the river, invaded Thrace, menacing even the straits of Propontis to the south and Macedonia to the southwest. The Empire, at least in theory, was still one, and so Constantine hurried to make up for the inefficiency of his Eastern colleague. At the time he was at Thessalonica and therefore very near to where the invasion had occurred. With his usual speed he rushed to battle and drove the invaders from Thrace. Licinius then began to protest. Thrace was under his government and Constantine had entered his territories without permission. The conqueror should, it would seem, not have driven back the invaders of the Empire, but allowed the flood of barbarians to occupy Asia Minor and further.

220. The "cold war" had turned from comedy to tragedy, and real war now broke out between the Augusti. The struggle developed rapidly. From what we have seen it was inevitable that from the beginning the war had a religious character. Without relying too much on the information given by Eusebius (*De vita Constant.*, ii, 3 ff.), it is certain that Licinius' army took on the role of avenger of the Empire's gods, while Constantine's army took on the work of defending the Cross. The material strength of the two sides was about equal. Constantine's army, however, followed the *labarum* (par. 167), which was escorted by a maniple of the bravest soldiers. Licinius, on the other hand, was accompanied by *victimarii*, magicians, fortunetellers, and others of his persuasion whom he had commanded before the battle to sacrifice with secret rites in the shadow of a wood so as to bring down the favor of the gods. The battle took place on July 3, and ended with the defeat of Licinius' troops. The encounter was near Adrianople where, only ten years before, Licinius had routed Maximin (par. 191). Some of the conquered troops surrendered, and the rest retreated with Licinius to Byzantium to continue the resistance.

This soon proved to be quite impossible. Almost at once the Constantinian fleet commanded by Crispus, his son, appeared before the city. Crispus was master of the sea, for he had dispersed Licinius' fleet which had already been damaged by a storm. The port was blocked and the city was besieged by land. Licinius hurriedly withdrew from Byzantium and went into Chalcedon. Meanwhile, a truce was being discussed which would have been welcomed by Constantine. Licinius, however, was only gaining time to prepare a new army. After a few weeks military operations were resumed. Licinius called for help with all the ceremonies of paganism, while Constantine put his trust in the God of the Christians. The next and last encounter was on September 17, near Chrysopolis (Scutari), and resulted in an even greater defeat for Licinius. The defeated were completely at the mercy of the conqueror.

Constantia put herself once more between the conquering brother and the conquered husband. Licinius was spared, but was sent off to Thessalonica.

What happened after this is not certain for we come into one of the usual dark periods of the life of Constantine. It would seem that the exile of Licinius lasted for some time, and that he was still alive and well in the year 324. It may be that Licinius obstinately continued to make plots and intrigue with the Goths even from Thessalonica. Other reasons have been given, such as a condemnation from the Senate, or else an explicit request of the army; whatever the motive, it is certain that in 324 Licinius was removed altogether.

The whole Roman Empire was now in the hands of Constantine and he had no rivals.

4. Foundation of Constantinople — Building in Palestine

221. The unity of the Roman Empire was now restored. Once more it had only one emperor and its immense territories were no longer divided between Augusti and Caesars. Was there a capital city of the Empire? Officially there was, for Rome was still surrounded with so much glory that no other city of the Empire could compare with it. The authority of Rome, however, had been decreasing ever since Diocletian had instituted the tetrarchy; the seats of the four dynasts, Nicomedia, Sirmium, Milan, and Treviri (par. 13), had taken over much of the administration and Rome had lost most of its influence on affairs.

Over the whole Empire the political axis had inclined gradually toward Eastern Europe, since the West always lacked more seriously any basis for political supremacy. Legionaries rarely came now from Italian towns, but from the North and especially the East, most of all from Illyricum. The lands beyond the eastern frontiers of the Empire were now better known and offered good openings of trade. Finally, while the towns of Greek civilization remained the inexhaustible source of knowledge and the arts for the Roman, the triumphal advance of Christianity gave a new importance to the East where the new religion had first arisen and been practiced. "Ex oriente lux." Rome was rapidly becoming a suburb of the rest of the Empire.

Seutonius relates (cf. *Divus Iulius*, 79) that Julius Caesar had already thought of transporting the capital of the Empire to Troy, encouraged by the legend which connected the origins of his *gens Iulia* with the Troy of Homer. Actually the legend had little to do with his plans —

there were clear practical reasons for the change of capital even then. Troy, near the western end of the Propontis (Sea of Marmara), was in the center of the Empire where sea and land routes between the East and the West crossed. Rome, after her lands had been so immensely extended, did not have this advantage. It is no surprise, therefore, to find that Constantine, perhaps unconsciously reverting to the idea of Julius Caesar, decided to transport the capital of the Empire to the banks of the Propontis. The only difference was that Constantine preferred Byzantium to Troy, the eastern end of the Propontis to the western. According to Byzantine authors this decision was made by the command of God (cf. Sozomenus, ii, 3; Zosimus, 11, 30; Cod. Theodos., xiii, 5, 7). An emperor so favored by the God of the Christians could not take so grave a decision without his special assistance.

222. After Constantine's brief visit at the Saxa Rubra in 315, he showed himself in Rome on the occasion of his decennials (par. 179). He had never lived in the city, but knew it very well and realized that it could never be the capital of his Empire. Everything was solemn in Rome; everything was ancient and sacred; a building could not be demolished or an arch taken down without removing at the same time a mass of honorable memories. Worse than this, the whole of Rome was marked by idolatry — the buildings and the institutions and customs — and it would not be possible to abolish such traditions without disturbing and perhaps paralyzing the life of the citizens. Constantine, by now quite alienated from pagan cults, despaired of ever making Rome his own city. It seemed much better to found an entirely new one and to place it on the shores of the Bosphorus; such a position reflected the changed conditions of the Empire. The new capital would arise at Byzantium.

Byzantium had been in existence for almost a millennium, but it had never grown to first importance. Its position in the vast rectangle of the Roman Empire was excellent, however, and superior to that of Troy. Situated at the eastern extremity of the Propontis, it communicated with the Pontus Euxinus (Black Sea) and with the lands to the east through the corridor of the Bosphorus, a stretch of sea about eighteen miles long and six hundred yards wide. A deep inlet, the Golden Horn, on the north isolated the city on a promontory pushing into the sea toward the entrance to the Bosphorus, Seraglio Point, and leaving at the rear a hilly terrain. The promontory was part of Europe, but the stretch of sea which separated the point of the promontory from the opposite coast was very narrow and the other side was Asia (Chrysopolis — Uskudar). The town was at the border of the two continents.

At this place where seas and continents met, there passed the roads to and from all parts of the world. Without counting the direct sea route through the Mediterranean and Hellespont (Dardanelles), very many roads joined Byzantium with southeastern Europe passing either through Constantia or Philippopolis or Thessalonica. From this last city the Via Egnatia crossed the present-day Balkans and ended at Durres from which ships could be taken to Brindisi. At Brindisi ended the Via Appia from Rome. Other roads stretched toward the western and eastern regions of Asia Minor and from there continued on to Armenia and India.

Byzantium, therefore, was neither the East nor the West; it was both. This reason and others mentioned earlier persuaded Constantine to build his capital there — the New Rome. This indeed was the official name of Constantinople until the end of the Middle Ages.

223. The oldest nucleus of Byzantium was on the extremity of the promontory Seraglio Point, and it was there that the ancient Acropolis had arisen. After various Greek governments, Byzantium came under Roman influence in the first century before Christ. Three centuries later it was besieged and taken by Septimius Severus for its support of his rival Pescennius Niger. The conqueror destroyed the ancient walls and constructed a larger town.

Christianity came to Byzantium in the second century, though more especially on the other side of the Golden Horn, which area was considered to be a suburb of the city. At the beginning of the fourth century there was at least one Christian church called "of Peace" (Irene) inside the old town.

The reconstruction of the city planned by Constantine was grandiose. The new walls were begun toward October of 326 and were built nearly two miles farther out than the walls of Septimius Severus. This increased the size of the town fivefold. A century later even this was too small, and Theodosius built another wall just over a mile outside that of Constantine.

The ancient agora near the Acropolis was greatly enlarged by Constantine and beautified with porticoes and statues; it was destined to the honor of Helena, the noble mother of the Emperor, and was to

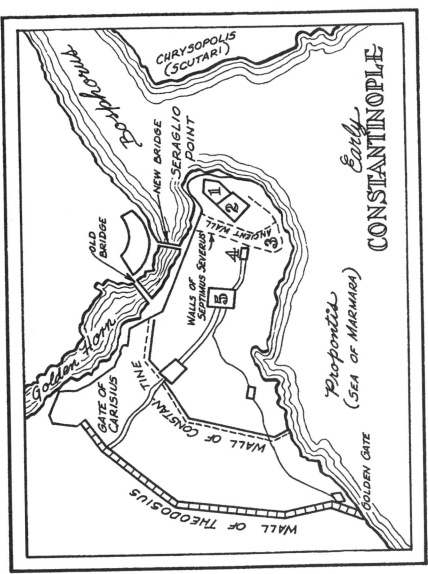

Early CONSTANTINOPLE

1. Ancient Acropolis; 2. Agora; 3. Hippodrome; 4. Forum of Constantine; 5. Forum of Theodosius

be called the Augusteum. The church of Irene in this part of the city was restored and enlarged; the same was done to the baths of Zeuxippus, which dated back to Septimius Severus. The Hippodrome which had been started by the latter, but never finished, was now completed, and became for many centuries the center of the popular life of the city.

At the place where, at one time, the principal gate of the walls of Severus stood, a great square was laid down called the Forum of Constantine. To the east of the Augusteum the Senate House was built, while farther to the south by the side of the Hippodrome arose the Sacred Palace of the Emperor. In later times, at a little distance from the Church of Irene, whose lack of space was soon apparent, was built another church dedicated to Wisdom (Sancta Sophia) and finished in 537.

In this group of buildings was the heart of the New Rome. Not without reason was it said that at Constantinople God had Sancta Sophia, the Emperor the Sacred Palace, and the people the Hippodrome.
224. A long street, the "Mese" or Triumphal Way, crossed the city from east to west. It started from the north of the Hippodrome on the western side of the Augusteum. As in the Roman Forum, the golden milestone was erected from which were counted the distances on the road which left the city by the Golden Gate near the sea. Another great road to the north left the city by the Gate of Carisius, near the place where Constantine had built the Church of the Apostles.

This was one of the fourteen churches which tradition ascribes to Constantine, and was certainly the most sumptuous. Eusebius (De vita Constantini, iv, 58–60) visited it just after it was completed and describes it with particular admiration. The church was built in the form of a cross, surrounded by porticoes with alcoves for various uses, and had a large courtyard open to the air where Constantine had prepared his tomb. The sarcophagus stood in the middle flanked on each side by six others dedicated to the twelve Apostles. Eusebius says that Constantine did this so that his body might be united with the honor of the Apostles and that he might share, after his death, in the prayers made there in their honor. One cannot judge now whether this was just a pleasant explanation by Eusebius. Certainly a visitor who saw the disposition of the thirteen sarcophagi would have quite naturally concluded that the one in the middle was not that of a "pari-apostle" — as Constantine was called in Byzantine tradition (par. 209) — but of an "arch-apostle." The arrangement, however, would suggest to most pagans the procession of a Roman consul flanked by his twelve lictors.

Notwithstanding the assertions of Eusebius, we must not think that the new city had a strictly Christian character without any pagan symbol or temple. In the first place, the beautification of the city was brought about largely with materials brought from every part of the Empire so that Jerome was able to say that in clothing Constantinople the rest of the world was left naked. Such materials would almost always be of pagan inspiration (par. 211). Furthermore, the ancient pagan temples continued, without doubt, to function in ancient Byzantium inside the walls of Septimius Severus.

The new city's population was gathered without much difficulty. To get them, various inducements were used, such as tax exemptions, privileges, and gifts. Besides, numerous officials in the court and government were obliged to reside in the city. Immigrants, therefore, came from Greek and Latin countries and in smaller numbers from the East. Even Germani and Slavs came to the city either as slaves or for commercial reasons. Ancient Byzantium had never reached a population of 30,000. By the time of Julian the Apostate, however, it had become larger than any other city of the Empire except Rome. In the fifth century it had reached half a million. The population continued to increase and led to further extension in the building of the city.

The Latin language, which was the official language for the government and the administration, never penetrated to the ordinary people, despite the efforts of Constantine and his successors. Greek became the common language and was the speech of New Rome. Even today the inhabitants of certain areas anciently Byzantine say they are speaking "Roman" when they speak Greek.

The building was done at such high speed that it was soon necessary to make repairs and replacements. The work was finished in 330; on May 11, with the utmost solemnity, New Rome was inaugurated.

225. The attraction of the East was felt by the Christians of the West even in spiritual affairs. For them the East was above all else Palestine, the land where Jesus Christ was born, lived, and died, and where their religion had produced the first seeds which had spread through the whole world. Their interest in Palestine was not only devotional, but also historical. We have certain evidence that Melito of Sardis, a learned writer in the second century, visited Palestine, having been drawn by

a pious and scholarly curiosity (cf. *Hist. Eccl.*, iv, 26, 14). The same was done in the following century by Alexander, a bishop in Cappadocia (cf. *ibid.*, vi, 11, 2), and there were without doubt others.

After the rebellion of Judea against Rome, Jerusalem was finally destroyed by Titus in the year 70; Palestine remained in straitened circumstances. Even more self-destroying was the rebellion of 132–135 under Bar-Kokebah, which was put down with considerable difficulty by the Emperor Hadrian. After this Judea was little more than desert land, we are told by Cassius Dio. The greater part of the population was either killed or deported, and Jews were forbidden under pain of death to set foot in Jerusalem. The city was reconstructed in such a way that the official desecration of the Holy City of Judaism was complete; on the site of the Temple was placed a statue of the Emperor Hadrian; the city's ancient name was changed to Aelia Capitolina (Colonia).

This official desecration affected the places especially venerated by Christians. On the western hill of the city, opposite to the one on which the Temple stood, Jesus Christ was crucified and buried. This was a little beyond the ancient walls of the city. This place was also profaned by a temple dedicated, according to Christian historians, to Aphrodite. Bethlehem, nine kilometers south of Jerusalem, was treated similarly. Pagans knew that the spot was venerated by Christians (cf. Justin, *Dialog. cum Tryph.*, 78; Origen, *Contra Celsum*, i, 51), and therefore the cult of the licentious Adonis-Thammuz was instituted, even using the cave where the Christ Child was laid.

226.   Nonetheless, the Christians were more fortunate than the Jews, for they were able to exercise some watch over their profaned holy places. Entry into Jerusalem was forbidden for Jews; but not for non-Jewish Christians, who were able to travel freely over the whole of Palestine. In any case, the primitive harshness of the prohibition could not long survive the requirements of life itself in Palestine; the strong Roman garrison at Jerusalem had to have contacts with neighboring regions, and so a mixed population gradually penetrated the devastated Judea, leading to a relaxation of the regulations. In this way the Christian community of Jerusalem soon came together again, and one of its more important members was Narcissus, a Greco-Roman who later became a bishop. Since he died a little after 212 at the age of 116 years, he was a living treasure house for the events of the Christian world from the times of Hadrian (cf. *Hist. Eccl.*, v, 12 and 23; vi, 9–

11). He certainly passed these on, for at an advanced age he received as coadjutor and successor in the see of Jerusalem Alexander of Cappadocia whom we have already met as a visitor in Palestine (par. 225).

Besides these two, there were other links in the chain of tradition; some of these have left written records. Hegesippus, of Jewish origin wrote, about the year 180, five books of *Memories* dealing especially with Palestinian Christianity; sections of this work have been preserved for us by Eusebius (cf. *Hist. Eccl.*, ii, 23, 3 ff.; iii, 32, 2 ff., iv, 8, 1–2; 11, 7; 22, 1–9). It is interesting that Hegesippus in his search for the doctrinal traditions of various Christian communities got as far as Rome under the pontificate of Anicetus in the reign of Marcus Aurelius.

The bishop Alexander of Cappadocia died in the persecution of Decius, and almost at the same time Origen died at Tyre. A few years later Eusebius of Caesarea was born who, with his archivial researches, seems to sum up the whole knowledge of antiquity. Besides the works we have already examined (pars. 71–73), Eusebius composed an Onomasticon where he treated of the various geographical and place names used in Holy Scripture; this work, of great utility even today, was translated and enlarged by Jerome. Through Eusebius we come to Constantine and Macarius, the bishop of Jerusalem who was the historical and topographical counselor of the Emperor in his construction work in Palestine.

227. With peace in the Church came the crowds of pilgrims to Palestine, and these increased more and more during the fourth century. Some of these left written records of what they had seen, and naturally the earliest documents are the most important. In 333, when Constantine was still alive, a pilgrim from Bordeaux visited the land of Christ, passing through Constantinople on the way there and through Rome and Milan on the way back; he drew up a small book of notes where he noted down briefly, but accurately, places and matters of interest (*Itinerarium Burdigalense*).

Even more important, though written after the death of Constantine, is the itinerary of a woman who seems to have been a Spaniard called Etheria or Egeria — at one time she was thought to have been Silvia of Aquitaine, the sister of Rufinus. Besides Palestine, Etheria visited Egypt, Sinai, and Mesopotamia spending three years on her travels. Her book, which has great value also for the Romance philologist for the vulgarisms it contains, seems to have been written at the end of the fourth century.

At the end of this same century a letter of Paula and Eustochius (in which the hand of Jerome can probably be seen) describes in passing the crowds of pilgrims in Palestine; it was written in Bethlehem about 386 or a little later, and is preserved in the letters of Jerome (Epist. 46). The letter is full of enthusiasm and points to the numbers that flock to the Holy Land from all parts of the world — from Gaul, Britain, Armenia, Persia, India, Ethiopia, Egypt, Pontus, Cappadocia, etc. — to visit the places holy to Christianity. Of these holy places a list is given beginning with Jerusalem and noting them as far north as Galilee. In all these districts, says the letter, there is nothing but peace, holiness, and brotherly love.

One understands that such opinions were possibly rather rosy and distant from reality from another letter written about 394 from Jerome to Paulinus (Epist. 58). The writer says, perhaps in one of his periods of bad humor, little to the good of Jerusalem. He remarks that one can be an excellent Christian without having been to Jerusalem. He says it is a noisy and crowded place where as in all cities one can find courtiers, garrison military, prostitutes, actors, and buffoons, and little peace and quiet. People come to Jerusalem from all parts of the world and they find there such crowds of men and women that they have to witness things they would do their best to avoid anywhere else. Jerome concludes with the advice that if anyone wishes to be perfect he should stay at home.

Perhaps the truth lies somewhere between the two letters quoted. 228. Eusebius speaks of the building done in Palestine, both in the area of Jerusalem and Bethlehem (De vita Constantini, iii, 25 ff.), and in that of Mambre (cf. ibid., 51 ff.). Naturally Constantine was the promoter and financial backer of the work, but the principal inspiration must have been the bishop of Jerusalem, Macarius (par. 226). The work around Bethlehem and Mambre was given much assistance by Constantine's mother Helena (par. 206), and his mother-in-law Eutropia, the widow of Maximian and mother of Maxentius and Fausta.

Work was begun after the Council of Nicaea in 325, and started first at Jerusalem and Bethlehem where Christ was born; where he died and was buried, and ascended into heaven from the Mount of Olives nearby. The close relation of Bethlehem, Jerusalem, and the

Mount of Olives is rightly emphasized by Eusebius (cf. *ibid.*, 41).

The transformation of Jerusalem into the Aelia Capitolina (Colonia) ordered by Hadrian (par. 225) caused the places where Christ died (Golgotha) and was buried (the Holy Sepulcher) to disappear. The two places, which were very close to each other, had been covered with earth and leveled. Aelia Capitolina had been built as a large rectangle, over 1000 yards north to south, and 650 yards east to west. The principal street, *cardo maximus*, ran from north to south, and about the center was the Forum with the usual buildings of a *colonia* such as the "capitol," the curia, law courts, and the like. The "capitol" and part of the forum had been placed on the artificial level obtained with the filling and leveling of Golgotha and the Holy Sepulcher. In the "capitol" were the statues of Jupiter, Juno, and another feminine divinity, which was either the Roman Minerva or else the licentious Eastern Astarte. This was the statue of Aphrodite referred to by Christian historians (par. 225), and they saw in its erection a purposed profanation of the Christian holy places.

This filling and leveling of the ground had actually led to considerable protection of the holy places. Their veneration had always remained in the hearts of the Christians of Jerusalem by means of the uninterrupted tradition we have already noticed (par. 226), and they were always able to say exactly where they could be found under the ground.

229. In the work on Golgotha and the Holy Sepulcher the first thing was to demolish the pagan temple, and then to carry away the earth which had been used for leveling the site. When this had been done the two holy places were in evidence. Constantine decided to enclose both spots under one vast basilica, the construction of which he entrusted to the architects Zenobius and Eustorgius who began in 326.

The basilica was formed of two principal buildings and two courtyards. The first building at the western end was the *Anastasis* (resurrection), a great rotunda about 124 feet in diameter; in the middle was enclosed the rock in which the tomb of Christ had been hewn and which had been the testimony of his resurrection — hence its official name. On the eastern side, the Anastasis had three gates which led into an internal courtyard flanked by columns. The southeastern corner of this held the rock of Golgotha or Calvary, which for architectural reasons was shaped and reduced to a cube. From the internal courtyard one climbed the rock by means of a short staircase; the top of

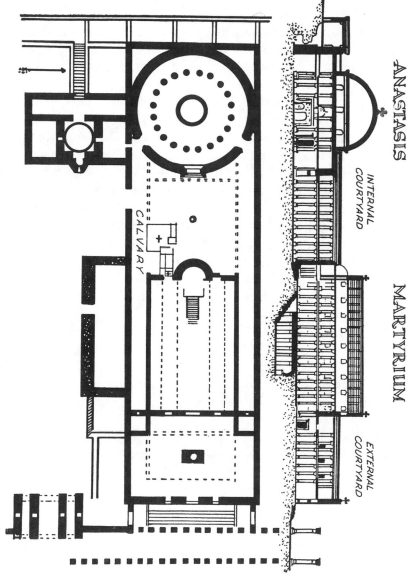

The Constantinian Basilica of the Holy Sepulcher. Upper: logitudinal section; Lower: general plan

ANASTASIS

INTERNAL
COURTYARD

MARTYRIUM

EXTERNAL
COURTYARD

CALVARY

the rock was enclosed by rails of silver and covered with mosaic paving.

On the eastern side of the internal courtyard were two doors leading to a basilica, 147 feet long and 29 feet wide, with five aisles dedicated to the Holy Cross. Here the instruments of the Passion were kept, consequently it was called the *Martyrium*.

To the east of the basilica there was another courtyard surrounded by porticoes; three doors led from the basilica to this external court. A flight of steps joined this with the *cardo maximus* of the city which passed by a little lower down.

It has been remarked that there is a certain architectural affinity between this building of Constantine in Jerusalem and the Mausoleum of St. Constantia in Rome (par. 207), which also dates back to the same period, and also with other buildings in Italy in later times.

According to a belief of the time, Christ had told his disciples what would happen at the end of the world and ascended into heaven from the Mount of Olives. Right at the top of the hill, about 363, was built an octagonal church to honor the actual spot of the Ascension. As early as 326, however, Constantine had erected a basilica a little lower on the hill over the cave where, it was believed, Christ had his last conversation with the disciples before his departure for heaven. This connection of the Constantinian basilica with the grotto is attested not only by Eusebius but also by the pilgrim of Bordeaux (par. 227). This basilica remained the principal sanctuary of the Mount of Olives and was called Eleona, which in Greek means sanctuary. The basilica, which had one apse and three naves, was about 100 feet long and about 58 feet wide. In front of it was an atrium on a slightly lower level and a propylaeum. There are some remains even today of the cave which was incorporated and covered by the basilica.

230.   The third place which claimed Constantine's attention was Bethlehem. Here, as in Jerusalem, the various idolatrous messes had to be first removed from the cave of the nativity (par. 225). In 326 a basilica was begun and finished certainly before 333, in which year it was visited by the pilgrim of Bordeaux. In front of the basilica was placed a very large atrium with four porticoes. Three doors from it led into the body of the basilica, which was patterned after another octagonal edifice. This latter measured about just over 25 feet on each of the eight sides and covered the cave of the Nativity. The latter remained visible, however, through a hole in the pavement which was surrounded by a balustrade and by a couple of steps along the bases of the sides. The

basilica joined to this building was of five naves, formed by four lines of monolithic columns. In the sixth century, under Justinian, the basilica was greatly changed. The octagonal building was removed and three apses were built in its place and other rearrangements were made in the atrium in front of the basilica. The basilica has more or less remained in this form to this day.

There was another place in Palestine not far from Jerusalem which attracted the attention of Constantine, although it was not strictly Christian in its interest. This was Mambre in southern Palestine, two and a half miles to the north of Hebron, famous in the history of the Hebrew patriarchs (Gen. 13:18; 14:13; 18:1; etc.). Here, at the place where there were terebinths (or oaks), Abraham had raised an altar. When Eutropia, the mother-in-law of Constantine, visited the place (par. 228), she found that idolatrous rites of all kinds were celebrated at the spot still called today *Haram Ramet el-Khalil* — Sanctuary of the Highness of the Friend (of God). The "friend" of God was Abraham who seemed to cleanse any superstition by his authority. Eutropia was very shocked and wrote immediately to her noble son-in-law, who ordered that all idolatrous objects were to be destroyed and that a Christian basilica was to be built in the place. The spot, however, had been considered sacred for thousands of years, certainly from the time of the Chanaanites and there were many buildings of different kinds and uses — among these could be noted particularly a sacred enclosure (*haram*) erected by Herod the Great. The tombs of Abraham, Isaac, Jacob, etc., were venerated there, as also a terebinth which was said to date from the beginning of the world. There were also a well and an altar attributed to Abraham. Visitors had freely added their own idols and other sacred objects. All this was now cleared away to make room for the basilica. Today, unfortunately, the basilica is no longer standing; recent excavations have found only a few remains of the enclosure of Herod.

Superstitious practices, however, did not cease for some centuries. It is probable that the followers of a Christian sect used to meet there to honor the Divinity which appeared to Abraham at Mambre under the appearance of three men (Gen. 18:2); they held that one of these was the Divine Word.

V. SCHISMS AND HERESIES

1. Donatism

231. The Roman Empire again had its ancient unity with a new capital. Christianity, however, in one region or another was losing its unity — its organization showed signs of breaking down and disputes were arising over matters of doctrine.

We have seen more than once that the greatest preoccupation of Constantine, the supreme head of the pagan Empire and "bishop of those outside," viz., the Christians (par. 209), was that there should be peace and concord among his subjects. He would expect this especially from the Christians, for they had received many favors from him and would therefore assist him in the government of the Empire by keeping the peace. The opposite happened. It was from his Christian subjects that Constantine saw the most dangerous threats to the public peace.

The two worst threats were Donatism and Arianism.

*　　*　　*

Donatism was conceived in the persecution. In Carthage, the metropolis of Christian Africa, during the episcopate of Mensurius, a body of opinion formed against the Bishop. Although this opposition was local in character it was looked on with a certain favor by the bishops of Numidia who were against the primacy of Carthage. The hostility had various causes; in Carthage itself it arose from personal envy mingled with religious motives; in Numidia similar reasons were complicated still more by ancient racial and political rivalries. Once the movement was set going, one cannot exclude long-standing social problems of the various peoples of the region. The influence of these, however, was purely secondary and not decisive as some scholars have thought.

We have already met Mensurius. It was he who avoided, by a stratagem, handing over of the Holy Scriptures (par. 83); and who, after refusing to surrender his deacon Felix, went to Rome to discuss the matter with Maxentius (par. 156). When the persecution slackened under the latter, meetings of bishops were held in Africa to repair in some way the damages of the persecution and to fill the gaps made in the episcopate. At Cirta where the bishop Paul with all his clergy had given so bad an example of pusillanimity (pars. 80–81), a meeting of about a dozen bishops was held in 305 to designate a successor to Paul. Secundus, bishop of Tigisi and dean of the bishops of Numidia, presided at the meeting.

232. Most of the bishops would better have stayed at home. All had some grisly secrets about their behavior in the recent persecution. One had been a real *traditor* and handed over the Holy Scriptures, even if he had stopped short of offering incense to idols; another had not given up the Scriptures but had thrown them into the fire. Then there was Purpurius, the bishop of Limata, an unusual pastor who had murdered two of his nephews and was inclined to use hardly empty threats when he could not get what he wanted. The past of Secundus, who presided, was not clear; he had received the command to surrender the Scriptures, but no one knew what he had done. He himself denied that he was a *traditor*, and the general opinion was that he had got out of the difficulty by some trick or other.

Notwithstanding all this, Secundus stirred up the episcopal wasps and suggested an investigation into their conduct during the persecution. The buzz could be heard all over Africa. Purpurius jumped to his feet and reminded the president what rumor said about him. This was not good, so Secundus changed his mind about the investigation and demanded silence.

At about this time there was an exchange of letters between Mensurius, the primate, and his dean, Secundus. At first sight these letters seem to be a discussion of topical questions, but between the lines of Secundus' letters we can see the opposition of the Numidians to the methods adopted toward imprisoned Christians. Mensurius had little time for fanatical Christians who had been put in prison for presenting themselves before magistrates, announcing that they possessed copies of the Scriptures and that they had no intention of handing them over (par. 82). There were other Christians who, burdened with debts or liable to the law for some reasons or another, had no reluctance to go to prison with the halo of a martyr where they were given generous assistance by their fellow Christians. Against all such persons Mensurius was obdurate; he ordered his deacon Caecilian to visit the prisons, dissuading the faithful from giving help to unworthy Christians. The reaction of ordinary Christians to this was understandable. If Mensurius was now persecuting the confessors of the faith, it was obvious that he himself must be a *traditor* of the Scriptures. His past was examined and it was decided that the trick by which Mensurius had avoided handing over the Scriptures to the police (par. 83) was no more than a clever story to hide a shameful fall.

In his letter to Secundus, Mensurius himself had told the story as if to give an example of how it was possible to keep a Christian conscience without running to stupidity and fanaticism. The reply of Secundus to this letter shows that he considered Mensurius was being "diplomatic" and was employing dissimulation and avoiding difficult points. Secundus was "diplomatic" in his turn, therefore, and recorded how violent the persecution had been in Numidia and how strong the Christians had been — they went to their death rather than surrender the Holy Scriptures. In regard to his own conduct, Secundus declares his innocence — he had handed over nothing.

Thus the affair stood. Many at Carthage and very many in Numidia considered Mensurius a crypto-*traditor*. The situation remained without change until Mensurius died on his way back from seeing Maxentius (par. 156).

233.   Before leaving for Rome the prudent Mensurius had seen to the safekeeping of the goods of the Church for which he was responsible. He entrusted precious objects to two aged members of his church who were to hand them to his successor in case he did not return. Since where money is concerned prudence is rarely excessive, he left a pious lady a list of what he had given into the keeping of the two men with instructions to hand the list to the next bishop of Carthage if he himself should not return. This was an excellent check on the trustees, especially since they were not told about the list. The way things turned out showed that Mensurius had not been too careful.

As soon as the death of Mensurius became known in Carthage preparations were set on foot for the election of a successor — in so delicate a situation a bishop in charge of the see was essential. The deacon Caecilian was elected and was immediately consecrated by three bishops who were — as was the custom — those nearest to the territory of the new bishop: Felix of Aptonga, Faustus of Thumbarbo, and

Novellus of Tignica. The choice of Caecilian, who had co-operated with Mensurius in the provisions against Christians who were in prison for fanaticism rather than faith, was not welcomed by the late bishop's many enemies in Carthage nor by his even more numerous opponents in Numidia.

Caecilian found a personal adversary in Carthage itself. This was a very influential matron called Lucilla who was blessed with vast wealth and superstition. She had already crossed swords with Caecilian when he was still a deacon for he had reproved her for kissing a bone — which only she said was of a martyr — before drinking the consecrated chalice. The two old men who had been entrusted with the precious vessels of the church by Mensurius were two more enemies of the bishop. They had already made plans to keep quiet about what had been entrusted to them, but the presentation of the list by the pious lady put them on the spot. "*Inde irae,*" especially in the direction of Caecilian. All this was sufficient to produce an opposition party to Caecilian in Carthage, which was led by two clerics, Botrus and Celestius, both of whom had dreams of being elected bishop of Carthage.

To strengthen their position they called on the bishops of Numidia, whose sentiments they well knew and who had some faithful supporters in Carthage itself. One of these was Donatus of *Casae Nigrae,* so called after his birthplace — a little-known town in Numidia.

234. It is from Donatus that the schism derives its name. Until the meeting at Carthage in 411 only one Donatus was spoken of; after that, however, we hear about two men called Donatus, the one from Casae Nigrae and the other who was at the head of the party and came to be called Donatus the Great. It seems that Augustine recognized two people. As far as we can see, however, there was actually only one Donatus. The multiplication was a trick of the Donatists who wished to conceal the not very honorable conduct of their leader during the persecution. Whenever Donatus the chief of the schism appears on the scene, therefore, he is always taken as the Donatus of Casae Nigrae.

When the Numidians were called to help their friends in Carthage, they were delighted and got to work immediately. Their dean, Secundus of Tigisi, came to Carthage with seventy bishops to make a stand against Caecilian, although his election and consecration had been perfectly in order and he was the primate of all Africa, and therefore of Numidia. If there were no legal arguments, however, there was no lack of anger and envy. Nor was financial assistance wanting to the opposition, since Lucilla of the "martyr's bone" fame was quite willing to use her fortune to avenge her slight.

The arguments brought against Caecilian were two — one ecclesiastical-juridical and the other of a theological nature. The first was based on the fact that the bishops of Numidia had not taken part in his consecration; the second alleged that Felix of Aptonga (par. 83) and his coconsecrators were unworthy ministers, since they had been *traditores* during the persecution. So far as the first charge is concerned, the method used at Caecilian's consecration was the one that had been used in Africa from the time of Cyprian and probably before. As for the accusation of *traditores*, this was pure calumny, as was evident from the very minute investigation which took place later. But even aside from this, the second objection presupposed the theological principle that the validity of a sacrament depended on the dignity and sanctity of the person conferring it, a principle not accepted even at this time, except by the Donatists (par. 241).

235. The Donatists, however, were not really concerned with canon law or theology, but with Caecilian. They refused to recognize him as primate. Since they were not able to use the buildings restored by Constantine to Caecilian (pars. 201–202), they met elsewhere and cited him to appear before them. The legitimate Bishop disregarded this, but declared that he was ready to be consecrated again by his enemies if they considered the earlier ceremony to have been invalid. This proposal — if it has come down to us correctly (cf. Optatus of Mileum, *De schismate Donat.*, i, 19) — was interpreted in an ironical sense already by St. Augustine and by some modern scholars as if the Bishop wished to demonstrate that his enemies had less right than any to inquire into the worthiness of the three consecrating bishops. Perhaps this interpretation is correct. It may be, however, that Caecilian wanted to show himself as condescending as possible, and at the same time to remove any basis for objection by his adversaries. The proposal was brought to the Donatist party and the reply was given by Purpurius in a manner natural to him: "Let him come; instead of laying our hands on him we will split his head open by way of penance."

Complete schism was decided upon and carried out immediately. A temporary administrator was put in Caecilian's place; Felix of Aptonga and his coconsecrators were formally declared *traditores*; for his behavior toward Christians imprisoned for reasons mentioned above Caecilian was noted as the enemy of the confessores and martyrs. An election was held in which a lector called Majorinus was named primate. Thus the Egerian nymph, Lucilla (par. 233), had her triumph for she saw her own candidate — he was also one of her servants — raised to the primacy of Carthage. She showed her appreciation with large donations in Carthage and in Numidia.

Official letters notified the whole of Africa of the new bishop, while Majorinus hurried to consecrate bishops in the various sees to provide opposition to the Catholics. This move was aided by the old opposition in Africa to Carthage, so that by the end of the year 321 the Donatist schism had a firm hold on proconsular Africa in smaller centers, especially in Numidia. Majorinus died not long after this, and in his place was elected Donatus the Great (par. 234).

It is for this reason that there was a certain ambiguity in the designation of the schismatics who were first the followers of Majorinus and then of Donatus. With the passage of time the latter gave his name to the movement.

236. Donatus was a man of no common qualities. He was educated, a convincing writer, and a fine speaker; nothing could be found wrong with his morals. He was, however, puffed up with pride and felt himself destined to command. In reality he was a born tribune, a people's leader who could draw the masses, uniting them when they were at loggerheads and giving direction to their wild power.

He had lived in Carthage during the time of Mensurius, but had remained in obscurity. When he was made bishop by his party he faced a very difficult task, but his ambition was excited by the knowledge that he was supported by the faithful and easily moved masses. The greatest difficulty for him was that the Catholics supporting Caecilian owned the churches and were under the official protection of the government. Constantine always dealt with Caecilian in African Church matters. What could be done? He could face the government with a rising of the people, or he could seek to change its policy by open protests and veiled threats. The first method was too risky and forthright — it could be kept in reserve for later. Thus he chose the second method.

Donatus (or his party, for precise data are wanting) must already have known how much Constantine feared disputes in the empire. Using this fear it was best to go directly to him, warn him of possible trouble, and show him how it could be avoided. The condition for this happy solution was that the Emperor should take on a certain office of protection toward the schismatics.

If this was the secret plan of Donatus (or his party), it could be objected that Constantine was neither a bishop nor a Christian and therefore had no right to interfere in the purely religious affairs of the Christians. *Caesari Caesaris, Dei Deo.* If there were any doubt on this matter, it is perfectly true that a few years later it was the scandalized Donatists who were asking: "What has the Emperor to do with the Church? [*Quid est imperatori cum ecclesia?*]" This cry, however, came after they had discovered that there was little or nothing to be got from him. It was the Donatists who at first turned obsequiously and devotedly to the Emperor and opened the doors of the Church to him.

News of what was happening to Christianity in Africa passed the seas and came first of all to Constantine himself. The Donatists sought support and publicity outside Africa and later in Rome itself formed a small community — the *montenses* with a bishop called Victor. But the rest of the Church kept out of the African dispute, and though it did nothing to help settle the affair, it recognized Caecilian as the primate of Africa and dealt with him only. Constantine followed the same method (though perhaps at first he did not realize the gravity of the situation) and remained faithful to Caecilian. Since he had been informed that the Catholic bishop of Carthage was exposed to intrigue and even violence from his enemies he authorized him to call on the protection of his proconsul Anulinus and vicar Patrick (*Hist. Eccl.*, x, 6, 4–5). This was simply a matter of public security, and not an interference in religious questions.

It was then that the Donatists attempted to go directly to Constantine.

THE SYNOD OF ROME

237. On April 15, 313, a few months after the disturbing meeting at Carthage, a delegation of Donatists presented itself to the consul Anulinus and offered him two letters, one open and the other sealed, with the request that he should forward them to the Emperor. They were sent off with a personal report of the Consul.

The open letter was a petition to Constantine (*preces ad Constantinum*) with which the Emperor was invited to intervene in the

Christian dispute in Africa. Constantine, said the letter, had had as father the Emperor who had been the only one not to persecute the Christians and had kept Gaul free from such cruelty. In Africa at the moment there was argument between the signatories of the letter and "the other bishops"; the petition asked that he should end such difficulties by nominating men to judge it from Gaul. Personal signatures were appended followed by a general designation of "the other bishops of the following of Majorinus." Some documents have "the following of Donatus," but it may be that this has been due to later scribes (par. 235 at the end).

The sealed letter, which has not come down to us, was probably a documentation of the rights of the Donatists and the wrongs of Caecilian: since the Donatists claimed that they were the Catholic Church it was entitled *Libellus ecclesiae catholicae criminum Caeciliani* — the Catholic Church's list of the crimes of Caecilian.

Can these two documents be taken as a clear invitation to Constantine to interfere in religious matters? If we accept the manner in which the petition is put, there is no definite request that Constantine should act as judge; this is to be the duty of the Gauls he elects for the purpose. In practice, however, so powerful an emperor would have been able to influence as he might wish both the judges and their decision. Even if the Emperor had not exactly been invited to come into the Church, he had been given the keys of the door. The Donatists would have done better to have cried as they did later — "What has the Emperor to do with the Church?"

Constantine received the appeal kindly and nominated as judges of the dispute three bishops of Gaul, Reticus of Autun, Maternus of Cologne, and Marinus of Arles; they were to assemble in Rome under the presidency of Miltiades, the bishop of Rome. A certain bishop called Mark, of whom we have no certain information, was to give assistance. Before this court each party in the dispute would be represented by a delegation of ten members (*Hist. Eccl.*, x, 5, 18–20). In his turn, the Bishop of Rome did not forget that he was the Pope and that he had behind him a long tradition of Roman synods. He therefore enlarged the court into a Roman synod in which not only the Pope and the three Gaulish bishops took part, but fifteen other bishops of various Italian regions (Ostia, Palestrina, Terracina, Milan, Pisa, Florence, Siena, Capua, Benevento, etc.); the numbers were thus raised to nineteen. Greater scope was thus given to the authority of the assembly and its neutrality and impartiality were guaranteed, for all the judges were non-Africans.

The delegations of the two parties arrived and at the head of the Donatists was Donatus himself.

238. There were three sessions from October 2 to 4, 313 in the *domus Faustae* at the Lateran (par. 179).

Since the purpose of the discussion was "the crimes of Caecilian," denounced in the letter, the Donatists were first invited to state precisely what these crimes were and to produce some proof. But from the start it appears that the accusers began to retreat and hesitate; perhaps they had not been expecting a proceeding so accurate and objective and were hoping to use the methods adopted at Carthage. According to St. Augustine — who handled the transcripts of the meeting in the first session — the accusers of "Caecilian refused to say anything against him." When they were asked if they intended to bring forward witnesses they feared that this might do little to assist their cause and so replied that they would bring them in on another day.

Donatus was very active. He detailed several charges, but when he was requested to bring proof he was not able. In this rather awkward situation he was subjected to questioning by the judges on his own personal conduct, which brought to light some interesting facts. It transpired that even before the quarrel with Caecilian, Donatus had caused commotions and secessions in the Christian community at Carthage. According to his own confession he had personally baptized Christians of the opposition and had laid hands on bishops who had fallen during the persecution with every show of reconsecrating them. Such behavior was quite contrary to the usual customs of the Church. After this had been revealed, the session was ended for the day.

The following day Caecilian's accusers, despite earlier promises, did not present themselves. At the third sitting there was no sign of them and so the commission decided to give sentence according to the facts which had been proved. All the judges, singly and unanimously, pronounced themselves in favor of Caecilian. The last to speak was the Pope Miltiades, who said: "Since Caecilian had not been accused in any way by those who came with Donatus in spite of their declaration against him, and since he [Caecilian] has therefore had nothing proved against him by Donatus, I believe that he ought to be left with the right of ecclesiastical communion and dignity of office." The only person condemned was Donatus; toward the bishops who had followed him, mercy was shown (through the influence, it seems, especially of Pope Miltiades). If they wished they could remain in the Catholic Church. If, however, there was already a bishop in their see, the one who had been consecrated second must retire and wait to be placed elsewhere.

To sum up, we find that the inquiry demanded from Constantine by the Donatists, and granted faithfully by him brought harm only to themselves. They demanded the condemnation of their adversaries, but none was condemned. The only person found guilty, on the other hand, was their leader who had come to accuse Caecilian. The Donatists were in the position of the snake charmer who had been bitten by a recalcitrant serpent.

239. The Donatists were not people to be disheartened by such a reverse. The following events show this clearly.

For the present they acted as unfortunate victims maintaining that the commission had not been fair. In the first place, they said that the Gaulish judges they had asked for had been ineffective since they had been lost among the large commission which had been packed by Miltiades. Second, they complained that the question which they considered the most important of all, the presumed unworthiness of Felix of Aptonga, the consecrator of Caecilian (par. 234), had not been discussed. More protests therefore followed — recriminations and further petitions to Constantine.

The Emperor was becoming annoyed with these troublesome Africans. With his usual fear of disorder, however, he did not wish to neglect any method of gaining peace. From Africa, moreover, reports from local magistrates kept reaching him which said that the movement was growing steadily and looked like the beginning of sedition. By now there were two definite parties: the "church of the martyrs," as the Donatists called themselves, using the name already chosen by the Meletians of Egypt (par. 95), and the "church of the *traditores*" as the Catholics of Caecilian were called by the Donatists. The quarrel was not just theoretical and theological but entered fanatically into daily life; city was divided from city, street from street, house from house; there were continual quarrels and fighting. This was anything but the Christian concord dreamed of by Constantine. There was nothing else but to try to solve the matter once more with seeming deference to the troublemakers.

The Emperor decided to act himself. This time he did not halt at the threshold of the church but went inside and acted as the Supreme Moderator. He had realized that it was not sufficient to be the "bishop of those outside" (par. 209), and tried to be the bishop of those inside. "Ahi, Constantin!"

THE COUNCIL OF ARLES

240. Without delay Constantine called another meeting. This was not to be a restricted synod as that of Rome, which had included only a few bishops of Gaul and Italy, but a large council which would represent, as largely as possible, the churches of the Western territories which were then under the dominion of Constantine.

But this was not all. Since the Donatists made a great fuss about the case of Felix of Aptonga on the pretext that it had not been examined separately, the Emperor ordered his vicar in Africa, toward the end of 313, to make a thorough investigation of the conduct of Felix during the persecution to see whether he had really been a *traditor* as the Donatists claimed. This investigation was really no more than a gracious condescension toward the Donatists, for even if he had been a *traditor*, his consecration of Caecilian would not have been invalid. Constantine wished to leave the Donatists no ground for complaints of any kind. The council was to be very large; the investigation of Felix was to be most searching. Once all this was over there could be no doubt as to which party was right and there would be no more trouble. The Emperor had genial illusions.

The council was held in Gaul, the region first proposed by the Donatists themselves. The members of the council were to meet on August 1, 314 at Arles; they were given the use of the public post for themselves and for a train of five officials. In all, the members were 45 or 46; the representatives of Gaul were the most numerous, being sixteen; nine came from Africa; six from Spain; three or perhaps four from Britain; one from Dalmatia; ten from Italy (Rome, Milan, Aquileia, etc.), including two of the islands (Syracuse and Cagliari). Constantine had ordered his vicar in Africa to send both Caecilian and Donatus with their supporters.

The behavior of the Donatists in the session must have been insolent and overbearing to a great degree, for the letter that the council sent at the end to Pope Sylvester presents them as *homines effrenatae mentis;* this would seem to say that they behaved like brigands. The seed was already there which later developed in Africa into the *circumcelliones,* typical brigands of Donatism. The council was not impressed, however, and decided on the various questions in accordance with the facts and ecclesiastical tradition. The result was that the Donatists as such were condemned and excommunicated.

241. Besides this action the council issued 22 canons on various points which had arisen in the dispute.

The most important, canon 13, concerned the *traditores* or "those who handed over" the Scriptures. It ordered that those who during the persecution had surrendered the Sacred Scriptures, the sacred vessels, or the names of brethren (par. 80) should be removed from the clerical state, the offense to be proved by public documentary evidence and not by simple accusation (*ex actis publicis . . . non verbis nudis*). If a *traditor* had performed ordinations to sacred orders, those who had been thus ordained should not be affected, provided that they were men of worthy conduct.

Canon 8 is also important. This declares that baptism given by heretics is valid, so long as it had been conferred in the name of the Trinity. In Africa it had been customary to rebaptize converts from heresy, a custom which went back to the times of the great Cyprian. After this decision by Arles the African Catholics ceased to do this, and followed the use of the other Western churches. With this they confirmed a wider principle — denied by the Donatists — that the validity of a sacrament does not depend on the dignity or sanctity of the person who confers it (par. 234).

The numbers present at the conference and its soundness of approach opened the eyes of a certain number of the Donatists who were not entirely in the grip of fanaticism; they abandoned the sect and joined Caecilian once more. The greater part of the Donatists, however, especially the leaders, remained unmoved. There was nothing else for these latter to do but to address new appeals and laments to the Emperor.

But another disaster had fallen upon them — the investigation of Felix of Aptonga had finished and the results were declared. The proconsul Aelianus had consulted documentary evidence and listened to witnesses both at Aptonga and at Carthage on what had happened to Felix in faraway 303, and he had come across some unexpected information. The Donatists who had made such a fuss over the presumed fall of Felix had attempted to suborn witnesses and change records. From Alfius Caecilian, who had been a duumvir of Aptonga in 303, they had tried to obtain through a third person a written declaration attesting that Felix had surrendered the Sacred Scriptures. Alfius had refused; he was a pagan, but honest. A friend of his called Augentius had left a letter in which he related the events of the sequestration which he had carried out in the church at that time, but the letter contained nothing compromising for Felix. This letter finished up in the hands of Ingentius, a public scribe and a convert to Donatism who made additions which showed Felix as a *traditor*. This was just what the Donatists wanted. After further complications the documents and witnesses were examined by Aelianus. He examined the letter and discarded as false the additions of Ingentius, which the latter admitted were due to his imagination. The least that could be done — and it was done — was to put Ingentius the forger in prison and keep him for the Emperor who had a personal interest in the affair. Thus the whole fabric of Donatist lies and exaggerations collapsed with the failure of their most important piece of evidence.

242.   Things were going badly for the Donatists. As they lost the favor of honest men, however, they increased in their obstinacy, for they did not lack the blindness usual to fanatics. This fanaticism made a deep impression on Constantine. He was not disturbed by the question of whether the sacraments worked *ex opere operato* or through the personal virtue of the ministers. What terrified him was to have Africa in a turmoil at his rear while Licinius was openly preparing for war (par. 214). The result of the Council of Arles had profoundly disillusioned him and at the end of it he had written a letter to the members of the council (Aeterna, religiosa, In Optatus of Mileum, Append. 5), in which he showed his displeasure quite clearly. When the Donatists once more began to address appeals to him he did not close his ears to their pleas, however, hoping that some agreement could be reached. He did not realize that this made him a cowardly weakling in the eyes of the Donatists, whereas the Catholics felt he was contradicting his self-appointed office of quasi-bishop. He called councils and synods, indeed, but paid little attention to their decisions.

Even after Licinius had been removed, Constantine waited a while before going to Rome (July, 315) to treat directly with Caecilian and Donatus who had been summoned there. For various reasons, however, the meeting could not take place until the following autumn in Milan when, with the leaders of the two parties with him, Constantine had a pleasing new idea. Since all the trouble could be traced to these two people would it not be a good thing to remove both of them without deciding who was in the right? True, an injustice would be done to the innocent one, but of what account was this compared to the peace of the Empire? It was sufficient to consider Caecilian and Donatus as nonexistent and to place a new pastor on the throne at Carthage.

The idea was ingenuous and showed how little Constantine knew about the spirit and the practice of the Church. He did not realize that such a solution would upset his own previous provisions, for it contradicted very clear decisions of the Synod of Rome and the Council of Arles. His preoccupation with public peace, however, did not allow him to see the matter clearly and he immediately set about carrying out his new plan. He detained both Caecilian and Donatus in Italy, sending them to Brescia and dispatched the bishops Eunomius and Olympius to Africa with the task of reconciling the two parties and of electing a new primate of Carthage.

243. Their mission was a complete failure. The two emissaries stayed in Africa about forty days probably between the end of 315 and the beginning of 316. They managed to reconcile a few Donatists while the rest refused their advances. The two bishops then turned to the followers of Caecilian and declared that these were the true Catholics for they were in communion with the Church all over the world. They recalled the decision of the Synod of Rome (they seemed to have paid no attention to the Council of Arles) and declared it completely valid. Thus the mission of the two peacemakers ended and things remained as they were before.

In fact, they got worse. Donatus managed to escape the vigilance of his guards and returned to Carthage. Caecilian followed him a little later and the quarrel between the two parties began once more with an ever greater fury. For Constantine the news from Africa became worse with every messenger. A report sent at the beginning of 316 from his vicar in Africa, Domitius Celsus, gave a grim picture of affairs. This document gave him food for thought. Extreme remedies for great evils — so Constantine decided to go and settle the matter personally. Surely the full weight of his imperial authority would put everything right once more.

The personal intervention in African Church affairs did not take place, for almost the whole of the year 316 was taken up with travels. But Constantine was not the man to abandon easily any idea which had to do with religious politics — in which he considered himself specially guided. During his journeys from place to place he thought over the question and studied the documents bearing on it.

Finally with a letter of November 10, 316, Constantine communicated to his vicar in Africa, Eumalius, the sentence he had decided upon and which he wished to be final. The Emperor declared that Caecilian was innocent and completely blameless of the faults attributed to him by his accusers.

The sentence was without doubt very just. Two observations should be made, however, in its regard: first, it was a sentence on strictly ecclesiastical matters by one who was not a bishop and not even a Christian; second, it merely repeated what had been proclaimed three years earlier by the bishops of the Synod of Rome and confirmed by the Council of Arles. The Emperor-Bishop had taken three years to reach a conclusion already long since decided by true bishops. Ahi, Constantin!

AFTER ARLES

244. At this point Constantine changed his attitude toward the Donatists. Since he had failed to obtain the desired settlement by peaceful means, he decided to regard them officially as seditious rebels and to use force against them.

Perhaps Constantine remembered what had happened during his own youth when Diocletian was persecuting the Manichaeans (par. 16). The situation was different, however. Manichaeanism was quite another thing from Christianity, and in any case Diocletian had never given any support to the Manichaeans. Donatism, on the other hand, was a question inside Christianity and of the followers of this religion Constantine had made himself protector. It is true that the Donatists had provoked fierce measures by their conduct, but it could also be asked whether the Church, of which Constantine was certainly not the head, had no disciplinary means whereby she could bring back rebellious children ad bonam frugem. And if she did possess them and had applied them without result, was it really opportune that the Emperor should intervene as a "secular arm"?

These questions are now more theoretical than practical. In the practice of the time Constantine acted not so much as a "secular arm," but as the custodian of public security and the supreme head of the police. The laws of the State were clear enough, and they had been broken many times by the Donatists; the Emperor therefore had the right to interfere. What form should his interference have taken? The violence of the Donatists extended beyond the religious field into civil order, for churches had been seized, regular worship impeded, the organization of religion made difficult, and so on. The matter was of mixed jurisdiction in which both the civil authorities and the conscience of individual subjects could have much to say. What could be done in face of such disorder?

The ideal would be to give freedom to the Donatists on condition that they should concede equal freedom to the Catholics. If the two groups could be isolated without force or evasion, then it would soon be seen which party would prevail. But for those times such a method was a mere dream, a utopia which would not occur to any ruler; far less was there any chance of its occurring to Constantine who had been completely disillusioned in his earlier peaceful attempts and was now convinced that he must resort to the *ius coercitionis*. This he did — and the dispute became insoluble. Violence resulted and blood was spilt, and so were provided the motives which have always driven dissenters to exasperation.

245. The Donatists reacted against Constantine's sentence as well as they could by falling back on the usual arguments. When, in the conference of Carthage in 411, the Catholics produced a copy of the letter written by Constantine to his vicar in Africa, Eumalius, to proclaim the innocence of Caecilian, the Donatists objected that the copy which had been taken from the archives did not bear the names of consuls. The objections were futile, for another copy was soon forthcoming with the desired names on it. Later the Donatists said that Constantine's decision had been taken at the suggestions of others, especially of Hosius. Without bothering about this charge, there was always the fact that the Donatists had been condemned by the Synod of Rome, the Council of Arles, the inquiry on Felix of Aptonga, and finally by the commissioners Eunomius and Olympius — all these were not Hosius. Finally, as a supreme argument against the Donatists there was the fact that the last person to condemn them had been that Emperor to whom they had so incautiously confided their problem (par. 237).

The Donatists resisted the repressive measures of Constantine with great tenacity. The basilicas which they had seized from the Catholics were now restored to the latter and so they built others. The Donatists were punished with exile and confiscation of their goods, and so they intensified their propaganda, extending it outside Africa. There were serious clashes when the imperial troops proceeded to Carthage to take over their basilicas. Those who resisted were overcome or killed, among them the Donatist bishop of Advocata.

Such incidents were not confined to Carthage and they were accompanied by sacking and looting as was to be expected. We can admit without difficulty that the Donatist women were not lacking in spirit (par. 109), but it is difficult to believe that they opposed physical force to the soldiers in service of the police. We have, on the other hand, information of the rape of Donatist women by soldiers.

The Donatists collected abundant material for their martyrologies. They convinced themselves more than ever that they were the "Church of the martyrs" (par. 239), the only true Church of Christ, completely divorced from the Church of the Catholic *traditores* who had shamefully given in to the Emperor. Full of pride, they increased their acts of hostility against the Catholics either by calumnious writings and anonymous letters, or by a strict boycott of anything which was Catholic. As a consequence, despite the protection of the government the Catholics especially in Numidia took hardly any part in civil life, were cut off from all social relationships, and were exposed to many reprisals. As *traditores* they were not given the normal civilities in the streets by the "sons of the martyrs."

246.   It was inevitable, however, that from time to time the Donatists would taste their own medicine. The persecution against them had not been long in progress when a scandal occurred which shook their church to its foundation and showed that its members were not all the "sons of martyrs," and it was the *traditores* who began it.

In 320 a serious quarrel arose between Silvanus, the Donatist bishop of Cirta (Constantina), and his deacon Nundinarius. The cause of the quarrel is not known, but Nundinarius said that he was being unjustly persecuted by Silvanus and the latter ended by excommunicating him. Nundinarius did not submit but sought support for his cause among the Donatist clergy; he passed to the attack and declared that he was in the position to reveal grave faults in the past conduct of Silvanus. This threat scared some of the Donatist prelates who never felt very secure in the face of such menaces. To avoid general recriminations they intervened between the bishop and the deacon endeavoring to bring them to some agreement. Nundinarius was not satisfied, however, and took his case to Zenophilus, the governor of Numidia. The Governor was pleased to be asked to arbitrate for he foresaw that much would come out which the Donatists would have preferred to have kept hidden. This would please the Governor and the Emperor for both of them had had quite enough of Donatists.

The Governor was not mistaken. The case was discussed in great detail on December 13, 320, and ancient official documents and witnesses were examined. We have already met the chief protagonist — the bishop Silvanus — on the occasion of the sequestration of church goods made in the church of Cirta by the curator Munatius Felix (pars. 80–81). At that time Silvanus was only a subdeacon, but the official documents of the sequestration now examined in court showed that he had co-operated zealously with the officials who had confiscated the Holy Scriptures at Cirta. He was, therefore, a true and formal *traditor*. Other things came out too. Silvanus had plotted with Purpurius, the bandit bishop of Limata whom we have also met before (par. 235), to steal some pipes of vinegar belonging to the treasury and to hide them in the temple of Serapis. Silvanus was found to have been paid to ordain a priest. Finally, it was discovered that the Numidians who had come to Carthage to keep the schism going were in the pay of the matron Lucilla (par. 235), and that some of them had put into their own pockets donations intended for the poor. The wickedest blow of all was that it was now learned that the bishops who had ordained Silvanus had themselves been *traditores*.

247. The results of the inquiry, now copied out and deposited in official archives, were the greatest moral blow the Donatists had received up to that time. The mortal strokes which the Donatists were aiming at the heads of the Catholics were now turned on themselves. And owing to the official and public character of the inquiry the Donatists were not able to make any real defense. They resorted to the usual vague excuses that such testimonies were inspired by the civil authorities and that the reality was quite different, and so on.

Silvanus was sent into exile, probably not for his embezzlement nor for ecclesiastical reasons, but as a police precaution against disorder. Later the Donatists said that his exile was inflicted because he had offended the Governor and because he would not come to an agreement with the Catholics. Before Silvanus, other important Donatists had already disappeared either by death or exile; thus the power of the sect diminished visibly as its reputation sagged more and more after the dreadful disclosures of the inquiry by Zenophilus.

As a consequence of this the Donatists changed tactics. Far from considering themselves conquered they became more boastful, and at the beginning of 321 sent a petition to Constantine asking consideration. The Emperor was even more than usually anxious for peace in his lands owing to the imminence of a new war with Licinius (par. 219), and so was pleased with this new move by the Donatists. On May 5, 321, he sent to Verinus, his vicar in Africa, a letter very harsh in form, but mild in substance, with which he conceded full liberty of conscience and worship to the Donatists. It was a real edict of tolerance. Thus the exiled Donatists returned to their fatherland as bumptious as before, and with the aureola of martyrs or at least of confessores.

It was easy to predict that there would be new disorders. Constantine tried to quiet the Donatists, and in 322 directed a letter to the Catholic bishops recommending that they have patience, and support with longanimity the provocations of the Donatists (cf. *Quod fides*, in *Optatus of Mileum*, Append. 9). Actually this letter would have been more valuable and of more authority if it had come from a bishop and not from a "Bishop-Emperor." Constantine had no difficulty in taking on the powers of bishops, but as before he was not successful.

For some time the Donatists preserved a certain exterior calm, but internally they had not lost their intransigeance which had been provoked and nourished by the long-standing weakness of the Emperor in their regard. At the time of Constantine's death the Donatist question was still as grave as ever. A little later the affair flared up into even greater disorder leading to the troubles of the *circumcelliones*.

2. Arianism

248. Donatism began as a dispute over Church discipline, whereas Arianism concerned theological matters. In time, both movements left their original course. A modern reader is surprised to see the far-reaching effects, both civil and political, of a theological controversy such as Arianism. Not only were learned scholars and churchmen involved in it, but even the rude populace who brought with them the partisanship and roughness which are companions of ignorance. Arianism flooded the whole Empire; it washed over the frontiers, overwhelming many barbarian peoples, and lasted for more than half a century. Jerome referring to a time when Arianism was forty years old was able to write: "the whole world wept and was amazed at being arian" (*Ad Luciferianos*, 19).

The reasons for the enormous success of Arianism were many, but one of the most decisive was the very popularity of theological dispute. All wanted to talk and give their opinions on matters of theology; they based their arguments on Sacred Scripture holding themselves all to be learned and competent to judge. A really learned man such as Jerome had good reason to complain of this invasion of his territory by presumptuous ignoramuses. If for the most part his protests fell unheeded he has at least given us the following spirited passage which breathes life at every sentence: "Builders, carpenters, workers in metal and wood, websters and fullers, makers of anything, cannot become expert without a teacher; physicians are trained by physicians: 'tractant fabrilia fabri.' The art of the Scripture is the only art which is claimed by all. 'Scribimus indocti doctique poemata passim.' It is the Scriptures which chattering old women, doting gossips, wordy sophists, everybody in fact, take to their own, tear to pieces, and teach to others what they have never learned. Some with ponderous brow boom out high-sounding words and issue philosophies on the sacred pages to an audience of featherbrained women. Others, alas, learn from the women what they teach to men; they make light of their task and with a certain facility of speech, even with boldness, explain to others what they cannot understand themselves" (*Ad Paulinum*, epist. 53, of the year 395–396). Just as nowadays everybody talks about sports or politics — even if they understand little of the first and know nothing about the other — so during the fourth century the streets and squares and houses rang with disputations in theology and Sacred Scripture.

Besides this popularity, there was another very good reason why Arianism grew so quickly — it soon became involved with cultural, regional, and above all political questions. So much so, indeed, that its primitive object was almost forgotten. From the time when Constantine and his sister Constantia entered the Arian controversy — followed more or less by the succeeding sovereigns of Byzantium — the original theological question, which had already suffered greatly from the logomachy of the people, remained bogged down in a slough of interests of all kinds except theological. The typical "byzantism" built up of sophisms, cunning, and implacable rivalries was already in full flower at the time of the Arian controversy. Everyone in the Empire was shouting loudly. If anyone of the imperial mob were asked what he was shouting about he would have been hard put for an answer. It seemed a repeat of the disturbance of the silversmiths at Ephesus where of the crowd — "some cried one thing and some another . . . and the greater part knew not for what cause they were come together" (Acts 19:32).

THE BEGINNINGS OF ARIUS

249. Arius saw to the diffusion of his doctrines among the common people with passages to be learned by heart. He was not the inventor of this method, for as early as the second and third centuries the Gnostic Bardesanes and his son Harmonius had propagated their theories among the Syrians by poetical composition. Ephraem the Syrian later opposed them in the same way, composing anti-Gnostic hymns and having them taught to the people by the "daughters of the promise" — women of ascetic life. But, besides writing, Arius did a great deal with his voice and he also received much help from the "daughters of the promise."

He was a native of Libya, but was living in Alexandria during the episcopate of Peter, the future martyr (par. 93 ff.), and during the schismatic machinations of Meletius. The Arius whom we then found among the followers of Meletius (par. 95) seems to have been the same Arius we are dealing with here. He left Meletius, however, and was ordained deacon by Peter about 308; then Arius' renewed support of the Meletians put him in opposition to Peter, and he was excommunicated by him. Achillas, Peter's successor, received him back, and in 311 ordained him a priest. Alexander, who succeeded Achillas in a few months, treated Arius benignly and placed him in charge of the church of Baucalis, one of the churches of Alexandria (cf. Epiphanius, Haeres., 68, 4: 69, 1–2), which had its own organization of faithful and inferior clergy with a priest in charge. These priests enjoyed a certain autonomy and acted particularly as teachers and interpreters of Sacred Scriptures.

The Bishop of Alexandria, however, kept a watch on their activities and the doctrine that they taught.

As a young man Arius was trained at the school of Lucian of Antioch, the future martyr (par. 132), or at least by the disciples of Lucian. Nevertheless, we cannot affirm with certainty that Arius preserved the general lines of Lucian's doctrine; he may have insisted on certain particular aspects and neglected others altogether. The first Arians certainly claimed, rightly or wrongly, to be following the teaching of Lucian, and called themselves his disciples ("Collucianists," par. 253).

250. Arius studied the Trinity, and particularly the relations between the Father and the Logos. In substance, the following was his system.

Only the Father is truly God. He is the only God and being eternal has not become ($\gamma\epsilon\nu\eta\tau\acute{o}s$) nor has he been generated ($\gamma\acute{\epsilon}\nu\nu\eta\tau os$). The two words were synonyms for Arius. The Logos (Word, Son) is only a creature although the first and most perfect among the creatures. The Father created him from nothing ($\grave{\epsilon}\xi$ $o\grave{v}\kappa$ $\check{o}\nu\tau\omega\nu$) and proceeded through him to the creation of inferior beings. The Logos, therefore, is not truly God, but is the demiurge or intermediary between God and creatures inferior to the Logos. There was a "when" at which the Logos did not exist ($\mathring{\eta}\nu$ $\check{o}\tau\epsilon$ $o\grave{v}\kappa$ $\mathring{\eta}\nu$) but he is "without time" ($\grave{a}\chi\rho\acute{o}\nu\omega s$) and "before the ages" ($\pi\rho\grave{o}$ $a\grave{\iota}\acute{\omega}\nu\omega\nu$). Vaguely one can give him the title of God both because he is the mediator between God and his creatures, and because God adopted him as his Son foreseeing his merits. The title, however, is not correct, for he is Son by grace ($\kappa a\tau\grave{a}$ $\chi\acute{a}\rho\iota\nu$) not by nature. By his will he is determined to good, but of himself he is free and able to change ($\tau\rho\epsilon\pi\tau\acute{o}s$). Not even the Holy Spirit is God. He is the first creature of the Logos and less noble than he. Jesus Christ was not God "made man" ($\grave{\epsilon}\nu a\nu\theta\rho\omega\pi\acute{\eta}\sigma as$), but the creature Logos "infleshed" ($\sigma a\rho\kappa\omega\theta\epsilon\grave{\iota}s$). Arius, in fact, took in the strictest sense the phrase in the Gospel "the word became flesh" (Jn. 1:14), and therefore affirmed that in Jesus Christ there was only the corporeal element of human nature (flesh) since the spiritual element ($\nu o\hat{v}s$) had been taken over by the Logos.

251. It is true that some points of this arrangement of the Trinity echo earlier doctrines of the subordinationists to be found in apologetics of the second century and in the catechetical school of Alexandria; the system on the whole, however, sounds rather like the school of Antioch, Paul of Samosata, and perhaps the Lucian we mentioned

earlier. In any case, the teachings of these people had either been explicitly condemned by the Church as those of Paul of Samosata or had been presented as the private opinions of a certain school without any intention of asserting for them the status of an official doctrine of the Church. In other words, these predecessors of Arius had presented their opinions as attempts at a philosophical interpretation of dogma, leaving to the Church the last official word in regard to the essence of the dogma itself. Arius, on the other hand, gave out his system as the official teaching of the Church. His predecessors considered the Church to be over them; Arius saw himself as over the Church. He founded his doctrine — or thought he did — on the Gospel, but naturally had not read the apothegm of St. Augustine: "I would not believe in the Gospel if I was not moved thereto by the authority of the Catholic Church" (*Contra epist. Manich.*, v, 6). Although this saying had not yet been written, it was already the practice of the Church where private opinion was always subordinate to her official teaching — *sensus ecclesiae*. Arius was wrong in disregarding the traditional teaching of the Church, and precisely because his system contradicted the *sensus ecclesiae* it roused remonstrance.

Arius was very expert in propaganda. His very physical appearance gave him authority. He was already advanced in years, very tall, with drawn features and a grave, recollected manner. Like the martyr Edesius (par. 124), he dressed in a manner to recall both the philosopher and ascete wearing a short tunic with sleeves and a small cloak over it. He was gentle in manner, his speech easy and persuasive, and he was obstinate in his opinions. It seems that he possessed great learning even in profane matters (cf. Epiphanius, *Haeres.*, 69, 3). His morals were excellent.

Availing himself of such qualities he diffused his doctrines at private meetings and during his explanations of Sacred Scripture to the people, and very soon he found many followers. Although many clerics and aristocratic ladies joined him, his greatest successes were among the sacred virgins. At Alexandria the women of ascetic life were at that time very numerous and powerful, and about seven hundred of them became ardent supporters of Arius and his doctrine. This was a great help in the spreading of Arianism, and its teachings became very well known.

252. The popularity of Arianism brought the obvious reaction. Perhaps in 323, perhaps a little before (certain dates are wanting), the attention of Bishop Alexander was drawn to the doctrines being preached by the priest of the church of Baucalis. These doctrines denied the divinity of Christ, and, therefore, attacked the central doctrine of Christianity. Later it was said that it was Meletius who denounced the doctrines of Arius to Alexander (cf. Epiphanius, *Haeres.*, 69, 3). This would have been very difficult for the Meletians, if only for the reason that they would not wish to cut a poor figure before their friends, the Arians (par. 95). It is much more probable that the denunciation came from Catholics who were scandalized by what was being preached at Baucalis (cf. Sozomenus in *Hist. Eccl.*, i, 15).

Alexander realized that he had to do something, but preferred to begin with persuasion. He called a meeting of the clergy to discuss the matter of the Trinity, in which all were asked to expound their own ideas and defend them. The bishops explained the traditional orthodox teaching affirming "unity to be in the Trinity" (cf. Socrates in *Hist. Eccl.*, i, 5). Arius replied violently to the accusation of his being a follower of Sabellius. He then passed to the exposition of his own system, producing the following proofs, among others, of his theory. If the Father begot the Son, the begotten had a beginning of existence; from this it is clear that there was a "time when there was not the Son" (ἦν ὅτε οὐκ ἦν ὁ υἱός); necessarily then he had the hypostasis from nothing (ἐξ οὐκ ὄντων ἔχειν αὐτὸν τὴν ὑπόστασιν) (cf. Socrates in *ibid.*).

This proof must have seemed clear and decisive to the disciples of Arius, for we know that they then went on to say to the women: "Ehi! Have you had sons before they were begotten? Certainly not. So neither God could have a Son before he had begotten him." With theology of this kind the women were easily gained for the party. This was enough for these disciples, since their real aim was to gain proselytes.

Arius found himself with sufficient support, and so refused to obey Alexander's order to abandon his doctrine. He knew that he was followed by most of the people and many clerics in Alexandria; and even outside Egypt he could count on the support of some of the bishops of Palestine and surrounding regions. At his refusal, Alexander acted against him. He called a council of the bishops of Egypt and Libya, and placed the case of the priest of Baucalis before them. A hundred bishops took part in this council and they condemned Arius almost unanimously. Only two refused to do so — Secundus of Ptolemais and Theonas of Marmarica. As a result of this decision six priests and six deacons of Alexandria and the two recalcitrant bishops were deposed. Later, two other priests and four deacons of Marmarica who had thrown in their lot with Arius were also deposed.

A firm supporter of Alexander in these provisions was his deacon, Athanasius, who was to figure for fifty years as the most tenacious defender of orthodoxy.

253. Seeing that he had not much to hope for from the Egyptian episcopacy, Arius moved to Palestine where he was certain of finding protector bishops, either in the country itself or in the lands to the north. At first he stayed at Caesarea in the shadow of Eusebius (par. 71), the fervent origenist, who, although he had not the same ideas on the Trinity as Arius, was sufficiently similar in his doctrine to be called by Jerome *principem Arianorum*. For the rest, the other bishops of the district probably thought with Eusebius — the work of Origen in Caesarea had left its marks. Eusebius sent a letter to his colleagues in favor of the priest of Baucalis, presenting him as the object of unjust persecution. Arius did not stay silent either, and one of his letters was directed to Eusebius, the bishop of Nicomedia.

This other Eusebius was much more important in the Arian controversy than his historian namesake. One can almost say that he was more Arian than Arius; he certainly acted as supreme strategist in the fight against orthodoxy. He did not have a great speculative mind, but was amazing in his practical industry. He was an undisputed master in arranging plots and intrigues. At first he had been bishop of Berytus (Beirut) in Phoenicia, but this was too rural for his ambitions, and about 318 he managed to get himself transferred to Nicomedia — the residence of the imperial court (for the same reason after the death of Constantine, he was transferred to Constantinople). At Nicomedia, Eusebius was favored by Constantia, the wife of Licinius and sister of Constantine, and soon became very powerful in the court. To have the "grey eminence" of Nicomedia in his favor meant that Arius had a patron of the greatest power. Arius took care to insure himself of this by his letter. In it (cf. Epiphanius, *Haeres.*, 69, 6; cf. Theodoretus in *Hist. Eccl.*, i, 5) Arius calls Eusebius "Collucianist" (par. 249). He wished this to be a proud reference to the first source of their common doctrine. To this letter Eusebius replied with a complete approval of Arian teaching which gave the highest hopes to its recipient. A little later, in fact, Arius transferred to Nicomedia so as to be near Eusebius.

A letter-writing office was set up there immediately from which letters went out in all directions to find supporters among the bishops of the Empire. The Bishop of Nicomedia wrote frequently to the Bishop of Alexandria, and invited Alexander to annul the condemnation of Arius. Arius himself wrote a letter to his own bishop, reported by Athanasius (cf. *De synodis*, 16), Epiphanius (cf. *Haeres.*, 69, 7), Hilary of Poitiers, and others, in which with much caution he explains his ideas on the Trinity. What is most amazing here is his affirmation that his teaching was perfectly in accord with what he had heard preached by his bishop in Alexandria. The letter in some documents is countersigned by followers of Arius, for it was sent around for the collection of such signatures.

In the face of this epistulary activity, Alexander organized his own attack. He sent to different bishops about seventy letters (cf. Epiphanius, *ibid.*, 4) more or less on the same lines. One of these was sent to Eusebius of Caesarea, who most certainly did not read it with satisfaction. Hilary of Poitiers says that Alexander notified Pope Sylvester that Arius' followers in Alexandria had been deposed.

254. Among all this activity Arius did not forget to keep the people with him, especially those of Alexandria. About this time in Nicomedia, he prepared a literary composition, probably of prose and verse, which was to be the most efficacious method of propaganda among the lower classes. Its title was *Thalia* (θαλία) which means "banquet," or "feast," and it was certainly calculated to please the vulgar. Athanasius says that the work followed the example of Sotades, cynical philosopher and satiric poet, who flourished between the fourth and fifth centuries before Christ. He was notorious for obscene writings and was imprisoned for them, and perhaps even executed. It seems that at the early part of the fourth century B.C. the various "thalia" were songs of orgies and debauchery. Very little has come down to us of the ancient Sotades, and unfortunately we have only a few fragments of the *Thalia* of Arius quoted by Athanasius.

He interspersed his principal work with secondary compositions intended to render the propaganda more efficacious. They were short songs in popular taste, and they became, along with the *Thalia*, the poetical repertory of the sailors, millers, travelers, vagabonds, and suchlike, which are the "ἄσματά τε ναυτικὰ καὶ ἐπιμύλια καὶ ὁδοιπορικά" mentioned by the Arian Philostorgius (cf. *Hist. Eccl.*, ii, 2). It appears also that Arius himself provided melodies and musical airs, thus giving the performers both words and music. Already in ancient times the Gnostics

Bardesanes and Harmonius and the orthodox Ephraem the Syrian had used similar methods of propaganda (par. 249), but all these had kept a high standard of quality. It was the prerogative of Arianism to bring in the taverns and worse places — it became a theology of the guitar. The "chattering old women" and the "doting gossips," whom Jerome has described engrossed in theological disputes on the streets and the squares of the town (par. 248), were following the teaching of these songs.

Naturally there were continual disputes between the Arian ballad singers and the orthodox Catholics of Alexandria, and the whole city was in an uproar. The pagans were pleased at all this for it made a laughingstock of the martyrs and confessors — the new protégés of the Emperor. Parodies were composed and executed in the theaters which served as "top of the bill's" and "latest attractions." "So scandalous did the situation become," says Eusebius of Caesarea, "that in the very theaters of the unbelievers the venerable teachings of God were exposed to the most shameful ridicule" (De vita Constant., ii, 61). An "intellectual" representative of the Arian party came into the picture, a certain Asterius of Cappadocia. He was a rhetorician whom Athanasius calls a "sophist with many heads" (De synodis, 18). He had become a Christian and had followed the teaching of Lucian of Antioch; during the persecution he had, however, fallen into apostasy. For this reason he was not admitted into the Arian clergy. But he did publish propaganda more or less everywhere in the East by talking and writing. Later he was answered by Marcellus of Ancyra (par. 272).

Meanwhile, pamphlets of accusations and insults crossed each other in all directions. Synods were held by both sides and mutual excommunications flashed across the Eastern sky. Everything was in disorder, and the trouble spread rapidly to Egypt, Palestine, and Syria.

255. As a further complication about this time, Arius returned unexpectedly to Alexandria. Since the attempts of Eusebius of Nicomedia and his other bishop-protectors had not persuaded the Bishop of Alexandria to re-establish the deposed priest of Baucalis, Arius now wished to obtain the same result by circumventing the obstacle of his own bishop. He, therefore, managed to convene in Caesarea under the presidency of his protector Eusebius a synod of Palestinian bishops who readily permitted Arius and those of his followers who found themselves in the same trouble to hold meetings of the faithful and exercise their ministry as before. They added the clause, however, that

they must remain subject to their bishop Alexander, and that they should request him to readmit them to the Church (cf. Sozomenus, i, 5).

This procedure was not only unheard of before, but also self-contradictory. The synod, in fact, had no jurisdiction over Alexandria or over Arius. Although they did recommend that he should make peace with his bishop, they conceded to a censured priest what only his legitimate bishop was able to give. But this concession was enough for Arius. He moved to Alexandria where he could build up his strength, not only with the backing of the synod, but also under the protection of the sailors, millers, and others who were busy spreading the musical theology of the *Thalia* and his other works.

This was the situation when Constantine intervened as he had done in the matter of the Donatists. With his final victory over Licinius (par. 220) he had become the only Augustus and the absolute ruler of the Empire. When he arrived at Nicomedia, he was informed minutely on the new religious controversy which augured so badly. His informer was quite probably Eusebius of Nicomedia, who was the bishop of the city and the most influential ecclesiastic of the court (par. 253). The light in which Constantine saw the controversy from the start shows that he had had it explained by a supporter of Arius such as Eusebius was.

Without doubt Constantine had been unfortunate in his relations with Christians. Every time he had a great political success the Christians seemed to produce another crisis. The Donatist controversy was by no means finished and now there was more trouble. If the first looked as though it might arouse the whole of Africa, this threatened to involve the whole Empire. When Constantine had got to know the principal lines of the dispute he acted with the speed he was accustomed to use on the battlefield — and with the inexperience of Christian affairs which we have already seen. As usual he began by attempting persuasion and compromise.

He had with him his trusted counselor Hosius (par. 204), and so he sent him with a letter directed to both Alexander and Arius — the condemning bishop and the condemned priest. If these two could be made to agree, the whole trouble would be over. Here also it is easy to see the hand of Eusebius in this, secretly attempting to help those of his own party. Apart from this, the letter shows us the true mentality of Constantine.

256. The letter has been preserved for us by Eusebius (cf. *De vita Constant.*, ii, 64–72). Its authenticity has recently been questioned, but the reasons given are not convincing. The characteristic qualities of Constantine appear quite clearly in the document — his great preoccupation with public peace and his even greater ignorance of theological questions.

The letter states that Augustus, having now gained the final victory in the Empire, would have expected to have found unity and concord among the Christians. Instead, he finds in the East even worse trouble than the already serious disputes and disorders in Africa. How have they arisen? Merely from a foolish incident. Alexander one day demands from his priests their opinion "on a certain part of the matters written in the law or rather on a part of a certain unprofitable question." Arius in his turn replied imprudently, saying what he ought not to think or at least what he ought not to say (cf. *ibid.*, 69). Having presented the origin of the controversy in this way (par. 252), the letter adds that the dissension has been formed from "small and useless contests of words" (*ibid.*, 71). Such things are "vulgar things and expected of foolish children, but not suited to the good sense of priests and prudent men" (*ibid.*). Constantine says more than once that the dispute is about "small and vastly unimportant matters." Are not all Christians agreed that they must believe in the one Supreme God, the Saviour of all? Surely this is enough without bothering about questions which are beyond the normal intellectual level of the people. Let each one think within himself what he wishes, but without losing concord and mutual respect for others. The philosophers, indeed, though they are followers of a particular school of thought, still keep to certain fundamental principles — for the rest they think as they wish. Let peace therefore return. Here Constantine breaks into a sentence straight from his heart: "Give back to me therefore calm days and nights without worry; in this way I also may have pleasure in the pure light and pleasure in a tranquil life for my remaining years" (*ibid.*, 72).

These touching words show very clearly his almost morbid anxiety for public peace. The earlier statements, however, on the foolishness of theological investigation demonstrate a complete lack of understanding — we feel we are listening to senseless ravings. Constantine was, by nature, unable to consider such questions (par. 210), and besides, to be perfectly fair, he did not have the two thousand years of experience that we have now. The person, however, who furnished the theological material of his letter, almost certainly Eusebius of Nicomedia, must have known very well that the Arian controversy did not consist in "small and useless contests of words," nor did it rest on "small and vastly unimportant matters," but was concerned with whether Jesus Christ the founder of Christianity was true God or a simple creature. This was anything but a "useless inquiry."

As easily seen, the letter did not achieve what it intended and the words spent by Hosius in presenting it were quite useless. It would seem that Hosius was not overly insistent, for he realized that he was asking the impossible as soon as he was on the spot. He endeavored, however, to be of some use by taking part in a synod at Alexandria in which some local matters were discussed, i.e., concerning the invalid ordination of the bishop Colluthos and the priest Ischyras. In this synod Sabellianism was once more condemned (par. 204).

What could be done in this dangerous situation? During the course of Donatism we saw that Constantine had a weakness for synods and councils, and it is therefore probable that he thought immediately of having a council. Some modern scholars, indeed, think that at this time — that is at the beginning of 325 — a synod was actually held in Antioch in which more than fifty bishops from the districts from Palestine to Cappadocia took part. From this meeting they say that the orthodox clergy first got the idea of a great council of the Church which would definitively solve the Arian dispute. Whether this synod at Antioch really took place we do not know — there is no evidence for it.

Whatever actually did happen, it is certain that at the beginning of 325 the idea of a great council was very much in Constantine's mind and that he was already arranging for it.

THE COUNCIL OF NICAEA

257. Did the first idea of the council arise in Constantine's mind quite spontaneously, or was it suggested to him by someone? According to Eusebius (cf. *De vita Constant.*, iii, 5-6), it was entirely due to Constantine. According to the Arian Philostorgius (cf. *Hist. Eccl.*, i, 7) the suggestion first came from Alexander of Alexandria, and was made to Hosius and other bishops in Nicomedia, whence it came quite naturally to Constantine. Rufinus also says that Constantine acted ex *sacerdotum sententia* (cf. *Hist. Eccl.*, i, 1), where he is perhaps alluding to the clerical counselors of the court with Hosius at their head. It may be that all these historians are right insofar as the situation gave rise to the same idea in several people, independent of one another.

This time, also, the Emperor acted on his own initiative. He called the council, sent the letters of invitation to the various bishops, and took the first place in the inaugural session. That the convocation of the council was the personal work of Constantine is affirmed by the members of the council themselves at the beginning of their synodal letter (cf. Socrates in *Hist. Eccl.*, i, 9; Theodoretus in *Hist. Eccl.*, i, 9, cf. 7). For the rest, none of the historians of the time who treat of the preparations for the council ever mention the Bishop of Rome; it was only later that he was named in the *Liber Pontificalis*, where it speaks of Pope Sylvester. This time also, therefore, the Emperor acted as "the bishop of those outside" (par. 209), and coming into the Church, arranged things even more firmly than in the Donatist controversy (pars. 237–239). This all happened not because he considered himself the head of the Church, but because of his usual preoccupation with keeping the peace in his lands. One can add that there was a lack of efficient safeguards in the Church against such a danger.

Since the danger was even graver this time, the meeting to discuss it was larger. Up to now there had been meetings of bishops of certain regions, or groups of regions, and they had considered matters common to the lands they represented. For example, the bishops of Egypt and Lybia met in Alexandria, those of Palestine in Caesarea, those of Syria and certain regions of Asia Minor in Antioch; when the distances were great then the interests of far-off places were not considered (except in exceptional cases such as had happened with Donatism). This time, however, bishops of the most remote parts of the Empire came together; Constantine placed at the disposition of the bishops the *cursus publicus*, the horses and carriages of the imperial post. For general convenience, the city of Nicaea close to Nicomedia was chosen as the place of meeting. This city was the dwelling of the Emperor and, therefore, gave him the opportunity of joining in without leaving the center of government. It had first been suggested that the council should meet at Ancyra in the center of Asia Minor, but this was too inconvenient for the bishops of Western Europe.

258. Ancient historians disagree on the actual number of bishops.

Later a conventional number was fixed. Different figures are given by three members of the council itself; Constantine says "more than 300 bishops" (Socrates, i, 9); Eusebius of Caesarea "more than 250" (*De vita Constant.*, iii, 8); Eustathius of Antioch "about 270" (Theodoretus, i, 7–8). From the time of Athanasius and Hilary the number has usually been given as 318. It is not known, however, how this number was arrived at. If it is due to symbolism — the 318 slaves of Abraham in Genesis 14:14 — it is hardly of historic value. Regardless of how many bishops there may actually have been, the Council of Nicaea in later writers became that of "the 318 Fathers."

The list of those who took part has come down to us both incomplete and in parts doubtful — the numbers and the names differ (cf. H. Gelzer, H. Hilgenfeld, O. Cuntz, *Patrum Nicaenorum nomina*, Leipzig, 1898). It is not certain, in fact, that minutes were taken of the official acts of the council. If they were taken, we have only the list just mentioned, the synodal letter, the canons, and the creed.

The most numerous representatives were from the whole of Asia Minor, Palestine with Phoenicia and Syria, Egypt with the Thebaid; there was less representation from Achaia and the modern Balkans. There were other isolated representatives, one from Persia, that is Jacob (or James) of Nisibis who, local tradition says, was accompanied by young Ephraem the Syrian; one from the Caucasus; one from the kingdom of the Bosphorus; two from Greater Armenia. Roman Africa was represented by Caecilian of Carthage; Spain by Hosius of Cordova; Gaul and Pannonia by a bishop each; Italy by a bishop from Calabria (now modern Apulia) and by two priests from Rome. Also present were many members of the lower clergy who had come in the company of bishops, or on their own.

It was a truly solemn assembly not only because of the size, which was the greatest to date in ecclesiastical meetings, but also because of the dignity of very many of the bishops. Some of them still showed the scars of the torments undergone during the persecution. There was Hosius (par. 204); the Egyptian Paphnutius, the bishop of the Upper Thebaid, whose right eye had been torn out and tendon of the left heel cut when he was condemned to the mines (par. 88); so great was Constantine's veneration for him that he kissed the empty eye socket each time he met him (Socrates, i, 11). Other famous cripples for the faith were Paul, the bishop of Neocaesarea on the Euphrates, who had been maimed by having both the tendons of the hands burned with a hot iron (Theodoretus, i, 77); Potamon, the bishop of Heraclea on the Nile, Amphion, bishop of Epiphania in Cilicia, and others. A singular figure was Spiridion, the bishop of Trimithus, on the island of Cyprus, who had been elected bishop while he was a shepherd and continued to work as a shepherd after his consecration. He was a man of extraordinary simplicity and great virtue; many miracles had been attributed to him and to his virgin daughter, Irene, who had died earlier (Socrates, i, 12). Other bishops, beginning with Eusebius of Caesarea, were eminent in their learning and doctrine.

259. After he has made a summary list of those taking part, our witness Eusebius adds: "the most well known bishop from Spain sat with the rest; the bishop, however, of the imperial city could not attend for reason of his advanced age, but some of his priests were there to speak for him (De vita Constant., iii, 7). There is no doubt that the unnamed Spaniard is Hosius, but what is the "imperial city"? Gelasius of Cyzicus (ii, 5), and others after him, believed that it was Constantinople, but in that year New Rome was still being built (par. 223), and therefore could not yet be described as the "imperial city." Without doubt the city must be Rome, as is expressly affirmed both by Sozomenus (i, 17) — by mistake he calls the bishop of Rome Julius instead of Sylvester — and by Theodoretus (i, 7). Sozomenus also gives the names of the two Roman priests, Vitus and Vincentius.

What was the relation between Hosius and the two Roman priests? Gelasius himself, the humble compiler at the end of the fifth century, says that Hosius, together with two priests, presided at the council in the name of Pope Sylvester. This sharing of the legation is not confirmed by any authoritative document before or after Gelasius. It is true that among the signatories of the council Hosius always occupies the first place and immediately after him come the signatures of the two Roman priests. But while the two priests declare that they are signing in the name of their bishop, Sylvester, Hosius appears to sign without mentioning any authority for which he stands.

There is little to be discovered from Eusebius about the working of the council. In one place (cf. De vita Constant., iii, 13) he says that when the ceremony of inauguration was over Constantine "gave the word to the presidents of the synod." Who were these "presidents"? Was there more than one? The grammatical plural used here does not necessarily show an actual plural, for it can be considered a "categorical plural," indicating in general whoever was at the head of the meeting.

There is a clear example in the evangelists Matthew (27:44) and Mark (15:32) who speak in the plural of thieves insulting Jesus on the cross, while Luke (23:39 sq.) refers to one thief.

Before Eusebius names these president(s), he says that when Constantine had entered and was seated, the bishop who sat immediately on his right made a brief speech of welcome and thanks (*De vita Constant.*, iii, 11). This bishop would seem without doubt to have been the most distinguished in the assembly, but unfortunately Eusebius does not tell us who he was. Was it Eusebius himself? Or Alexander of Alexandria? Or Eustathius the newly elected bishop of Antioch? Both early authorities and the modern historians of the council have championed one of these three with fairly reasonable proof in all cases. But in none can there be more than probability, and so it is useless to pursue the matter. It is certain, in any case, that this first speaker was not Hosius or one of the Roman priests.

260. The inauguration of the council took place on May 20, 325, according to Socrates (i, 13). Other documents give a date a month later, but it would seem that they are referring to the end of the council.

Constantine made a great show of the affair, and treated the members of the council with sincere deference and royal munificence. Besides its religious importance, the council had great import politically, for it seemed to renew the "catholic" nationhood of the Roman Empire. The inauguration was in a very large hall of the imperial palace. The bishops, seated on both sides, awaited in silence the arrival of the Emperor. Constantine appeared, preceded by a few officials, all of whom were Christians; he was clothed in the imperial purple embroidered with gold. With the modest manner reserved by him for such occasions (pars. 60, 176), he went to his place. An elevated throne of gold had been placed at the end of the hall, but he did not use it until he had invited the bishops to take their seats. After all were seated the unnamed bishop made his speech of welcome.

Constantine was a good speaker, and replied in Latin; he could just as easily have replied in Greek, but Latin was the official language of the Empire (par. 224). His words were immediately translated into Greek. It was a sober discourse in the Christian spirit, with his usual preoccupation for the public peace (cf. Eusebius, *De vita Constant.*, iii, 12). The discussion then opened.

From what Sozomenus tells us (i, 17) it seems that the bishops had already met among themselves to select the arguments for these discussions, and perhaps also to agree on procedure. In these preliminaries Arius was also interrogated; though his bishop Alexander was present, the most effective member of this meeting was Athanasius, the deacon of Alexandria.

When the public discussion began some say that Constantine took part in it. But this happened, especially at the beginning, either to start the particular discussion, or in an attempt to reconcile opponents. In theological argument, however, the Emperor was careful to keep his mouth shut; he was intelligent and understood that this was not his territory. Had he spoken it would be interesting to know what he would have said since he had already characterized the Arian question as an "empty search" arising from "small and empty disputes over words," and "not suited to the good sense of priests and prudent men" (par. 256).

In the official discussion Arius was heard more than once (cf. Rufinus, i, 5; Sozomenus, i, 19); and it seems that he expounded his system of the Trinity faithfully and frankly. He had, indeed, powerful patrons to help and defend him, such as Eusebius of Nicomedia, Eusebius of Caesarea, Paulinus of Tyre, the local bishop of Nicaea, Theognis, and others. The words of Arius were sufficient to give a true picture of the situation; to help things along, however, passages of his *Thalia* were read. This reading, according to Athanasius, aroused lively indignation in the greater part of the assembly, and many closed their ears to its sordid string of blasphemies.

At this point the fate of Arius and his doctrine was, to all intents and purposes, decided. Since he taught that the Logos was not truly God, but a creature of God made from nothing, and that there was a "when" when the Logos did not exist (par. 250), his doctrine was proved heretical since it contradicted what the official Church had always taught (par. 251).

261. This was negative. The positive work of the council was to come when, in opposition to the heretical doctrine of Arius, the orthodox teaching on the Trinity had to be formulated, which up to this time had not been set down in detail. This was a very difficult task, for followers of different schools and members of various civilizations had to agree.

The defenders of Arius grouped themselves more or less openly around Eusebius of Nicomedia (the "Eusebians" of ancient historians), and they began by bringing forward a confession of faith contained — it would seem — in a letter of Eusebius himself, proposing it as a basis for discussion. This was so obviously heretical, however, that those present condemned it immediately, and the letter was torn up at the meeting (cf. Theodoretus, i, 7–8; Ambrose, De fide, iii, 15, in Migne, Patr. Lat., xvi, 614).

It was the intention of the council to formulate the doctrine that the Logos was God and the true Son of God, and it proposed to do this by using the terms found in Sacred Scripture, which were acceptable to everyone. But it was quickly found that such terminology would be insufficient. The Arians would have accepted such a formulary, but they added that from various passages of Scripture it was proved that men were the sons of God, created to the image of God (cf. Athanasius, De decretis nicaenae synod., 19–20; Epist. ad Afros, 5). Thus they would accept in a large and metaphorical sense the doctrine of the Logos which was taught by the orthodox in a strict and ontological manner.

Eusebius of Caesarea spoke. He was, as usual, helpful to the Arians, though not wholeheartedly committed to their cause. He was always anxious to find a middle way, and thus show himself as a peacemaker to the Emperor. He proposed, as a basis of discussion, the baptismal creed used in Caesarea, but coming originally from Rome. Eusebius himself tells, in a letter directed to his people in Caesarea, how this was received. The text has been handed down to us, not by himself but by other historians (cf. Socrates, i, 8; Theodoretus, i, 12; Gelaius of Cyzicus, ii, 34; Athanasius, De decretis nicaenae synod., 3). The letter, however, contains the usual omissions and dissimulations of which Eusebius was the master. To hear him it would seem that the creed which he had proposed was then definitively approved by the council and supported by Constantine. In reality, the creed approved by the council contained certain points of fundamental importance that Eusebius' text could not have contained. The more important of these was the word "consubstantial."

Constantine made this word a sine qua non. If the creed did not affirm that the Logos was "consubstantial" with the Father then it ought not to be approved. But who suggested this word? It was certainly not Constantine himself, who was no theologian (par. 256). It must, therefore, have been one of his most authoritative and influential counselors.

262. At that time the word already had a long history. It had been used by Paul of Samosata, the author of Modalism, which taught that the Logos was the same "substance" as the Father, but in a different modality. His doctrine, however, had been condemned in the Synod of Antioch in 269. This synod, in fact, had interpreted Paul's doctrine in the sense that the Logos was not only the same "substance" or "essence" as the Father but also the same "person." This denied any real distinction between the Logos and the Father. On the other hand, toward 263, a discussion had arisen between Pope Dionysius of Rome and Bishop Dionysius of Alexandria concerning the use of the term "consubstantial," which had come into common Catholic use in Rome, while Dionysius of Alexandria had avoided using it. The Bishop of Alexandria had been reproved for this by the Bishop of Rome.

The truth is that at those times the word "consubstantial" and other terms connected with it, for example, "hypostasis," had not the precise and unequivocal sense that they gained later — especially after the Christological struggles of the fifth century. Athanasius himself was able to affirm that the "hypostasis is essence," ἡ ὑπόστασις οὐσία ἐστίν (*Epistula ad Afros,* 4; in Migne, *Patr. Gr.,* 26, 1036), but he gave the term a meaning quite different from that given it later by the Nestorians or the Monophysites. The word "consubstantial" (ὁμοούσιος: "same essence") signifies etymologically that one essence can be predicated of two distinct hypostasis. But in the case of the Divine Trinity, what was the meaning of the word "essence" — οὐσία? Paul of Samosata had interpreted it in the sense of "person"; therefore, for him the Logos was the same person as the Father, although in a different mode (Modalism).

The pope Dionysius, however, interpreted it according to the Roman tradition in the sense of "nature." He understood, therefore, that the Logos was of the same nature as the Father. In such a tradition the Logos was "consubstantial" with the Father insofar as he was of the same "substance" or "nature" (ὀυσία) of the Father, although not the same person.

The West, however, which used the term "consubstantial" quite happily, and the East, which did not like it, were both under the influence of struggles which had taken place in their territories during the preceding century. The East had fought against Sabellius and Paul of Samosata, who denied any real distinction in the Trinity. The West had been influenced much less by these heresies, and its greatest preoccupation had been to safeguard the perfect divinity of the Logos who, although distinct from the Father, was one true God like Him. 263. At the Council of Nicaea there were present bishops who, although they were perfectly orthodox, had leanings toward the teachings of Origen or Lucian of Antioch. There were present others, equally orthodox, who did not concern themselves with schools, but were supremely occupied with upholding the traditional faith of the Church (cf. Sozomen, i, 17), beginning with the unity of God and the divinity of the Logos. On each of these groups the term "consubstantial" made a different impression. The Origenists and the Lucianists were interested to see whether or not the unity of God and the divinity of the Logos could be reconciled with their particular school. The Traditionalists examined the matter closely to see if the term was supported by Sacred Scripture or by the documents of orthodox tradition.

There was nothing to be found in Scripture for in it the word "consubstantial" is never used for the Trinity. This deficiency would have been of little moment, indeed, if the word had had some practical value in expressing orthodox tradition and if it had already been generally used in the Church. The word had indeed been used in Rome by certain Greek writers, including Origen; its sense, however, remained equivocal, since it could refer to the unity of "nature" or the unity of "person."

Under such conditions the question would remain unsettled if a new factor did not enter the discussion, saving the question from a lingering death by putting it on the way to a practical solution. This factor had to be outside the predominant parties in the Council, that is, independent of the schools and tendencies of the eastern Mediterranean which in general balanced each other. The only thing was to find some western — that is, Roman — factor.

Philostorgius the Arian (i, 7) attributes the choice of the term "consubstantial" to the conversations which Alexander of Alexandria had before the council with Hosius and the other bishops who were with him in the imperial court of Nicomedia. For his part, the orthodox Athanasius (cf. *Hist. Arianorum ad monachos*, 42) seems to say somewhat more than Philostorgius, for he affirms that Hosius was the one who expounded the faith (established) in Nicaea. The natural explanation of these words is that they allude to the most delicate and important term included in the Nicene creed — "consubstantial."

These various indications tally well with our earlier considerations. Hosius and the two priests sent by Pope Sylvester represented the West and Rome, and this placed them apart from the contending parties and above the struggle. If, therefore, Constantine imposed the word "consubstantial" as a *conditio sine qua non* for the approbation of the Creed (par. 261), then he did this almost certainly at the suggestion of Hosius, his most trusted theological adviser.

264. The intervention of Constantine was decisive, not because he proposed new theological arguments, but because he had power behind him. Acting as the chief of the forces of public security the Emperor threatened exile to any who refused to sign the Creed in the form approved by the council with the inclusion of the word "consubstantial." Before this threat the adversaries of the Creed gave in, whether they were Lucianists or Philo-Arians — none of them had very strong vertebrae anyway. The only dissentients were Arius, two Libyan bishops, Theonas of Marmarico, and Secundus of Ptolemais, along with some priests of Alexandria who were friends of Arius. These were immediately sent into exile in Illyricum. The others avoided the penalty by signing the Creed, albeit with hesitation and mixed feelings. Among these halfhearted signatories were Eusebius of Nicomedia, Theognis of Nicaea (par. 260), and also, it is superfluous to say, Eusebius of Caesarea, the Talleyrand of the Constantinian court. It is likewise unnecessary to add that these men kept their counsel in expectation of better times.

Arian sources, in later years (Philostorgius, i, 8) relate that Eusebius of Nicomedia, Theognis, and certain others did not sign the authentic text bearing the term "consubstantial" but an altered text bearing the words "of similar essence" (ὁμοιούσιος; cf. par. 262). This story has all the earmarks of a pitiful invention which was only intended to cover up the inglorious capitulations of the Arian leaders.

265. It is not certain who actually composed the Creed approved by the council. This is, in any case, of secondary importance. Athanasius and Philostorgius say that it was done by Alexander of Alexandria and Hosius — especially the latter. According to Hilary of Poitiers, Athanasius had a hand in it. Basil (cf. *Epist.*, 81) says that the deacon or priest Hermogenes, who was later the bishop of Caesarea in Cappadocia, had the task of writing out the text and reading it to the council. It is permissible to think that various people helped, and that there were successive revisions; it is also probable that the basis of its formulation, besides the text of Caesarea proposed by Eusebius (par. 261), was the baptismal creed in use at Jerusalem.

The Nicene Creed is reported by various sources (cf. Socrates, i, 8; Theodoretus, i, 12; iv, 3; Athanasius, *De decretis nicaenae synod.*; Gelasius of Cyzicus, ii, 35; etc.) which differ slightly. They are again different from the text which the Council of Chalcedon in 451 obtained direct from the Church at Nicaea. We give here the text recorded by the most authoritative historian of the council, Socrates, putting variants in parentheses:

"We believe in one God only, the Father, Omnipotent maker of all things, visible and invisible. And in one Lord only, Jesus Christ, the Son of God, the only begotten of the Father, that is from the essence of the Father, (God from God, Light from Light) true God from True God; begotten not made, consubstantial with the Father by whom were made all things (whether in heaven or on the earth). Who for us men and for our salvation came down, was made flesh, became man, suffered, rose the third day, went up to heaven and will come to judge the living and dead; and in the Holy Spirit."

"Those then who say that there was a 'when' at which he did not exist; or that before he was begotten he did not exist; or that he was made from nothing or from another hypostasis (ὑποστάσεως) or essence (ὀυσίας), or that the Son of God is a created being, changeable or variable; those the catholic (and divine apostolic) church condemns."

266. After the question of Arius the council turned to other urgent matters, especially the affair of Meletius and the schism caused by him (par. 95).

Officially, for the moment, the schismatics were reconciled. In reality, however, the divisions remained, and had led to other disorders. Athanasius who knew all about it speaks of this reconciliation with plain hostility (cf. *Apolog. contra Arianos*, 71), for he realized that it was mostly fictitious. It was not that he thought the council had done wrong in being so indulgent, but that he considered such kindness was not the best method with rebels and schemers. Later events proved Athanasius right. It would not be very dangerous to suppose that in this matter the council also acted through the inspiration and suggestions of Constantine, who was always thinking of peace and quiet at all costs. However it may have been, Meletius was left with the episcopal dignity in his town of Lycopolis, but was forbidden to exercise his powers. This would suggest that some other bishop was put in his place, if there was not already a Catholic one in the town. The clergy ordained by Meletius in all parts of Egypt were allowed to continue, provided that they joined the Catholic clergy and remained subordinate to them. Before this they had had to undergo a ceremony which seems to have been a new imposition of hands (cf. Socrates, i, 9; Theodoretus, i, 9). When a Catholic bishop died he was to be replaced by a Meletian reconciled and approved by the metropolitan Alexander. In this way the full incorporation of Meletians in the Catholic clergy would gradually be achieved.

267. The next matter to be discussed was the date on which Easter was to be celebrated. The Christian feast had grown up in connection with the Hebrew Pasch when Jesus Christ had been killed. The Hebrew celebration always fell on the fourteenth day of the Hebrew month Nisan (March-April), that is, at the full moon of the month which was the first of the year and was a lunar one like the rest of the Jewish calendar. In the beginning the Christians celebrated their Easter on the same day as the Hebrew Pasch. But from the time of Pope Victor the custom had come in of transferring it to the Sunday after the 14th Nisan. There was a further difficulty in deciding the exact dates of the month Nisan, for the Jews did this in a very empirical way without taking account of the equinox on March 21. The Jewish custom was followed by many Christian communities in Syria, with Antioch at their head, and also in Mesopotamia and perhaps even in Cilicia. The uncertain methods of the Jews, however, led to grave practical inconvenience and the community at Alexandria had decided on their own method of fixing the date of Easter. They disregarded the Jewish dating and took the equinox into account. The Christian Easter must fall not only after the 14th Nisan, but also after the equinox. This system had been adopted by Southern, Western, and Northern Christians and also by some in the East, except for those mentioned earlier. This variation of the time when Easter was celebrated meant that frequently one community was in mourning and penance for the Passion of Christ when another was in joy and exultation at His Resurrection (such a discrepancy still occurs between the Church of Milan and that of Rome in regard to the beginning of the Lenten fast). A precise decree of the council removed this difficulty by obliging all Christian communities to follow the custom of Alexandria. The decree was generally carried out, but here and there there were exceptions. John Chrysostom, in one of his sermons, mentions Christians who still followed the ancient use of Antioch.

After Arianism and the date of Easter there were still various questions of discipline. The council attended to these with twenty canons. They were all topical regulations, provoked by contemporary circumstances and not intended as a complete legislation. The canons group themselves around four matters: the remnants of old schisms and heresies; the results of the last persecution under Licinius; discipline of the clergy; and questions of ecclesiastical jurisdiction. Here are the canons in short.

268. 1. Admission to the clerical state is forbidden for voluntary eunuchs.

2. It is also forbidden to neophytes.

3. Members of the clergy must not keep in their house a woman who is not their mother, sister, aunt, or a woman above all suspicion.

4. It is prescribed that the bishop should be consecrated by his colleagues in the province; if all are not able to be present, there must be at least three and absentees must give their consent to the consecration in writing; the metropolitan bishop must authorize the induction.

5. A person who has been excommunicated in one place must not be reconciled in another. If anyone wishes to appeal against a penalty which he feels is unjust, he can do so; the bishops of a province must meet twice a year, before Lent and in the autumn, to examine these appeals.

6. The rights and pre-eminence of certain ancient sees, such as those of Alexandria and Antioch, are to be preserved. The bishop of Alexandria is to keep his rights over the churches of Egypt, Libya, and Pentapolis "since this is customary also to the bishop of Rome."

7. The prerogatives of the bishop of Aelia Capitolina (Jerusalem) are to be preserved, but without interference with the rights of the metropolitan (Caesarea).

8. The Novatians who wish to be reconciled are to be received, but on condition that they declare in writing that they accept the dogmas of the Catholic Church, and that they will accept people who have married a second time and reconciled *lapsi.*

9. Anyone who is found guilty of crime before ordination is to be deposed from the clerical state.

10. The ecclesiastical *lapsus* (during the persecution of Licinius) is also to be deposed.

11. The *lapsi* who fell without any threat or danger will remain eleven years in the state of penitents, passing through the various degrees of this condition.

12. The *lapsi* who at first resigned their offices under the government for the sake of their faith but then despising the grace (of martyrdom) have taken them back or asked for them once more are to be punished more severely. Nevertheless the bishops are allowed to shorten the period of penitence if this seems to cause great hardship.

13. The Viaticum (of the Eucharist) is to be given to all the dying who ask for it; it must not be given without previous examination of the case.

14. Those who fell (into idolatry) are to be deprived, for three years, of the right of praying with the catechumens.

15. Bishops, priests, and deacons must not pass from one church to another.

16. Clerics belonging to one church must not be received into another. If a bishop ordains a cleric of another church without the consent of the candidate's bishop, the ordination will be illicit.

17. Clerics who practice usury are to be deposed.

18. Deacons are not to sit with the priests and are not to distribute the Eucharist to them.

19. The followers of Paul of Samosata who return to the Catholic Church are to be rebaptized. After this their clerics may be ordained once more and exercise their offices in the Catholic Church. Similar dispositions are to be observed for deaconesses.

20. The ancient custom must be observed of praying standing, and not kneeling on Sundays and in the fifty days after Easter.

These canons were accepted in all the churches of the East and the West, and were included in the official collections of ecclesiastical legislation where they were given first place. This honor had not been given to the canons of earlier councils of the East or the West — earlier canons had had force only in certain regions.

269. With these labors the council had finished its task, and after a month's session it ended, perhaps on June 19 (par. 260). On the occasion of the formal closure, Constantine gave a solemn banquet to the members of the council — it was also the twentieth anniversary of his assumption of the imperial power.

In describing this banquet, Eusebius of Caesarea takes on a lyrical tone (cf. *De vita Constant.*, iii, 15). He did indeed recite for the occasion a panegyric in praise of the Emperor, and his description is obviously based on what he said at the time. As the bishops entered, the soldiers of the guard formed up along the two sides of the hall and presented their gleaming arms. The most distinguished bishops sat at Constantine's table and the others took their places at tables arranged down the hall. All this could hardly have seemed real to many of those taking part — one of them asked if this was the beginning of the kingdom of Christ on earth. So the story goes. We hope that there were few who could identify the kingdom of Christ with the power of Constantine in so Eusebian and foolish a way. All, however, could recall that those shining swords and lances only fifteen years before had pierced the living flesh of the martyrs. Through the merits of the fallen heroes there was now feasting and the Emperor was able to kiss with reverence the mutilated limbs of the survivors there present.

Rich gifts were distributed to the bishops, and plentiful alms for the poor of their churches. When the day of separation came, Constantine — who made speeches willingly — made one to those who were leaving, recommending as usual peace and harmony. He also urged other virtues worthy of bishops such as a zeal for the conversion of the unbelievers. Like Galerius on his deathbed, he asked all to pray for him (par. 154).

Even if official minutes were not taken at the council (par. 258) its decisions were certainly carried to the principal churches by messengers. A message was sent from the council itself to the church of Alexandria (cf. Socrates, i, 9; Theodoretus, i, 9; Gelasius of Cyzicus, ii, 33). Constantine, who had convened the council and had partly seen to its direction, felt he ought to do the same with the Eastern churches (cf. Eusebius, *De vita Constant.*, iii, 17–20; Socrates, i, 9) and with the church of Alexandria (cf. Socrates, i, 9; Gelasius, ii, 37). The doubts raised by recent scholars on the authenticity of these letters have very little basis in fact.

270. Constantine felt satisfied with the work of the Council of Nicaea. Arianism had been condemned; its author was in exile; all the bishops

of the council, except for two, had signed the creed. Victory seemed complete. In his message to the church of Alexandria he announced solemnly that every division and all discord had been dispelled from the splendor of the truth by the will of God.

Looking more closely, however, we can see that the reality was quite different. A critical observer would have seen that even if almost all the bishops had signed, many heads of important Christian communities had done so without internal consent and sometimes with sheer dislike. They were not able to withstand the Emperor, for his wish was more powerful than any theological argument for these courtier bishops. Chief among the critics were Eusebius of Nicomedia, Theognis of Nicaea, and Eusebius of Caesarea (par. 264). The first two were rough and intolerant, and the third was subtle and adaptable; all three were more or less favorable to Arius and convinced that the term "consubstantial" was erroneous.

The first two, keeping their forced silence for only a short time, soon began to show their favor to those condemned in the council. Constantine, however, was too enthusiastic about his work at Nicaea, and could not allow it to be spoiled so quickly. The two nonconformists were sent into exile in Gaul, and two other bishops were elected to their sees. Another nonconformist, but not so obvious, was Theodotus of Laodicea in Syria, who showed his feelings by his speeches and favors to the Arians. With him, Constantine was not so harsh. He merely wrote him a letter of warning without referring to the unpleasant example of the two exiled bishops. All this happened toward the end of the very year in which the council had been held. The shortness of the time which elapsed before trouble began again was very instructive for those who wished to learn.

Eusebius of Caesarea was more astute and very wary; he avoided the imprudence of his two exiled colleagues. He saw that the time was not suitable for open revolt, and so keeping his true feelings to himself, he shut himself up to work in the archives at Caesarea. Thus, because he avoided any clash with Constantine, the Emperor came to esteem him more and more as the most learned man of his times. Among other things the Emperor entrusted to him, as the most expert in such matters, the preparation of fifty copies of the whole of Sacred Scripture in Greek, of which the churches of newly built Constantinople had need (cf. De vita Constant., iv, 26–37).

AFTER NICAEA

271. It was destiny, however, that whenever Constantine meddled in Church affairs, he only made matters worse. This happened in the case of the Donatists, and so also now with the Arians. After Nicaea, Arianism was only apparently put down, and it continued to spread and grow, notwithstanding the imperial measures taken against it. The last years of the Emperor's life were saddened by Arianism. He never achieved the peace for which he so much longed.

Arianism, from Nicaea until the death of Constantine, resembles a tangled thicket from the exploration of which it is very difficult to extricate oneself. We are therefore forced to present the events in a form of list — a dry chronicle.

Already in the two years after the council there were many letters in circulation, written by bishops who had signed the decisions of the council — many of them show special unhappiness and distaste for the word "consubstantial." The orthodox Eustathius of Antioch accused Eusebius of Caesarea of contradicting the decision of Nicaea, and he was answered by the counteraccusation of Sabellianism (cf. Socrates, i, 23).

In 328, Eusebius of Nicomedia and Theognis of Nicaea were called back from their exile (par. 270) and restored to their sees. Probably Constantine decided to do this through the intercession of Licinius' widow, his sister Constantia, who had particular respect for Eusebius.

After his return, Eusebius of Nicomedia once more took up his work against the decisions of the council, directing his energies especially toward Antioch where the orthodox bishop Eustathius was faced with a strong opposition party of the disciples of Lucian.

Also in 328 Bishop Alexander died in Alexandria, and on June 7 Athanasius was elected in his place. Both were great champions of the Nicene decrees.

About 330 the work of Eusebius of Nicomedia showed fruit in Antioch. He had regained the confidence of the wavering Constantine, and managed to blacken Eustathius of Antioch in the Emperor's sight by theological pretexts, and perhaps by accusing him of speaking with little respect of the Empress's mother Helena by referring to her earlier life (par. 11). The result was that a synod, in which Eusebius of Nicomedia and his namesake of Caesarea with other bishops favorable to Arianism took part, deposed Eustathius. Constantine then sent him into exile where he died a little later. In his place after various events — among which is notable the refusal of Eusebius of Caesarea to accept the see of Antioch, bringing high praise for his modesty from Constantine — a priest of Caesarea in Cappadocia called Euphronius was elected. He was anti-Nicene.

272. Between 331 and 332 grave disorders, provoked by the Meletians and the Arians, occurred in Alexandria. Despite the Nicaean decrees (par. 266), the Meletians were not really reunited with the Catholics, and from the death of Meletius about the year 326 they had been led by John Arkaph, the bishop of Memphis. For their part, the Arians stirred up trouble hoping for an amnesty for Arius. Eusebius of Nicomedia fanned the flames in Egypt from a safe distance.

Despite all this, Constantine clung firmly to his Council of Nicaea and its condemnation of Arius. About this time a campaign was launched against Marcellus, the bishop of Ancyra. It lasted for some time. This solid defender of Nicaea had attacked among others Asterius, the "intellectual" of Arianism (par. 254), and had written a work against him, though without formulating very precisely the orthodox doctrine. Constantine ordered a synod of court bishops to be held at Constantinople to examine the book. They found the book infected with Sabellianism and condemned it. Marcellus was sent into exile. Eusebius of Caesarea, to strengthen the condemnation, wrote a work, *Contra Marcellum*, and went over much the same ground in another writing, *De ecclesiastica theologia*.

Toward the beginning of 332, the Meletian bishop John Arkaph sent to the imperial court four of his suffragans, Ision, Eudemon, Callinicus, and Jeracammon, to accuse Athanasius of imposing a tribute of linen tunics on the Egyptians. This accusation was immediately shown to be false by Athanasius' own friends in court. New accusations were then made: that Athanasius had broken a chalice which a priest called Ischares used for the Eucharist and — a very telling charge — that he had given money to a certain Philomen suspected of treason. Constantine called Athanasius to court. Athanasius answered the summons and, with the help of Ablavius the prefect of the praetorian guard, proved himself innocent on all charges without much difficulty. He was back at Alexandria by the Easter of 332.

Constantine was very much irritated with the troublesome Egyptians, whether Arians or Meletians. He gave Athanasius a letter containing grave threats to those who broke the public peace, with special mention of the Meletians (cf. Athanasius, *Apolog. contra Arianos*, 61–62). About a year later he sent to Alexandria two officials of the court, Syncletius and Gaudentius, with two letters. In one directed to the bishops, he ordered drastic action to be taken against the writings of Arius and his followers who were called "Porphyrians." The other letter, directed to Arius and his followers, is very long and vehement and is partly a reply to a manifesto sent by Arius, in which he had boasted of the numbers of his party. At the end — changing the tone unexpectedly — he invites Arius to come to court to justify himself before the "man of God." The "man of God" was Constantine (the two letters are found, respectively, in Socrates, i, 9; Gelasius of Cizicum, ii, 37; iii, init.).

273. Arius, suspecting a trick, did not come. Instead, feeling secure in the protection of Constantia, the Emperor's sister, he continued to work quietly for his own ends at court. During 334 Constantia warmly recommended to Constantine a priest under her protection who was a secret follower of Arius. This priest spoke favorably to the Emperor about his leader showing him to be perfectly orthodox, but persecuted by jealous enemies. When Constantia fell ill she asked her brother as a last consolation before she died to save the Empire by ceasing to persecute the innocent and by recalling the exiled (cf. Rufinus, i, 11; Socrates, i, 25; Sozomenus, ii, 27).

This last request had its effect. Constantine sent Arius a letter dated November 27 — it would seem of 334 — which contained a new invitation couched in pleasant terms. Arius presented himself with Euzoios, his ally in doctrine and exile. He left with the Emperor a wary profession of faith (cf. Socrates, i, 26; Sozomenus, ii, 27) which could be interpreted either in the Arian or the orthodox sense but which did not contain the word "consubstantial." Constantine was content, revoked his sentence of exile, and ordered that Arius should be readmitted to his rank in the clergy. Arius' ecclesiastical superior, Athanasius, however, refused to accept him. On the other hand, the mild character of his profession of faith (as the Arians understood it) lost to Arius a certain number of his followers who considered that he had changed his doctrine.

The refusal of Athanasius to receive Arius back was not well received in court. The Arians and the Meletians of Egypt took advantage of this to bring forward old and new accusations against the prime defender of Nicaea. Once again we hear of the broken chalice of Ischares (par. 272); of a Meletian bishop called Arsenius who lost a hand and was then killed by order of Athanasius. There were other stories of this kind. Constantine was particularly impressed by the accusation about Ischares and Arsenius and instructed his stepbrother to make inquiries. The result of the inquiry was that Ischares made a written declaration that his chalice had not been broken. Arsenius was found quite alive, and with both hands, in an Egyptian monastery where he had been hidden by the Meletians.

A synod had already been fixed at Caesarea in Palestine to give the final blow to Athanasius. Since all the charges had collapsed it was called off and Constantine sent Athanasius a letter full of praise for him and of blame for his calumniators. After this John Arkaph was reconciled with Athanasius; Constantine also sent a letter praising him and inviting him to court (cf. documents in Athanasius, *Apolog. contra Arianos*, 64–70).

After a short time, however, at the beginning of 335, trouble began once more. Arkaph, now in court, had plotted with other Meletians and Arians against Athanasius. The Emperor, to quiet all controversy, had recourse to his usual idea of a council.

THE COUNCIL OF TYRE

274. The moment seemed suitable for a council. This year, 335, marked the tenth anniversary of Nicaea and the thirtieth of Constantine's accession. In addition, the Basilica of the Holy Sepulcher in Jerusalem (par. 229) was now finished and had to be consecrated. It was ordered, therefore, that before the consecration of the new basilica a council should be held at Tyre not far to the north of Jerusalem. Thus, every disagreement would be removed. Acting once more like a bishop, Constantine, in a letter (cf. *De vita Constant.*, iv, 42), presented the council with a program of its labors. Concord must be restored; the Emperor would co-operate with the efforts of the bishops and any who refused to appear before them would be dragged there by the police. It is easy to see that this last ordinance was directed especially at Athanasius.

The council met in July. Constantine did not take part, but sent as his representative the Count Flavius Dionysius who — with a good force of troops — was to act much the same part as that which Constantine played at Nicaea. The most ardent supporters of Arius presented themselves; with the old ones, such as Eusebius of Nicomedia, Eusebius of Caesarea, Theognis of Nicaea, and others, there were new followers such as the two young bishops of Pannonia, Ursacius of Singidunum (Belgrade) and Valens of Mursa, who were both to be very prominent Arians of the future. Neutrals and those favoring Athanasius, such as Alexander of Thessalonica, were very few. In all about sixty bishops took part in the council (cf. Socrates, i, 28).

Athanasius left Alexandria on July 10, accompanied by about fifty Egyptian bishops. They were not admitted to the council, however, and only Athanasius was allowed to appear in the role of defendant. Theological matters were not brought up but the usual accusations (Ischares, Arsenius) were adduced both by Meletians and by Arians and other new charges were leveled. Athanasius was said to have ordered five Meletian bishops to be struck; to have deposed and replaced Callinicus, the Meletian bishop of Pelusium; to have used frequent violence against ex-Meletian bishops. Later it was said, but it seems without foundation, that Athanasius was accused by a woman of assault (cf. Rufinus, i, 17).

Athanasius defended himself as best he could. The case of Arsenius collapsed, for Arsenius himself was the living proof of Athanasius' innocence. In the matter of Ischares it was decided to send a commission to Egypt to make inquiries. The commission was chosen from the enemies of Athanasius, and this drew protests not only from Bishop Alexander of Thessalonica, but also from Dionysius, the imperial commissar, although he was not favorable to Athanasius. The commission set off, however, and on its arrival in Egypt was helped in every way by Philagrius the prefect. The testimony of those defending Athanasius was not heard and the commission returned to Tyre with a very one-sided case against Athanasius.

275. The council now lost all semblance of order. Athanasius was shouted down when he tried to speak, and was spat on by the members of the council. He was accused of being possessed by the devil, and his life was threatened. To avoid this danger, the imperial officials got him out of the council chamber by a secret door. Athanasius set sail for Constantinople to confer with the Emperor.

In his absence the council cast sentence on him. He was deposed from his see and must never appear in Alexandria again. John Arkaph and the other Meletians removed by Athanasius were put back. Information of this action was given both to the Emperor and to the principal churches.

After considerable difficulty, Athanasius finally managed to have a conference with the Emperor at Constantinople, and to inform him of the true state of affairs. The Emperor was taken aback, but did not yet give up his trust in the Council of Tyre. He called the bishops of the council to see him at Constantinople (cf. Athanasius, *Apolog. contra Arianos*, 86). This invitation was not welcomed by most of the bishops who disappeared from the stage; only the trustees of Constantine came to see him — the two Eusebiuses, with a few others. They did not repeat the accusations of the late council in regard to the cases of Ischares and Arsenius. They now said that Athanasius had hindered the transport of grain from Alexandria to Constantinople. As soon as this charge was mentioned the Emperor felt for his new capital and lost all common sense and justice. Without further inquiry he sent Athanasius into exile at Treviri a long way away from the seat of trouble.

Meanwhile, the bishops of the council moved to Jerusalem to consecrate the new basilica on September 14. On this occasion they absolved Arius from all censure and restored his ecclesiastical position. A letter was sent to all the churches of Alexandria and to Egypt, the Thebaid, Libya, and Pentapolis explaining what had been done at Jerusalem and ordering it to be recognized (cf. Athanasius, *Apolog. contra Arianos*, 84; *De synodis*, 21).

THE DEATH OF ARIUS

276. After all this it must have seemed to the members of the Tyre-Jerusalem Council that the old troubles were at an end. Arius had conquered and his adversary Athanasius was in exile.

Looked at impartially it was obvious that they had solved nothing, but had only changed the line of argument. Instead of the old theological question of whether the "Logos" was "consubstantial" with the Father or not, the question now was whether Athanasius had broken the chalice of Ischares and cut off the hand of Arsenius. Just as too much enthusiasm can lead a losing card player to arrange the deal when he sees his chance, so also it is true that little can be gained by attempting to lie in hot blood. Here also the same lesson could have been learned — scarcely two years after his defeat at Tyre Athanasius returned, in 337, to Alexandria as the rightful bishop.

The first person to realize the consequences of the council was the one who had got the idea of a council in the first place — Constantine. It had been quite easy for him to send Athanasius into exile far away in Treviri where the Emperor had lived for many years and Athanasius had never been; it was not quite so easy to put right the situation in Alexandria and the affairs of Arius himself.

At Alexandria the Arians had made a great noise — far more noise than their number warranted. When the orthodox Catholics found out what had happened to their Bishop, whom they liked very much, they began to make a noise too — quite as loud as their opponents. There were demonstrations in the churches and squares; petitions were sent to the Emperor begging the return of the exile; connected with these petitions was the great Anthony, the famous hermit who during the persecution had appeared to help the martyrs (par. 111), and who now fought for the persecuted (cf. Sozomenus, ii, 31). Anthony wrote several times on the matter to Constantine and the Emperor — who honored him enough to ask by letters his prayers for himself and his children — was not able to leave unanswered his letters in defense of Athanasius. But his reply was that of a simple but obstinate man who found himself in difficulty. He said that an assembly of such learned bishops could not have been mistaken, and that the condemned man had merited his punishment by his quarreling and insolence. The Emperor was even firmer with the people of Alexandria, especially clerics and pious women. He wrote recommending calm, since the sentence could not be changed. And, to emphasize his recommendation, he had some of the clergy imprisoned or exiled.

Meanwhile, elated by their successes, even the Meletians began to agitate and John Arkaph began intrigues to increase his power. But for him also things went wrong, for he was sent into exile and the Arians who regarded him as a valuable friend could do nothing to help him.

277. It was difficult for Constantine to put Arius in his place, for the latter had his own plans. He had triumphed at last, and his whole desire was to enjoy his victory in Alexandria whence his opponent had

now been driven. Such a wish was natural to a man like Arius. We do not know for certain exactly what did happen.

According to our usual informants (cf. Rufinus, i, 12–13; Socrates, i, 37; Sozomenus, ii, 29) Arius went with some of his supporters to Alexandria. There, however, the Catholics would not receive him in their churches, and his arrival was a signal for uproar in the city. This was the last thing that Constantine wanted, and so to quiet things down the Emperor called Arius to Constantinople to give an explanation of the disorders. He said he would give him a greater satisfaction than that which had been denied him in Alexandria. If he had not been received in the churches there, Arius would be received in the church of Constantinople, the capital of the Empire.

Constantine, however, always personally faithful to the Council of Nicaea, wished to assure himself first that the faith of Arius was orthodox and in conformity with the decrees of Nicaea. He therefore made him make a signed declaration of this. The Emperor-theologian was then satisfied, and called in the bishop of Constantinople, Alexander, and ordered him to receive Arius in his church. The Bishop was orthodox, and although he did not give an answer to the Emperor decided that he would not receive Arius. He gave an open refusal to Eusebius of Nicomedia and other protectors of Arius who were urging him with prayers and menaces.

It was the afternoon of a Saturday in 336, and the following Sunday Arius was to be received in the church. During that afternoon — or according to other sources, the following morning — Arius was walking with some friends around the city showing himself off before his great triumph. At a certain point he felt the needs of nature and he asked if there were any conveniences near at hand. He was near the great column of porphyry which rose in the Forum of Constantine (pars. 223–224) and he was shown to a place behind the Forum. He went in and left a servant outside. After some time, shouting of people was heard inside, and when the servant went in he found Arius stretched out on the ground surrounded by his bowels. He was already dead.

This is the traditional story on which, as was natural, various additions were made later. Athanasius, the great opponent of the dead man, says nothing of the visit of Arius to Alexandria but speaks of his death with noble reserve on two occasions in the *Epistola ad Serapionem de morte Arii* (in Migne, *Patr. Gr.*, 25, 685–689), which is wholly concerned with the matter and also in the *Epistola ad episcopos Aegypti et Libyae,* 19 (*ibid.,* 581). At the time, Athanasius was in exile at Treviri, but a priest of his called Macarius was in Constantinople, and Athanasius got his information from him.

Of the tragic event other orthodox writers speak later, such as Epiphanius, Gregory of Nazianzen, Ambrose, and Gaudentius. But their historical reliability in this matter is not very great. For their part the Arians who had suffered a great public moral blow by this death, started the rumor that their leader's end had been caused by the witchcraft of his enemies.

VI. THE DEATH OF THE NEOPHYTE

278. The life of Constantine was drawing to a close, and his final years were far from tranquil. In the last eleven years of his life, from the Council of Nicaea, he shed much blood including some of his own family and colleagues. For the suppression of his father-in-law (pars. 66–67) and that of his brother-in-law (par. 220) good reasons could be given, but for the killings in the last years of his life it is difficult to find a reason. These acts, apart from being very unpleasant in themselves, are covered by the veil which we have already found in the life of Constantine. The crimes are in semidarkness and we can barely see the actual deeds and nothing of the motives for which they were committed, nor even of the advantages of them to their author. We will confine ourselves to the victims to be found in his own family.

The first victim was Crispus, the son of Constantine and Minervina (par. 63). He was born about 303, was nominated Caesar in 317, and had been consul three times, the last in 324. He was a disciple of Lactantius (par. 74), and had fought victoriously against the Alemanni. In the war against Licinius he had acted worthily in command of the fleet (par. 220). His was a rising star, and he seemed destined for greatness. Unexpectedly he came to an eclipse and disappeared forever. A little while after the Council of Nicaea he was sent by his father to Gaul, but on the way he died of poison at Pola (Ammianus Marcellinus, xiv, 11, 20). The ancient historians ignore the motive of this death and there are some who say frankly that the reasons for it had to remain secret (cf. Aurelius Victor, *De Caesar.*, 41, 11). Almost all writers connect the death of Crispus with that of Fausta, Constantine's wife, a few months later.

It was said that Fausta had fallen in love with her stepson, but since he repelled her advances she had calumniated him before Constantine and accused him of attempting to take her by force. After the death of Crispus, however, the Empress Helena learned of the calumny and told Constantine. Then Fausta died by being suffocated in the bath. This information is given by pagan historians (cf. Zosimus, ii, 10, 29) to which Christian authors have added.

279. Of the Christian authors, Eusebius of Caesarea, the one who was the best informed of any, shows himself more astute and servile than ever, for he pretends to know nothing about the whole affair and keeps silent though he does make it obvious that he is not uninformed (cf. De vita Constant., i, 47). Sozomenus (i, 5) mentions the matter but connects it with a legend from pagan sources. This legend states that Constantine was filled with remorse at his murder of Crispus and went to a philosopher who told him that there could be no expiation for his crime. He then turned to Christian bishops who promised him full pardon, provided he asked for baptism. The Arian Philostorgius (ii, 4) says that Constantine killed Crispus through the calumnies of his stepmother, and that the latter was murdered in the bath in her turn when she was caught in the act of adultery with one of the courtiers.

All these ancient stories are suspect, however, since they may very easily be under the influence of the myth of the incestuous love of Phaedra and Hippolytus, a story known very well to the ancient pagans. It would seem too coincidental that the myth should be repeated in the persons of two important people in the imperial court. We need not spend much energy, therefore, in finding arguments against such a solution though they might easily be true. Looking at the matter impartially and historically it is not necessary that because the two deaths took place very close together in time one should have caused the other.

The fact is that we do not know today the true motives of the double tragedy, since the ancients knew little anyway. The Constantinian mists were functioning perfectly on this occasion. There is no worth in the modern conjectures. Some have thought to see political motives in the murder of Crispus, as if Constantine wanted to disembarrass himself of a rival who threatened either himself personally or the sons he had had by Fausta. One could always inquire whether the young Crispus was so dangerous a rival for Constantine who had conquered so many Caesars and Augusti. In any case, if Crispus was killed for this reason, why was Fausta killed also? Thinking the matter over it would seem more prudent to conclude that of the truth of these two sad events ignoramus et ignorabimus.

Even darker is the affair of Licinian Licinius. He was the illegitimate son of the Augustus Licinius, but he had been adopted by his wife,

Constantia, Constantine's sister. When his father died he was little more than twelve years of age. After killing his father, Constantine persecuted the boy, first putting him in prison in different places in conditions by no means easy and finally putting him to death. Why should he have been so cruel to a defenseless and innocent boy? Did the hatred of the father continue in the son and in the hatred for his adoptive mother? As in other cases, we have to confess that we do not know the motive for this murder. If we were to turn psychiatric, we could think that in these years Constantine passed through a crisis of suspicion and distrust — a very frequent disease in despots and tyrants — which made him discover plots and threats where there were none. **280.** These domestic upsets seem to have cleared after a few years and Constantine was able once more to enjoy a certain spiritual tranquillity. The Empire was safe in his hands, and there were no grave threats either inside or outside its boundaries.

Embassies arrived at the imperial courts from remote countries to present their respects and gifts. When he describes these embassies, Eusebius of Caesarea takes on his lyric tone once more, but he is worthy of credence for he is describing things which he has actually seen (*De vita Constant.*, iv, 7). He himself met groups of barbarians in the precincts of the imperial palace, diversified by their manner and decorations, their hair styles and beards; some were fierce looking, others of great stature; others were red-faced, some whiter than snow while others were of mixed race. These foreigners, as they are shown in paintings, paid homage to the Emperor with the rarest things of their own countries — diadems of precious stones, flaxen-haired slaves, barbaric garments woven with gold and flowers, horses, shields, long lances, arrows, and valuable cabinets.

Among others, an embassy came from the King of Persia which brought rich gifts, and received in return gifts even richer. Certainly in this exchange both sides were saying to themselves words very similar to those said earlier: "*Timeo Danaos et dona ferentes.*" In Persia Shapur II (310–380) was in the middle of his long reign which saw one of the most cruel persecutions of the Christians in that land. He was the son of Hormizdas, the son of the Narses who had been conquered by Galerius (par. 18). While he was still being nursed by his mother, at the end of 309, the magicians of the court had seen to his election as king and to his reception of the royal insignia in a special ceremony. Hence, he was born almost with the scepter in his hand. Quite naturally from his earliest years he had dreams of revenge on the Roman Empire to cancel out the memory of the defeat suffered by his grandfather and to get back the five provinces lost at that time. These ideas were favored in the court by the magi and by his ebionitic queen mother, Ephra Hormiz, who were as unfriendly to Constantine as to Christianity. On the other hand, it was too risky at the moment to attack Constantine in his enormous empire. It was better to await a favorable turn, and meanwhile to keep up the outward friendship with the Roman Empire which had dragged on until that time.

The Persian embassy came to Constantine, but its coming did not improve relations. Constantine was known among the Persians, also, as the great protector of Christianity. Indeed, when the embassy went back they took with them not only gifts from the Emperor, but also a letter from him to the King Shapur (De vita Constant., iv, 9:13) in which the writer presented himself as the sincere worshiper of the God of the Christians, and urged the King to treat his Christian subjects kindly.

Nothing could have been more calculated to worsen the suspicions of the Persian King. The King considered that the Roman Emperor, under the pretext of religion, wished to meddle in the affairs of Persia, and that he must certainly be preparing a great coup against his rival kingdom. King Shapur decided to get ready.

281. Events began to happen quickly. The Persians became menacing at the frontiers. Constantine, as was his custom, instead of leaving the initiative to the enemy took it himself and began to prepare for war. Among all his other victories, he said (De vita Constant., iv, 56) he had not yet had one against the Persians. The preparations were far reaching and precise, and they covered a very strong expeditionary force and the government of the Empire. Constantine, as if he wished to live again the glorious expeditions of his youth, had decided to take personal command of the expedition and was therefore forced to leave the government of the State to his relatives and trusted assistants. His son Constantius was already on the Euphrates to spy on the enemy, and to prepare the way for the army.

Notice of these extraordinary preparations got to the ears of the Persians, who did not expect so forceful an answer to their threats on the border. They were so terrified that to avoid invasion they endeavored to reach an agreement with Constantine. Constantine did not refuse the offer, since as Eusebius says (cf. *ibid.*, 57) he was a lover of peace and Easter was near. The principal reason, however, was certainly that he was not in good health and had realized sadly that he was no longer as suited to warlike expeditions as he had been years before.

Time passed and the Emperor still remained in Constantinople. Easter came, but his health grew steadily worse, and the sick man thought more and more on religious things. After the first days of Easter time he became dangerously ill and was carried to the thermal waters of Drepanum, recently named Helenopolis in honor of his mother Helena, where the memory of the martyr Lucian was preserved (par. 132). The water cure did nothing for the invalid, and Constantine realized that his time was approaching. He then decided to go through with what he had always put off — he announced that he wished to become a Christian officially.

This time at least there were no political reasons. His soul, conscious of many faults, would soon present itself in the presence of God. On this occasion Eusebius of Caesarea found full sincerity of expression. When the Emperor "realized that he was at the end of his life, he decided that this was the time when he must purify himself from all the faults of which he had been guilty; he had faith that he could cleanse himself with a saving washing 'from all the sin that he had committed in mortal life'" (*ibid.*, 61). There, in the place sacred to the martyr Lucian, mentally recalling his mother, he knelt on the pavement, and confessing his sins implored the mercy of God.

It is quite possible that on that occasion the penitent had the same sentiments as a grandson of Constantia the Empress, who referred to his death in battle while hardened with "horrible sins" by affirming:

> After I had lost myself
> with two mortal wounds, I gave myself
> weeping to Him who pardons willingly.
>
> Horrible were my sins
> but the infinite Goodness has so wide an embrace
> that it enfolds all that turn to it.
>
> (*Purgatory*, iii, 118–123)

282. Eusebius continues: "in that very place he was made worthy for the first time of praying with the others by the laying on of hands." These words allude to the ceremony with which catechumens were received into the Church as we know from contemporary documents (see the long note of Valesius on this passage). From that moment, therefore, Constantine was officially a member of the Christian Church although only a catechumen (par. 204). Before he had been the "bishop of those outside" (par. 209); now he had made a proper entry into the Church and had become one of "those inside."

After he had done this, Constantine felt much consoled. A little later he had himself taken to his villa of Achyron, a suburb of Nicomedia, where he awaited his fate with serenity. The feast of Pentecost was approaching on which it was the custom to solemnly administer baptism to the catechumens. The neophytes, after they had received the sacrament, put on their white garments and wore them for seven days. Constantine called together several bishops and asked to be baptized. He confided in them that he had hoped to go through this ceremony in the River Jordan where Jesus himself had been baptized, but since God wished otherwise he did not intend to put off any longer his full entry into the Church.

His desire was instantly fulfilled. Baptism was administered and the ceremony was presided over by Eusebius of Nicomedia, the bishop who had never abandoned Constantine. The Emperor's baptism was, therefore, by Arian hands.

On May 22, 337, toward midday the Emperor died.

The body was clothed with the white garments of a neophyte and placed in a gold sarcophagus, which was taken to Constantinople; and there the "apostle" Emperor was given a most solemn funeral and buried in the tomb which he had prepared for himself (par. 224). 283. To extend the funeral honors, commemorative medals were struck. On them, with a mixture of Christianity and paganism, the dead man was shown in a chariot which was taking him into the sky to be received at the right hand of the Divine Majesty.

For his part, Eusebius of Caesarea hurried to write that biography of Constantine which could be compared to the moon which turns its sunlit parts to the earth while never showing the shadows (par. 73). This tame biographer must be allowed some excuse however. If it is difficult today after sixteen centuries to give a balanced judgment on the person and the work of the dead Emperor, it was even more difficult for other reasons to give judgment immediately after his death when a thousand passions and interests were in conflict and when the "revolution" begun by him was only partly under way.

Confusion followed his death. Constantine had arranged the imperial succession with a precision which recalled that of Diocletian, but this time also little or no attention was paid to it. The sun had gone and the satellites left their orbits. Civil uprisings, military plots, and court intrigues brought death to many of the family and counselors of the late emperor and the ancient struggles for succession were revived.

If the dead Emperor had been able to raise his head from his gold sarcophagus at the sight of slaughtered relatives and friends he could well have exclaimed like another famous king: "Après moi le déluge"!

284. Constantine is a person of the highest importance in the history of the Roman Empire, and in the story of the Christian Church. He really changed the natural course of events.

He had very good, but not prodigious, natural gifts. He was tall, strong, and vigorous, and had sympathetic looks and an affable manner. He had no time for abstract speculation and subtlety of thought, but had a very acute power of observation. He made his decisions with rapidity, but often on the basis of summary and approximate information. On the battlefield he was a very brave fighter and an excellent tactician; in strategy he was among the greatest of Roman emperors, worthy of comparison with Aurelian. Besides military affairs, he had had a novitiate in civil government with his father, Constantius, and then in the court of Diocletian. The experience he gained there accompanied him for the rest of his life.

He came to know Christianity at first very vaguely from his parents, Constantius and Helena, and then at the court of Diocletian. This second contact left a profound impression on him, for it came at the outbreak of the great persecution. A zealous seeker of ideas and facts, the young man was able to see with his own eyes the things of which a deep religious faith was capable.

He had great personal ambition, and from the beginning knew how to restrain it by good sense and until the opportune moment. Although he was one of the last of the dynasts of the tetrarchy, he managed to work his way up among them and finally dislodge all competitors — he held back until the chance came, and was capable of waiting with almost Oriental passivity. When he did find himself at the top of the ladder without any opponents, he became almost morbidly preoccupied with tranquillity and peace in his dominions. This was merely another aspect of his native ambition — a desire to keep what he had worked so hard to obtain. He was not deaf to flattery if it was done skillfully. He had sudden and inexplicable fits of cruelty caused perhaps by political jealousy, perhaps by human passion. As a civil ruler he occupied himself seriously in the well-being of his subjects, and a great part of his legislation was in favor of the poor and badly situated people such as slaves and abandoned children. In this the influence of Christian principles is clear.

285. The greatest importance of Constantine is in the religious field where he was a true innovator. Before him it was inconceivable that there could be a Roman Empire which would ignore or neglect the traditional gods. There had been, it is true, tolerance for foreign religions; every subject of the Empire could quite easily be a *parcus deorum cultor* like Horace, or even discard the whole pantheon as Lucretius had done. The constitution of the Empire, however, had remained as it was in ancient times — essentially religious and tied up with the cult of the gods. Constantine for the first time distinguished the man from the citizen. To the man he left liberty of conscience; from the citizen he asked no more than the practice of a given cult, either for the gods of Rome or for Christ or for any other gods. Every religion was to sustain itself by its own strength without the support of the Empire. In this way the marriage between the Empire and the Roman religion broke up and the divorce between the two ancient spouses was made official. Now even the Emperor himself was able to discard the religion of Rome and accept in its place — a thing inconceivable for Tertullian — the religion of Christ.

Naturally, for innumerable practical reasons, the divorce did not take place at one blow. Constantine, therefore, continued to be the *pontifex maximus* of the cult of Rome and did not denounce other pagan ceremonies. There were simple official ceremonies which were backed by the force of tradition and were practiced without any internal assent to their significance.

Personally Constantine inclined more and more to Christianity. He did not do this by profound philosophical reflection, but by his acute practical intuitive powers. He saw in Christianity the religion of the future — the only religion which was going to survive the decadence and collapse of paganism. He was brought to the threshold of Christianity by the vague solar monotheism which was popular at his time and which he perhaps inherited from his father. He stayed on this threshold, however, until the last weeks of his life although he had a profound and sincere sympathy for Christianity. This sympathy was not completely disinterested. If it was not caused, it was certainly increased by the marvelous success which rewarded his political and military efforts. These successes, conducted *instinctu divinitatis*, persuaded him more and more that he was under the protection of the God of the Christians, that he was the "man of God" (par. 272).

286. When Constantine, without crossing the threshold, wanted to interfere directly with what was going on inside the Church he found himself in a completely new world where he soon lost himself and made bad mistakes.

He really knew very little about Christianity, and hardly anything about the theology, traditions, and disciplinary spirit of the Catholic Church. Despite this, right from the beginning of his absolute government he found himself involved in questions of ecclesiastical discipline and complicated theology. The weakest side of his religious politics was precisely this personal relation with the Catholic Church, while the most praiseworthy was that which defined the relations between paganism and Christianity.

He mixed himself up with the internal affairs of the Church, however, mainly because he was formally invited to do so — as when the Donatists had recourse to him to settle their troubles. He was not unwilling to do so, however. He felt himself at the head of an immense empire, and urged on by his preoccupation with peace considered it his duty to intervene. In any case was he not the "man of God," the "bishop of those outside"? From "outside" to "inside" the distance was very short or, better, seemed very short to him. He therefore entered and acted. When he was inside he acted as he would have done outside, and so like the soldier he was he called his officers for briefing before the battle or called together the governors of a certain region; and like an absolute ruler gave them their orders. This was done now by one who was neither a bishop nor a Christian and by one so inexpert in theological questions that he regarded as futile and useless the discussions of the doctrine of Arius. Yet the whole responsibility in this was not his. He was still, unconsciously in some part, a pagan in mind for whom no part of the Empire's land or life was closed to the head of the Empire.

287. It has been justly remarked (cf. Duchesne) that the intervention of Constantine in purely ecclesiastical questions usually complicated them further. Obviously one cannot be certain what would have happened if he had not intervened. At least, however, in theory we may ask if the very grave questions of Donatism and Arianism, which Con-

stantine took so much to heart but which he left substantially unsolved or even more complicated, would not have been settled more speedily and completely had he not interfered with so many synods, councils, exiles, and despotic persecution. The Church with its internal vitality purely religious in origin had already overcome the most dangerous crises in the past as those of Gnosticism, Modalism, and the heresy of Origen. In Peter's house everything was put right by the occupants without the work of any Caesar appearing in the family as a major domo. No emperor had then called councils, exiled orthodox bishops like Athanasius and Eustathius, or preferred heretical ones like the two courtiers Eusebius of Nicomedia and Eusebius of Caesarea.

One must say that the Council of Nicaea produced some good at least by giving a profession of faith. This is true. But this orthodox symbol was immediately subjected to a process of corruption as a result of the peculiar circumstances in which it was composed until it was finally denied completely to lead to the catastrophe of Rimini. If other ways had been followed, an orthodox profession of faith would likewise have been obtained, but without the police methods, without persecution, without fratricidal quarrels, the sad consequences of which continued for many centuries.

To Caesar Constantine finally gave that which was Caesar's and so far all was well. But he considered it his duty far too often to go into the house of Peter to arrange things there. "Ahi! Constantin . . ."

SOURCES

The most important historical sources of this period are given in paragraphs 68–78. Others of lesser importance are —

EUTROPIUS — *Breviarium ab Urbe condita* (Leipzig, 1887) — relates events until the middle of the fourth century. It was translated into Greek, rearranged and added to at various periods, and was very popular during the Middle Ages.

AMMIANUS MARCELLINUS — *Rerum gestarum libri* (Berlin, 1910). Books XIV–XXXI are still extant and take in the years 353–378. The author is a pagan though not particularly biased.

Panegyrici latini veteres (ed. Bahrens, Leipzig, 1911). These are turgid court discourses of which Nos. VI, VII, VIII, IX, X were given in Gaul in the years 307, 310, 311, 313, and 321.

ZOSIMUS — Ἰστορία νέα (*New History*) (Leipzig, 1837). There are six books of which II–IV treat of the fourth century. His account of Diocletian has been lost. Zosimus was a convinced pagan and hostile to Christianity.

During the fifth century Church histories were written by Socrates the Scholastic, Sozomen, and Theodoret of Cyrus. These histories were compiled for the most part from earlier writings although some original matter is found, especially in Socrates. Philostorgius is clearly Arian. Gelasius of Cyzicus is somewhat later and both he and Philostorgius are of little historical value. The Spaniard Paul Orosius wrote about the year 418 for apologetic reasons his *History against the Pagans* — there is some new material for the period from 378 on.

The following notes are given with reference to the appropriate paragraphs —

7–8 — The story by Eucherius of Lyons of the martyrs of Agaunum is found in RUINART, *Acta Martyrum* (ed. 1731), pp. 241–244; the Passion together with the story given by Eucherius in the *Acta Sanctorum Septembris*, vi (1867), pp. 308–403, 895–926; also in *Monum. Germ. Hist. Script. Rer. Meroving.*, iii, pp. 20–41 (ed. Krusch); there is an index of other documents in *Bioblioth. Hagiogr. Lat.*, 5737–5764.

42 — The Acts of Maximilian are in RUINART, *Acta Martyrum* (ed. 1731), pp. 263–264.

43–44 — The Acts of Marcellus and the Passion of Cassian are in RUINART, *Acta Martyrum* (ed. 1731), pp. 265–267.

72 — The extant writings of Eusebius are gathered in MIGNE, *Patrologia Graeca*, Vols. 19–24. Of the three works spoken of in the book — *Ecclesiastical History, Martyrs of Palestine,* and *Life of Constantine* — there

are critical editions in *Die griechischen christlichen Schriftsteller der ersten drei Jahrhunderten* (Leipzig), 9, 1–3 (*ibid.*, 1903, 1908, 1909), and 7 (*ibid.*, 1902).

73 — A recent lengthy study of the documents contained in the *Life of Constantine* is that of I. DANIELE, *I documenti costantiniani della 'Vita Constantini' di Eusebio di Cesarea*, in *Analecta Gregoriana*, xiii (Roma, 1938). The author defends the integral authenticity of the documents but apart from this he gives a full treatment to the opposite opinion (Crivellucci, Schultze, Mancini, Batiffol) with considerable information.

More recent is P. FRANCHI DE' CAVALIERI, *Eusebio non è l'autore della 'Vita Constantini'?* in *Constantiniana*, pp. 51–65, in *Studi e Testi*, 171 (1953), especially against the negative opinion of H. Gregoire.

74 — The writings of Lactantius are in MIGNE, *Patrologia Latina*, Vols. 6–7. There is a critical edition but not without errors in *Corpus Scriptorum Ecclesiasticorum Latinorum* of Vienna, xix and xxvii (1890–1897).

75–78 — Various scholars have contributed to the studies of the *Acts* and *Passions* and in general to the immense quantity of hagiographical material particularly Ruinart with his collection *Acta primorum martyrum sincera et selecta* (Paris, 1689, and elsewhere in later years). The most noteworthy of the scholars are Bollandists, a college of Jesuits called thus from their founder John Bolland (1596–1665). In spite of various troubles and frequent moves the college has worked from the sixteenth century until the present day but is still a long way from having finished its work. During its life it has produced the *Acta Sanctorum* which examines material on the lives of the saints for each day according to the months of the year. The month of November has now been reached. The original edition printed at Antwerp, Tongerloo, and Brussels is made up of about seventy volumes in folio, the first two of which appeared in 1643: later editions come from Venice and Paris. By the Bollandists are also published the *Analecta Bollandiana*, a quarterly review (from 1882) which publishes studies, texts, and catalogues of manuscripts; besides this there are the *Subsidia Hagiographica*, a similar series to the *Analecta* but more voluminous.

80 — The verbal transcript of the confiscation at Cirta is preserved in the *Gesta apud Zenophilum consularem* which is to be found with other documents in the appendix of the work *De schismate donatistarum* against Parmenianus by Optatus of Mileum (in *Corp. Script. Eccl. Lat.*, xxvi, 185 ff.; MIGNE, *Patr. Lat.*, 43, 794 ff.; cf. AUGUSTINE, *Contra Cresconium*, iii, 29–30).

93–94 — The canons of Peter of Alexandria are in MIGNE, *Patr. Graec.*, 18, 467 ff.

96 — Augustine refers to Marcellinus in *De unico baptismate*, 16. Cf. *Contra litt. Petiliani*, ii, 202; *Breviculus Collactionis cum Donat.*, iii, 34–36 (all in Migne, *Patr. Lat.*, 43).

100 — The *Passion of Fabius* is to be found in *Analecta Bolland.*, ix (1890), 123 ff. Cf. P. FRANCHI DE' CAVALIERI, *S. Fabio vessillifero*, in *Studi e Testi*, 65 (1935), 101 ff.

101 — The *Acts* of Crispina are in RUINART, *Acta Martyrum* (ed. 1731), pp. 395–396; P. FRANCHI DE' CAVALIERI, *Osservazioni sopra gli Atti di S. Crispina*, in *Studi e Testi*, 9 (1902), 24–35; *ibid.*, pp. 32–35, a new text of the *Acts*. The passages of Augustine on Crispina are in *Enarrat. in psalm. 120, 13; 137, 3, 14 and 17; Sermones 286 and 254*.

102–108 — The *Passion* of Saturninus and Companions is in RUINART, *Acta Martyrum* (ed. 1731), p. 338 ff. Cf. P. FRANCHI DE' CAVALIERI, *La 'Passio' dei martiri abitinensi*, in *Studi e Test*, 65 (1935), 3–71; *ibid.*, pp. 49–71, a new text of the *Passion*.

109 — The *Passion* of Maxima and Companions is in *Analecta Bolland.*, ix (1890), 110 ff. Cf. P. FRANCHI DE' CAVALIERI, *Della Passio sanctarum Maximae, Donatillae et Secundae*, in *Studi e Testi*, 65 (1935), 75 ff.

114–119 — The *Acts* of Phileas and Philoromus are in RUINART, *Acta Martyrum* (ed. 1731), pp. 434–436.

131 — On the authenticity of the second homily on Pelagius attributed to John Chrysostom cf. P. FRANCHI DE' CAVALIERI, in *Studi e Testi*, 65 (1935), 281–303.

136 — The Greek text of the *Acts* of St. Agape and Companions has been edited by P. FRANCHI DE' CAVALIERI, *Il testo greco originale degli Atti delle SS. Agape, Irene e Chione*, in *Studi e Testi*, 9 (1902), pp. 3–19. The Latin text in the translation of Sirletus can be found in RUINART, *Acta Martyrum* (ed. 1731), pp. 348–351.

138 — The *Passion* of Philip of Heracleia and Companions is in RUINART, *Acta Martyrum* (ed. 1731), pp. 364–373. Cf. P. FRANCHI DE' CAVALIERI, *Intorno alla Passio S. Philippi Ep. Heracleae*, in *Studi e Testi*, 27 (1915), pp. 97–103; see also *Studi e Testi*, 19 (1908), pp. 124–130.

142 — The *Passion* of Irenaeus of Sirmium is in RUINART, *Acta Martyrum* (ed. 1731), pp. 356–358.

143 — The *Passion* of Sinerus is in RUINART, *Acta Martyrum* (ed. 1731), pp. 433–444. For discoveries in the cemetery of Sinerus at Sirmium cf. G. B. DE' ROSSI, in *Bullett. Archeol. Crist.*, 1885, p. 144 ff.

144 — The *Passion* of the Four Crowned Martyrs in *Acta Sanctorum Novembris* iii (1910), pp. 765–784; the *Acts* are preceded by a learned introduction (pp. 748–765) by H. Delehaye. For questions arising from the *Acts* cf. P. FRANCHI DE' CAVALIERI, *I Santi Quattro*, in *Studi e Testi*, 24 (1912), pp. 57–66; H. DELEHAYE, *Le culte des Quatre Couronnés à Rome*, in *Analecta Bolland.*, xxxii, pp. 67–71; for the geographical background see N. VULIĆ, *Quelques observations sur la Passio SS. Quattuor Coronatorum* in *Riv. Arch. Crist.*, xi (1934), pp. 156–159.

145 — There is mention of Montanus in the *Passion* of Irenaeus of Sirmium (see paragraph 142); the stories given with greater detail in some martyrologies are very uncertain. The *Passion* of Pollio is in RUINART, *Acta Martyrum* (ed. 1731), pp. 359–360. The *Passion* of Quirinus of Siscia is in RUINART, *ibid.*, pp. 437–439. The *Passion* of Florianus is in *Acta Sanctorum Maii* i (1680), pp. 461–467.

146 — The only *Passion* of Afra is in Ruinart, *Acta Martyrum* (ed. 1731), pp. 400–401; together with her conversion in *Monum. Germ. Hist. Script. Rer. Meroving.*, iii, pp. 55–64 (ed. Krusch). Cf. Duchesne, *La Passion de sainte Afra*, in *Analecta Bollandiana*, xvii (1898), pp. 433–437.

148 — For Agnes, cf. P. Franchi de' Cavalieri, *S. Agnese nella tradizione e nella legenda* (Rome, 1899); id., *Hagiographica*, in *Studi e Testi*, 19 (1908), pp. 141–164. The duplication of Agnes (for which see paragraph 78) was proposed by Fl. Jubaru, *Sainte Agnès vierge et martyre de la voie Nomentane d'après de nouvelles recherches* (Paris, 1907).

149 — The *Acts* of Euplius are in Ruinart, *Acta Martyrum* (ed. 1731), pp. 361–363. Cf. P. Franchi de' Cavalieri, *Note agiografiche, S. Euplo*, in *Studi e Testi*, 49 (1928), pp. 1–54 (cf. 239–240).

217–218 — The *Passion* of the Forty Martyrs with their testament is in O. L. Gebhardt, *Acta martyrum selecta*, pp. 166–181 (cf. *Acta Sanctorum Martii ii*, p. 12 ff.). For other ancient records and connected questions cf. P. Franchi de' Cavalieri, *I santi Quaranta martiri di Sebastia*, in *Studi e Testi*, 49 (1928), pp. 155–184, which develops and supersedes the earlier study by the same author, *I quaranta martiri di Sebaste*, *ibid.*, 22 (1909), pp. 64–70.

331–347 — The chief sources for the history of Donatism are the writings of Optatus of Mileum (cf. note to paragraph 80) and those of Augustine; these and other less important sources are listed and studied by L. Duchesne, *Le dossier du donatisme* (in *Mélanges d'archéologie et d'histoire publiés par l'École Française de Rome*, x, 1890, pp. 589–650) and in greater detail and with a full historical background by P. Monceaux, *Histoire littéraire de l'Afrique chrétienne*, Vols. IV–VII (Paris, 1912–1923).

BIBLIOGRAPHICAL NOTES

After this necessary list of sources it does not seem important to give a true bibliography for various reasons. So many are the studies in general and on certain sections of this period that their bare enumeration would take up a large space. Even so such a list would inevitably be incomplete and in any case would be of interest only to a few specialists. These already know that they can find copious bibliographies in the following publications:

The Cambridge Ancient History — Vol. XII: *The Imperial Crisis and Recovery A.D. 193–324* (Cambridge, 1939).

The Cambridge Mediaeval History — Vol. I: *The Christian Roman Empire and the Foundation of the Teutonic Kingdoms* (ibid., 1936).

FRANCHI DE' CAVALIERI, P. — *Constantiniana*, in *Studi e Testi*, 171 (1953).

We must mention especially the following earlier works —

LE NAIN DE TILLEMONET, L. S., *Histoire des Empereurs et des autres princes qui ont régné durant les six premiers siècles de l'Église*, Vol. 6 (Paris, 1690–1738, and elsewhere afterward); by the same author, *Memoires pour servir à l'histoire ecclésiastique des six premiers siècles* in 16 volumes (Paris, 1693–1712, and elsewhere later); both these works in spite of their early date are very useful in modern times because of their extraordinary knowledge of the sources and the faithful use made of them.

GIBBON, E., *The History of the Decline and Fall of the Roman Empire* in six volumes (London, 1776–1788, with many reprintings and translations: London, 1909–1913; Turin, 1926–1927). The author, first a Protestant, then a Catholic, and then a Protestant once more, is under the influence of Jansenism and Voltaire and displays a clearly anti-Christian spirit. The first part of his work which extends over the years A.D. 180–641 is rich in information and balanced judgment; the second part for the years 641–1453 is much inferior and is spoiled by a studied depreciation of Byzantine Christianity.

INDEX

Numbers refer to paragraphs.

297

If you have enjoyed this book, consider making your next selection from among the following . . .

At your Bookdealer or direct from the Publisher.
Call Toll-Free 1-800-437-5876.

Prices subject to change.

ABOUT THE AUTHOR

Abbot Giuseppe Ricciotti (1890-1964) was a biblical scholar and orientalist who taught Hebrew and comparative Semitics (1926-27) at Genoa and at various times oriental history at the University of Rome. From 1950 to 1960, he taught Church history at the University of Bari.

Born in Rome, he entered the Congregation of Canons Regular of the Lateran in 1906 and was ordained in 1913. From 1935 to 1946 he was Procurator General of his religious congregation, receiving the title of Abbot in 1938.

His scholarly publications include works on Syriac literature and studies on particular periods of Church history, plus scholarly commentaries on various books of the Bible. He is known in the English-speaking world for a number of his books that were translated into English, notably *The Life of Christ* (1947), *Paul the Apostle* (1953), *The Acts of the Apostles* (1958), *The Age of Martyrs* (1959) and *Julian the Apostate* (1960). He is famous in Italy for having aroused extraordinary interest in the study of the Bible throughout that country. His works are remarkable for their reliable information and their clear and attractive style. (Source: *The New Catholic Encyclopedia,* 1967).